Daphne du Maurier

author of
REBECCA
MY COUSIN RACHEL
JAMAICA INN
and many more classic bestsellers, has
now created a spellbinding historical saga.

"Daphne du Maurier's prose is as swift as
a rapier. She is one of the most entertaining writers of the century."

Chicago Daily News

"A poignant glimpse into England's his-
toric past. GOLDEN LADS brings the
Elizabethan period alive."

Charleston Evening Post

"A fascinating maelstrom of uppercrust
and titled Englishmen. . . . Careful in
detail and splendid in the telling."

Columbus Dispatch

Other Avon books by
Daphne du Maurier

Daphne du Maurier

GOLDEN LADS

Sir Francis Bacon, Anthony Bacon
and their friends

 AVON
PUBLISHERS OF BARD, CAMELOT, DISCUS, EQUINOX AND FLARE BOOKS

AVON BOOKS
A division of
The Hearst Corporation
959 Eighth Avenue
New York, New York 10019

ISBN: 0-380-00786-X

First Avon Printing, August, 1976

AVON TRADEMARK REG. U.S. PAT. OFF. AND IN
OTHER COUNTRIES, MARCA REGISTRADA,
HECHO EN U.S.A.

Printed in the U.S.A.

Feare no more the heate o' th' Sun,
Nor the furious Winters rages,
Thou thy worldly task hast don,
Home art gon, and tane thy wages.
Golden Lads, and Girles all must,
As Chimney-Sweepers come to dust.

WILLIAM SHAKESPEARE

Acknowledgements

My grateful thanks to the Countess of Verulam for her courtesy in receiving my son and myself at Gorhambury; to Mrs King for answering my many questions about the original Tudor building; and to Monsieur Méras, chief archivist at Montauban, for entertaining us, showing us the old city, and producing the documents concerning Anthony Bacon. Above all, my immense gratitude to Joan St George Saunders and her team of assistants at Writers' and Speakers' Research for the work which they carried out for me over a period of eighteen months, with a special thought for the late Mrs Pugh, who took over the particularly difficult job of transcribing so many letters from Lady Bacon. Finally, I am indebted to Sheila Bush for editing my manuscript with such patience and perception.

D. du M.

Contents

PART ONE

Chapter 1

When Anthony Cooke became tutor to Prince Edward, the heir to the throne, in the closing years of King Henry VIII, he and his family of nine—five daughters and four sons—knew very well that life henceforward, for all of them, would no longer be the quiet, studious affair that it had been in the past, within the safe precincts of their home at Gidea Hall in Essex, the only rivalry permitted that of sister against sister, brother against brother, and who could translate the swiftest a page from Latin, Greek, Italian or Hebrew. It would be instead a process of manœuvre, of political judgement, of precise timing, with the ability to hold the confidence of the Prince's uncle, Lord Edward Seymour, the surest step to winning the affection of the future King himself. "Give me a child until he is seven, and he will be mine forever," the Spanish founder of the Jesuits, Ignatius Loyola, is reputed to have said; and considering his new pupil, delicate, thoughtful, wise beyond his years but inclined to obstinacy, Anthony Cooke wondered which of his own five daughters was most fitted to aid him in the task of moulding the character of England's future sovereign.

His choice fell upon his second daughter, Ann, then in her seventeenth year. His eldest girl, Mildred, two years older, was equally brilliant at Greek and Latin; but, possibly better favoured in her personal appearance, was more likely to make an early and advantageous marriage. Instructed as she was to her finger-tips in the Protestant faith, with a healthy abhorrence of all things Catholic, Ann could hardly fail to impress upon her royal charge the absolute necessity of holding firm to all the tenets and maxims of the reformed church.

Ann, fond though she was of her elder sister, felt a small sense of triumph that the choice had fallen upon herself.

3

Devotion to her father was paramount; he was almost
equal to God in her eyes, and the belief that she was his
favorite daughter seemed to her now proven. Adhering
firmly to the doctrine of predestination, she felt that the
hand of the Almighty was upon her; she had been chosen
from among her sisters to interpret the Holy Word to the
King's son. Proud, plump and determined, Ann Cooke set
forth for Court in the wake of her father, her envious
younger brothers and sisters waving farewell.

King Henry, already a sick man, and harried by affairs
of state, had no time to spare for yet another of his son's
attendants, and Ann arrived at Court to find that, although
her father commanded Prince Edward's attention for three
or four hours a day, she herself was obliged to share her
duties as governess with other equally scholastic ladies of
her own age or even younger, amongst them the Prince's
cousins, the Ladies Seymour, whose aptitude in writing
Latin verse excelled that of either Ann herself or her sister
Mildred. It was a chastening experience to find them
fluttering around the Prince with Latin and Greek tags
upon their tongues and a cousinly air of intimacy into the
bargain.

She decided to concentrate her powers upon religious
instruction, but here again there was apt to be distraction,
for no sooner had she caught the young Prince's attention
with a dissertation upon Calvin, a matter very close to her
heart, than she would be interrupted by the arrival of his
nurse with broth, or the physician would come to examine
his chest, which was said to be weak, or worse still one of
his Seymour uncles would arrive with a pet dog, and the
Prince, with a wan smile but a stubborn air, would an-
nounce to his governess that he had had enough of learning for the day. Ann appealed to her father for advice, but
he could give her little comfort, for he was himself sub-
ordinate to the Prince's chief tutor, the famous scholar
John Cheke, who had more important matters on his mind.
Not only was he involved in endless controversy with his
learned contemporaries about the pronunciation of the
Greek language, but he was anxious to secure the future
of his widowed son-in-law William Cecil, an extremely
able young man of five-and-twenty. Cheke's daughter had
died a few years previously, leaving an infant son named
Thomas; and Cecil was now hovering on the fringe of

Court society in the hope that his father-in-law might say a word for him in the right circles.

Cheke intimated to Anthony Cooke that young William Cecil would go far, and only needed to marry again—preferably a young woman who combined brains with beauty —to find himself in the forefront of those jostling for place in the corridors of power. Anthony Cooke found an early opportunity of falling in with young Cecil, who did indeed seem to be exceedingly able, far-sighted and agreeable, and on the first suitable occasion presented his daughter Ann. The meeting did not go well, William Cecil, whose outlook was political rather than religious, showing little interest in Ann's customary tirades against the odious practices of the Romanists. It was after this encounter that Anthony Cooke suggested to his daughter that her sister Mildred might care to relieve her for a few weeks in her capacity as governess at Court, while Ann herself would benefit from the fresh air of Essex. The exchange was made, and Mildred, slim, fair-haired, keen-eyed, and although sharply intelligent a better listener than her younger sister, made her debut at Court and was immediately liked by all, especially by William Cecil.

It came as a shock, and possibly not entirely a pleasant one, when Anthony Cooke arrived at Gidea Hall to tell his family that their sister Mildred was betrothed to William Cecil. He had given the happy pair his blessing, and the marriage would take place in December. There was general rejoicing, in which of course Ann joined; nevertheless, she could not but be aware that in a certain sense Mildred had stolen a march on her. She had found herself a husband in a short space of time, which was naturally the ultimate hope of all young women, scholarly or otherwise, and not just any young man, as her father explained to them, but one of the most promising of his generation. He had no title and as yet little land, but these would come, and appointments too, and he could not have wished a better match for his eldest daughter.

The wedding on December 25th 1546 had hardly been solemnised, the celebrations ended, when King Henry VIII fell mortally sick, and died on January 28th. Prince Edward, nine years old, was crowned in Westminster Abbey, his uncle Edward Seymour, now Duke of Somerset, became Lord Protector, and those who had won his favour during the preceding months found promotion in their turn. Anthony Cooke was made a Knight of the Bath, and later in the year he was returned as Member of Parliament for Shoreham. John Cheke became Provost of Cambridge, but the education of the young King remained in his hands. William Cecil was elected Member of Parliament for his family borough of Stamford, and the following year the Lord Protector Somerset made him his Master of Requests. His wife Mildred was not so fortunate. Her first baby died, as did subsequent infants, and a number of years passed before she produced two daughters who lived, naming them Anne and Elizabeth after her sisters.

Once King Edward had been crowned the royal training intensified. He was deemed too adult to need women about him, and Ann Cooke, who had perhaps hoped to return to Court once Mildred was married, found herself remaining at home with ample time to continue the translation from Italian into English of twenty-five sermons upon the predestination and election of God, with which she had consoled herself after her return to Gidea Hall. Her presence was often needed, however, at her sister Cecil's bedside, with the frequent still-born babies and the miscarriages, and the two became closer to one another as companions than they had ever been at home. And as William Cecil was constantly at the command of the Lord Protector Somerset, Mildred was glad to forget the anxiety of being wife to a politician, around whom storm clouds were gathering, if only by reading aloud to Ann the works of Chrysostom and Gregory Nazianzen.

The next few years were crucial for Cecil's political future. The Lord Protector had enemies, the chief of whom was the Earl of Warwick, and in October 1549 Somerset fell from power and was committed to the Tower. William Cecil followed him, but was soon released. Fortunately his father-in-law, Anthony Cooke, did not become involved. There was a patched-up truce the following February between Somerset and his rival Warwick, and Cecil took advantage of this to make overtures to the latter, whose star seemed in the ascendant. Eight months later Warwick made himself Duke of Northumberland, and William Cecil was knighted, at the same time gaining the post of Secretary of State to the young King.

The truce between the rivals was short-lived, for in the

latter part of 1551 the Duke of Northumberland brought a trumped-up charge of treason against the Duke of Somerset, and in January 1552 the boy-King was obliged to sign his uncle's death warrant. Sir William Cecil, now firmly established as one of Northumberland's henchmen, could do nothing to save his former patron.

It was some time during this year that Ann Cooke, once again called to minister to Mildred's household during her sister's pregnancy, was introduced to one of her brother-in-law's closest friends, the rising lawyer Nicholas Bacon. Son of a yeoman farmer in Suffolk, Nicholas Bacon had entered Corpus Christi, Cambridge, at the age of thirteen. He took his B.A. at seventeen, coming third out of the whole university. Some few years later, deciding upon the law as a career, he was admitted to Gray's Inn. Called to the bar in 1533, when he was twenty-four, he rose rapidly in his profession and became solicitor of the Court of Augmentations in 1537, the particular work of his department being to administer the various manors, lands and estates that had been forfeit to the Crown at the dissolution of the monasteries.

He was not above dealing in property himself, and by the time he was forty owned estates in Suffolk, Norfolk, Essex and Middlesex, besides several tenements in London. He had married well. His wife, the daughter of a well-to-do London mercer, had borne him three sons and three daughters; and the mansion he had started building for her and for his family at Redgrave, Suffolk, on the site of a monastic hunting lodge, was still in the process of completion when he met Ann Cooke at William Cecil's establishment at Burghley in Northamptonshire, an even more imposing edifice than Redgrave. There was no doubt about it, the two men thought alike, in politics and in other matters; they had risen from comparative obscurity to positions of authority by their own efforts and by keeping a prudent watch on the turn of events; and they both realised that in the rapidly changing world of the mid-sixteenth century one false step on the ladder of power which they were climbing might bring disgrace, or even death.

Ann Cooke took to her brother-in-law's friend immediately. He was only some six or seven years younger than her father, and this was a recommendation in itself. As a lawyer it amused him to argue with her, albeit he did it with courtesy and deference; and if he winked at William Cecil as he did so she was not aware of the fact. She liked older men, and Nicholas Bacon at forty-one was well set-up, even powerfully built, with a witty turn of phrase and a sense of humour; but what appealed to Ann most was his staunch defence of all things Protestant. When he asked her to visit Redgrave and help his already ailing wife with her brood of boys and girls, in the still unfinished mansion, she needed no prompting from her sister Mildred to accept. The decision changed her life.

Redgrave Hall, with its spacious rooms set in a park surrounded by woodlands, reminded her of her mother's home Milton, also in Northamptonshire, which her grandfather Sir William Fitzwilliam had bought at the beginning of the century. Perhaps the association was unfortunate. Sir William had been Cardinal Wolsey's Treasurer, and after the Cardinal's disgrace in 1530 had had the temerity to entertain the fallen prelate for five days at Milton. Although Ann, his daughter, enjoyed relating the story on every possible occasion, as reflecting past glory, it was something her own daughter and namesake preferred to forget.

Jane Bacon was a frail creature, only too willing to hand over some of her responsibility to an able-bodied young woman of four-and-twenty, for six children, between the ages of thirteen and three, were more than she could manage. She did not realise that she was handing over to a successor who would take her place as wife and stepmother. In October of 1552 Jane Bacon was still living; in the spring of the following year her tomb was being erected; and shortly afterwards Ann Cooke became the second wife of Nicholas Bacon and mistress of Redgrave Hall. She had made as good a match as her sister Mildred.

She had only a few months to accustom herself to the pleasures and pains of her new status before clouds threatened to darken the serenity of married life, just as they had done for William Cecil and Mildred during their first years together. The young King Edward VI died on 6th July 1553, having only a few weeks before, at the instigation of the Duke of Northumberland, altered the succession from his Catholic sister Princess Mary to his Protestant cousin Lady Jane Grey, bride of Northumberland's own son Lord Guilford Dudley. Opinion in the country was instantly divided: some rallied to Northumberland; the majority, even though non-Catholic, to the Princess Mary. William Cecil had been a witness to the document in favour of Lady Jane, though even at the time of signing he knew that Northumberland's move was a tactical error. Sir Anthony Cooke, ardent Protestant that he was, also declared himself for Lady Jane.

Nicholas Bacon, aware that the attempt to deprive the rightful heir, Princess Mary, of the succession would prove disastrous, withdrew prudently to Redgrave. His position as Treasurer to Gray's Inn and Attorney of the Court of Wards did not appear to be at stake, but he foresaw that Princess Mary and her supporters, should they march to London from her house in Norfolk—and this was their declared intention—must pass through Cambridge and Bury St Edmund's and halt at Framlingham Castle, a short distance from Redgrave. Therefore landowners and their ladies, Protestants as well as Catholics, should be prepared to show loyalty.

It was possibly the only time in their lives that Nicholas and Ann Bacon had a serious disagreement on political matters. The decision, either way, might cost them their heads. Ann, fiercely loyal to the Protestant faith and to her father, would have moved instantly to London. Nicholas Bacon, who knew Jane's and Northumberland's cause to be doomed to failure, told his wife firmly and gravely that she should go with him to Framlingham and offer their services to the Princess Mary. He did not tell her that in his pocket was a farewell letter from her brother-in-law William Cecil, with directions that it should be delivered to his wife Mildred should Cecil's life be forfeit. Ann had sworn to honour and obey her husband. They went to Framlingham.

Mary was proclaimed Queen on July 20th, exactly a fortnight after her brother Edward's death. The Duke of Northumberland, Lord Guilford Dudley and Lady Jane were committed to the Tower, as was Sir Anthony Cooke. William Cecil, who was still Secretary of State, had been sent to Ipswich with papers for the new Queen to sign before she started out on her triumphant journey to the capital. Nicholas Bacon, already at Ipswich with his wife Ann, knew that the letter in his possession need never be delivered. William Cecil, glancing at the little group of ladies waiting upon Queen Mary, saw that Ann Bacon was of the company. If heads were to roll during the coming reign, neither William Cecil's nor Nicholas Bacon's would be amongst them.

The months that followed were probably the most agonising and humiliating of Ann Bacon's life, and were to leave a lasting impression upon her. Her husband was safe, but he had lost stature in her eyes; loyalty to a mortal princess had proved stronger than his belief in a Protestant God. The father she revered and loved was a prisoner, and her greatest fear was that the axe would fall upon him as it did later upon Northumberland, the Dudleys, and many of their friends. In the event he was spared, and managed to leave the country and reach Strasbourg, where he remained for four years.

Nicholas Bacon was allowed to continue in his position as Attorney of the Court of Wards, but he was forbidden to leave the country, lest he should make common cause with Protestant exiles abroad. He divided his time between Bedfords, a house on the Gidea Hall estate, Redgrave in Suffolk, and his London house in Noble Street, Foster Lane. It was at one of these three that Ann gave birth to her first baby, a daughter, and, like her sister Mildred, she too knew the full sorrow of bringing a child into the world and losing it a few months later. She wondered, afterwards, whether the choice of the name Mary for the little girl, which her husband Nicholas had insisted would be wise amd diplomatic, was the reason for the child's untimely death. Surely, she argued, the God she worshipped must have been displeased that an infant, dedicated by its mother to His service, should have been named for a Catholic queen.

Chapter 2

While the axe fell on Protestant heads, and the fires of Smithfield burnt their bodies, Nicholas Bacon, like his brother-in-law William Cecil, took care not to become too involved in public affairs. Both remained for the most part in the country, making additions to their estates at Redgrave and Burghley, dabbling with other properties, buying, selling, leasing, the modest incomes on which they had started out in life gradually doubling, trebling in size. Sheep-farming was another profitable concern—Bacon, the son of a yeoman farmer, could advise William Cecil on this—and through his position as Attorney of the Court of Wards he was able to purchase certain wardships himself. The custom was that every minor who was heir to land held by the old feudal knight service became, on the death of his father, a ward of the Crown. The Crown held the land and the rights of marriage, but through the Court of Wards was empowered to offer the wardship to the highest bidder. Although Nicholas Bacon later protested strongly against the abuses that frequently occurred in this marketing of minors, it was nevertheless a sound form of investment.

Meanwhile, he had three sons of his own to educate and put through Cambridge before entering them for Gray's Inn. The great school chamber at Redgrave was hardly large enough for Nicholas, Nathaniel and Edward, let alone a sprinkling of wards. The supervision of the hall, the great parlour, the little parlour, some twenty rooms for the use of the family and an equal number for the servants, with dry kitchens, wet kitchens, pantry and bakehouse—though not the outbuildings, the fish-ponds and the deer-park— had taken a toll of his first wife's health, along with bearing six children, and Nicholas Bacon resolved that it must not do the same to his second wife Ann.

11

Nevertheless, she found the role of stepmother onerous. None of the boys was academically inclined or interested in book-learning, and as for sitting down and reading a page of Greek or Latin, or listening to a sermon, they turned sullen at once, and made every excuse to withdraw. Nicholas, already conscious of his position as eldest son and heir to Redgrave, turned most of his attention to farming, while Nathaniel had a good head for figures. Edward was amenable enough, but no intellectual. As to the girls, she saw to it that they were trained in the usual feminine accomplishments, and would know how to order their own households when the time arrived and a good match was arranged for them; meanwhile they made poor companions, the conversation between the sisters on a much lower level than it had been in the old days with her own sisters at Gidea Hall. If only her ill-named little daughter had lived, she would doubtless have lisped her way through the Greek alphabet before she had turned eighteen months.

Then Ann became pregnant again, and to her joy this baby also proved to be a girl, who would take the place of the poor dead Mary. William Cecil was godfather. The child was christened Susan, and surely there could be nothing unlucky in that. The Cecils and the Bacons exchanged visits, and while the brothers-in-law admired each other's properties of Burghley and Redgrave—which was now finally completed—resolving perhaps to add yet another wing on returning home and so astonish one another on a subsequent visit, the sisters were able to test the precocity of little Susan against Mildred's small daughter Anne— which was the better-grown, who was likely to walk first. When their husbands were well out of earshot, they exclaimed over the difficulty of disciplining stepsons, young Thomas Cecil being as indifferent to his books as Nicholas and Nathaniel Bacon. It would be very different, they agreed, should the sisters themselves be blessed with sons at some future date.

In the summer of 1557 there was sickness in both families. The Cecils were at their house in Wimbledon and the Bacons apparently at Bedfords in Essex, close to Gidea Hall. The younger Cooke sisters, Elizabeth and Margaret, were also staying at Wimbledon under Mildred's wing. They were both of them to make good marriages the following year: Elizabeth to Thomas Hoby, a promising diplomat and a close friend of William Cecil's, who had inherited Bisham estate from his half-brother Philip, ambassador to the Imperial Court during the reigns of Henry VIII and Edward VI; and Margaret to Sir Ralph Rowlett, a wealthy landowner in Hertfordshire. The middle sister, Katherine, may have gone abroad with her father, where she would have met another Protestant exile, Sir Henry Killigrew. In any event she was married to him a few years later. On August 18th 1557 a letter from Nicholas Bacon to William Cecil gives the family news.

"I and my wife thank you of your letter, and are glad that my sister Margaret hath for health's sake gotten liberty, and of my sister Elizabeth's recovery; your goddaughter, thanks be to God, is somewhat amended, her fits being more easy, but not delivered of any. It is a double tertian [ague] that holds her, and her nurse has a single, but it is gone clearly."

Ann adds a postscript.

"We at Bedfords are no less glad of Wimbledon's welfare and especially of little Nan, trusting for all this shrewd fever to see her and mine playfellows many times. Thus wishing continuance of all good things to you at once because your man hasteth away and my husband to dinner,

"Your loving sister,
"A. Bacon."

Alas, the cousins were never to be playfellows. Anne Cecil, the little Nan of the letter, survived, but Susan Bacon did not. The figures of the two small sisters, Mary and Susan Bacon, can be seen stamped on the family tree of Nicholas and Ann Bacon, wearing flounced dresses and small caps on their heads, Mary holding a feeding bottle, Susan carrying a doll in her right hand.

This second death was an even greater blow to their mother than the first. Susan had lived longer than Mary and had won her heart, showing such promise; how had Ann sinned, how had she offended God? She took no pleasure any longer in the great house at Redgrave, which seemed more and more to belong to her stepchildren, and found greater peace, if peace was possible in an age when Catholicism triumphed and the Queen had the Spanish King as consort, in her husband's London house. Her beloved father was still abroad, helped financially by his son-in-law Bacon, who arranged the sale of a manor on his behalf. Cooke's other son-in-law, Cecil, as surveyor to the lands of the Princess Elizabeth, was able to pay discreet visits to Hatfield, where the Princess had her establishment; far-sighted as ever, he knew that Queen Mary was a sick, possibly a dying woman, and that to win the trust and esteem of her successor was a necessary step not only in his own career and those of his relatives and friends, but for the future safety of the realm.

Ann Bacon was too sick at heart to look ahead to the time when her brother-in-law and her husband might rise to favour under yet another sovereign. More than three hundred Protestant martyrs had been burnt at the stake, and it was said that bystanders, from pity at their sufferings, sometimes attached bags of gunpowder to the necks of the victims so that they might die swiftly and not endure the fierce torture of the flames. Great and humble, none had done wrong except to hold firm to the Reformed faith. How, she wondered, could she bear to bring yet another child into the world, very possibly to die in infancy like its sisters, or, if it survived, fated to be brought up in an England where Protestants were persecuted and burnt as heretics, where men like her father and John Cheke were forced to live abroad, bereft of status, penniless?

When their son was born in 1558, the month and birthplace alike unrecorded, and they named him Anthony, it was as though her father called to her from exile across the seas and bade her take courage. The child would live, must live. Delicate from birth like his sisters, still she would rear him, cosset him, guide him, nurture him in the faith that had so long sustained her, train him in infancy, discipline him in boyhood, so that when, God willing, he reached man's estate he would prove the embodiment of all the qualities she prized. Should he become a great Reforming preacher, possibly even another Calvin, it would be to his mother that he would owe his strength of character, his zeal.

If the boy's arrival gave renewed faith to Ann, the year of his birth brought a change of fortune to Nicholas Bacon, to the Cecil family, and to the great mass of the English people. Queen Mary died on November 17th, and joy was overwhelming throughout the kingdom. The dread of Spanish tyranny was at an end. The exiles could return from abroad.

William Cecil became Secretary of State, and on December 22nd, a month after Elizabeth's accession, the new Queen made Nicholas Bacon Lord Keeper of the Great Seal and a member of the privy council, and knighted him for good measure. Prudently, sagaciously, the brothers-in-law had climbed the political ladder side by side and had reached the top.

Her father safe home in England, her husband firmly installed in a position of great authority, with the duties of a Lord Chancellor combining also recommendations in Church matters—his close friend Matthew Parker was shortly afterwards enthroned as Archbishop of Canterbury, achieving with almost Baconian discretion the alteration from the Roman Mass to an Anglican Holy Communion—Ann's rejoicing was subdued by yet another family tragedy. Her youngest sister Margaret, who had been married only a few months before, died very suddenly barely a fortnight before Nicholas was appointed Keeper of the Great Seal. Margaret, who had been Sir Ralph Rowlett's second wife, was buried beside her predecessor, and soon afterwards Nicholas Bacon was negotiating with the bereaved widower for his manor of Gorhambury. Now that he had become Lord Keeper, the dignity of his position necessitated a further elevation in his mode of living. He had sold the house in Noble Street and leased York House by Charing Cross, with a fine frontage down to the river, but he needed a country property as well, and one that was nearer to London than Redgrave in Suffolk. Ralph Rowlett's farmlands, close to St Albans in Hertfordshire, would suit him very well, and he could indulge his hobby of building by erecting a new house on the site of the existing one.

His eldest son Nicholas, now nineteen, was ripe for marriage, and negotiations were soon under way to procure for him an heiress who would bring him money and land as well. Young Nicholas and his bride could live at Redgrave, and his father would settle the entail upon him and any sons he might produce. His remaining children by his first wife should also be settled well as time went on, and make equally good marriages; but now, as Lord Keeper, living in York House with a large retinue of retainers, almost like a miniature Court, Sir Nicholas Bacon felt that he owed it to his second wife Ann, who had stood by him during the troublous reign of the late Queen, to build a house for her which, unlike Redgrave, she could feel would be her own, and the inheritance of their young son Anthony, if God was pleased to spare him—and that the delicate boy might not survive must sometimes have seemed agonizingly possible. When the boy was about two years old Sir Nicholas Bacon wrote in a letter dated June 17th 1560 that his son "was recovering from a dangerous fever". Seven months later Ann gave birth to a second son, born at York House and baptised Francis on January 25th at St Martin-in-the-Fields. Anthony now had a blood-brother to compete for his mother's affection.

The building of the new mansion at Gorhambury did not start until 1563 and took some five years to complete, so the early years of the little boys were spent at York House. They cannot have seen much of their father, who was by now heavily engaged in affairs of State, and at times opposed to the advice given to Queen Elizabeth by his brother-in-law William Cecil. He was against aiding the Protestants in Scotland to rebel against their Catholic Queen Mary, a course urged by the Secretary of State, and suggested that delay would be more prudent until it was clearly seen what action France would take. Two years later Sir Nicholas was pressing for an alliance with the Protestant King Anthony of Navarre, who was in conflict with Catherine de Medici, the Catholic Regent of France.

Speaking on home affairs, at the opening of Parliament in 1563, Bacon professed himself disturbed by the laxity of religious observances in the country. Ann Bacon very naturally endorsed her husband's opinion: prayers in her own household opened and closed the day, the little boys no sooner up on their legs in the morning than they were down again upon their knees, and woe betide Anthony if he toppled over from sheer exhaustion, or was more likely pinched where it most hurt by his mischievous younger brother. Rows of servants, ranging from steward to scullion, attended with bowed heads, the major-domo being Sir Nicholas Bacon's own cousin, imported from Suffolk to act as treasurer and hold the purse-strings. Later, at Gorhambury, a chaplain became a regular member of the household, one of these being Robert Johnson, a Puritan who was later suspended from duty for being a Nonconformist. Nicholas Bacon, tolerant in so many ways, was not entirely unshaken by the influence of his second wife. "Nothing should be advised or done," he said in one of his speeches, "that might in any way breed or nourish any kind of idolatry or superstition, so heed must be taken lest, by licentious or loose handling, any occasion were given whereby contempt or irreverent behavior towards God and godly things might creep in."

This was the kind of sentiment, Ann Bacon felt, which must surely atone for her husband's years of silence when Queen Mary reigned. Fired by his friend John Jewel, Bishop of Salisbury, who had written in Latin a lengthy *Apologia for the Church of England* as a counter-blast to the many Catholic treatises published abroad, she undertook the task of translating the *Apologia* into English, so that the common people might read it. When she had finished she sent the results to Bishop Jewel and to the Archbishop of Canterbury, together with a letter in Greek to the former. Both prelates were astonished at the accuracy of the translation and the modesty of the sender. "She had done pleasure," wrote the Archbishop, "to the author of the Latin book, in delivering him, by her clear translation, from the perils of ambiguous and doubtful constructions." She had also "raised up great comfort to her friends, and had furnished her own conscience joyfully with the fruit of her labour, in so occupying her time. Which must needs redound to the encouragement of noble youth in their good education, and to spend their time and knowledge in godly exercise, she having delivered them so singular a precedent." The work was printed in 1564.

The little boys, Anthony and Francis, were now obliged to listen not only to their mother's translation of the Italian sermons, begun so many years ago, but to Bishop Jewel's *Apologia* as well. This in addition to other sermons, besides the compulsory lessons in Latin and Greek. What a relief to run down to the Thames and watch the gay life of the river instead! Fishermen spreading their nets, watermen ferrying folk from bank to bank, barges travelling downstream towards London Bridge, the washerwomen thumping their linen on flat stones.

Or better still to journey by coach to Gorhambury with their father, when he could spare the time, and watch the progress of their new country home. Quarrymen, bricklayers, tile-makers, masons, and as the house took shape the carpenters and joiners appeared, glaziers, plasterers, a whole tribe of workmen with ladders and barrows, laughing, joking, singing, good-naturedly permitting the small brothers to climb up and down, to dirty their hands, to tear their stockings, while Sir Nicholas stood some way off, discussing his plan for the lay-out of the gardens, which he hoped would rival those of his brother-in-law William Cecil at Burghley.

He decided that Gorhambury should be built of flint and stone, the rooms compact, the main front facing south, about 115 feet long, flanked by octagonal towers. In the centre would be a porch and archway passing through a cloister into a court, and at the north end of the court the hall. East of the hall he would have buttery and kitchens, and to the west a chapel. East and west of the court would be the main rooms of the house. Above the main entry his family motto would be inscribed just as it was at Redgrave, *Mediocria firma* (Moderate things endure). And when the work was completed he would inscribe in stone

> *Haec cum perfecit Nicolaus tecta Baconus,*
> *Elizabeth regni lustra fuerit duo,*
> *Factus equis magni custos ipse sigilli,*
> *Gloria sit soli tota tributa Deo.*

A strking amenity was the system which involved bringing water through a leaden pipe 1¼ miles from its source up to the higher ground on which the mansion stood. The pumping engine must have had considerable force to do its work satisfactorily. Nicholas Bacon may well have borrowed this idea from his brother-in-law Sir Thomas Hoby, who had done the same thing at Bisham. Possibly Elizabeth Hoby, discussing household matters with her sister Ann Bacon as a change from her own Latin and Greek verse—for she herself was no mean performer—

may have suggested the innovation. In any event, the house was ready for the family to take up residence in 1568, in time for Anthony's tenth birthday.

The long cloister, with the great gallery above, was added nearly eight years later, in order to impress the Queen when she visited Gorhambury for the second time, since she had observed to her host, on an earlier visit, "My Lord Keeper, what a little house you have gotten," to which he made his famous reply, "My house is well, Madam, but you have made me too great for my house."

Tradition ascribes the fine terra-cotta busts of Sir Nicholas and his lady to the time of one of the Queen's two visits, and suggests that the bust of the small boy that was found alongside them in the gallery must be that of their younger son Francis. Yet the costume of all three busts would seem to be 1565 or thereabouts. If so, then the bust would be of Anthony. In 1565 he would have been seven years old, which the appearance of the boy in the bust suggests. Whether Anthony or Francis, the boy has a strong likeness to his mother about the nose and mouth, though the eyes are different, more slanted, like those of the Lord Keeper. Sir Nicholas would have been fifty-four in 1565 and Ann thirty seven, and certainly these appear to be the ages of husband and wife as represented by the busts. The question of the boy's identity, whether Anthony or Francis, will probably never be solved.

The Lord Keeper had time to sit for an artist during that particular period, and to supervise the building of Gorhambury, for he had fallen temporarily under the Queen's displeasure and been banished from Court. A pamphlet on the succession had been published, passing over the claims of Mary Stuart of Scotland in favour of Lady Catherine Grey, sister of the unfortunate Lady Jane, and the Lord Keeper was said either to have published the pamphlet under a pseudonym or to be compromised in some way in its issue. The Queen was furious, told him the succession was none of his affair, and warned him that if he meddled further he would be dismissed from her service. Sir Nicholas, discomfited, retired to the country, and when some months later he was restored to the royal favour he declared himself as upholding the claims of the House of Stuart, but not that of the Scottish Queen herself, who had forfeited her rights by her actions.

Meantime, with her stepsons thankfully adult and no longer any responsibility of hers—Nicholas at Redgrave married to his heiress, Nathaniel settled at the manor his father had bought for him at Stiffkey in Norfolk and married likewise to yet another Anne, the natural daughter of the Queen's financier Sir Thomas Gresham, and Edward mixing in doubtful company at Gray's Inn—Ann Bacon was able to concentrate on the education of her own two boys.

Sometimes at York House, sometimes at Gorhambury, occasionally perhaps with their grandfather Sir Anthony Cooke at Gidea Hall (where he entertained the Queen in 1568, having rebuilt his house, inspired possibly by the creative efforts of his sons-in-laws Cecil, Bacon and Hoby), the boys do not appear to have received any formal education outside the home. Certainly, as sons of the Lord Keeper, they would have been well informed of current events, both in their own country and across the sea: the escape of Mary Queen of Scotland, imprisoned in Lochleven Castle, into England, for instance, and their father's anxiety lest her influence should harm the cause of Protestantism in England. Occasionally his speeches annoyed the Queen, and once she told him that his councils were like himself, rash and dangerous—a strange rebuke to such a prudent man.

The boys would hear discussions about confusion in France, with Catholics and Huguenots continually at each other's throats, and Queen Catherine de Medici still holding the reins of power and having total sway over her son, the young Charles IX. It is less likely that Court gossip came to their ears, for their mother would have kept them out of the way of hearing it. Her two sons were never allowed to forget the little sisters who had gone before and now, robed in white, looked down from heaven upon their brothers. The image this conjured was not altogether consoling, disturbing privacy, as Anthony approached puberty. He was aware that his mother's eye was continually upon him, probing, accusing, insisting that he should set a better example to young Francis, who, slippery as mercury, was able to efface himself when they heard her footstep outside their room. He was an avid reader, but there were certain books she frowned upon—the French poets Ronsard and du Bellay, and the Italian Petrarch, and Anthony was obliged to conceal from her the fact that he preferred his uncle Hoby's translation of Castiglione's *Il Cortegiano,* an account of the life and education of a gentleman at the ducal court of Urbino, to her own tracts. Nor did she approve of his habit of hanging about the stables, and laughing and chatting with stable-boys and grooms. Both boys were too free and easy in their manners, and this must be curbed.

No one could be more suited to do this than the Dutch schoolmaster at the St Albans grammar school, a Presbyterian, who would come across to Gorhambury when his duties permitted and instill some of his own piety into her wayward sons. Especially as her own household chaplain Robert Johnson had been admonished by the Archbishop of Canterbury for not subscribing to the Prayer Book, and in his excellent defence had said, "Sir Nicholas Bacon needs Christian help regarding his youthful retinue, among whom all manner of vices do increase apace, and zeal, virtue, and the true fear of God decrease through lack of due admonition and instruction."

Small wonder that Anthony, at fourteen, suffered some sort of psychological illness. He said in after years that he had nearly lost the sight of both eyes at this time, but gave no explanation of the cause.

There is no record of the elder boy being present when the Queen paid her first visit to Gorhambury in 1572 and remarked that the house was small, but young Francis was undoubtedly there, for it was upon this occasion that the Queen, asking his age, was told by the precocious eleven-year-old, "Just three years younger than your Majesty's happy reign"—a remark that would have been repeated in triumph by his gratified mother to her sister Mildred, whose only surviving son Robert was now seven, and although very much undersized, with one shoulder higher than the other, was reputedly as quick-witted as his cousin.

His father, William Cecil, had been created Baron Burghley of Burghley the preceding year, and in November 1572 was appointed to the post of Lord Treasurer to the Queen. The Cecils were riding high: Mildred, as Lady Burghley, would take precedence over Lady Bacon, and their great house of Theobalds, Cheshunt—William having purchased an estate there from a Hertfordshire landowner

Robert Burbage, in 1564—bid fair to rival Gorhambury. Sir Nicholas Bacon certainly had to build a cloister and a long gallery on to his own house if he was to keep in step with his brother-in-law.

In any event, the Lord Keeper decided that it was time Anthony entered university. It might be that his health would improve at Cambridge and, placed in the care of Bishop Whitgift, Master of Trinity, he would make better progress in his studies. Francis, although he would be barely twelve in April, should accompany his brother, if only to keep him out of mischief at home. The younger boy was too pert in many ways, too fond of airing his knowledge. So in April 1573 Anthony and Francis Bacon, along with Edward Tyrrell, one of the Lord Keeper's wards, entered Trinity College, Cambridge, lodging under the Master's roof.

Chapter 3

The Bacon brothers remained at Trinity for approximately three years, apart from one long break from August 1574 until the following March, when the university appears to have been closed because of plague. No records exist of their studies, the progress they made, or whether they proved themselves to be intellectually in advance of their fellows. The only documents extant are the account books of John Whitgift, Master of Trinity College, and in these ledgers the careful and orderly Bishop, later to hold the see of Canterbury itself, noted down every expense from candles and sacks of coals to mending apparel and garters. No item was too minute to be included, no sum judged too trifling to insert, and from these accounts it is possible to glean something of the life led by the boys, what they read, how they dressed, their amusements when not at study, and how often they fell sick.

The cold, crisp air of Cambridge was perhaps not so healthy as the Lord Keeper had hoped, for very soon after their arrival the Master was paying out twelve shillings and sixpence for "Anthonie being syck", and then ten shillings and threepence more "in the tyme of hys syckness." Almost immediately afterwards there is a bill for three pairs of shoes and for bringing a cloak-bag from London—one of the grooms, perhaps, coming post-haste from York House—but by then Anthony must have been on his feet again, for the Master was obliged to buy two bows, arrows, quivers, and shooting-gloves, as well as arrows for Mr Tyrrell. Ann Bacon would have clicked her tongue in disapproval. No books? Yes, Titus Livius, Cicero, and the orations of Demosthenes, also Homer's *Iliad* and Caesar. So a certain amount of study was being done. Horse-play between-times, very evidently, for there is "mending a doublet for Anthony" and "mending a gowne for Tyrrell", then "mending curtains" and tables and desks in their room, and young Francis was obliged to have "oyle" for his neck and "meate when he was syck," so Anthony was not the only one to be cosseted by the Master.

The word "commons" occurs frequently, referring to the daily dinner eaten in hall with the other scholars, but breakfasts were taken in their own rooms, where heating and lighting were extra. There are bills for their own coal-houses and woodhouses, where the locks were always getting broken, while candles and candlesticks were one of the heaviest items marked on the ledger. More reading was done in the autumn and winter terms; there are two Aristotles and two Platos in the autumn account for 1573, a Xenophon, a Latin Bible for Anthony, and, making respite from this intensive study, "stringes for a lute". (In later years Anthony was to possess not only a lute but the virginals as well, which suggests that he was the musician on this occasion.)

A fourth companion joined them in the latter part of the year, a Mr Griffiths, and then a Mr Whitaker. The bills for suppers increased and the candles burnt fiercely too. Needless to say, after one of these supper celebrations "Anthonie syck" appears, and 23s. 6d. had to be spent "in the tyme of Anthonies syckness for meate and other things". The lad was generous with his purse, for in January of the following year, 1574, we have "gyvne by Anthonie at the christening of Mr Anger his childe, fifteen shillings". Then, to make up for lost time when ill, "a standing desk for Anthonie studie, with fyve shelves, a cubbert of waynscot, peynted clothes, and a chare".

Eighteen shillings for a breast of mutton and boiled mutton seems dear, but possibly here was another celebration, for following upon the feast, or perhaps in honour of it, are shoes for all the boys, the lining of three hats, the mending of their hose, and best of all "a yard of mockado to make them sclalions". Mockado (and this on the good authority of the late Ivor Brown) was mohair, but sclalions defeats interpretation. The image that presents itself is of three lively lads, new-shod and hosed and wearing beaver hats, with yards of mockado somewhere about their persons, all slightly the worse for tippling, and Anthony, his Latin Bible put aside, strumming upon the re-strung lute.

The year progresses, with mention of cloak-bags from

London, three dinners and suppers before young Mr Whitaker went home, and "meate from the Dolphin whiles Anthonie was syck". Also "almond mylke for Anthonie". The apothecary's bill was 15s. A mouse-trap and an "eurinall" are odd items to be entered side by side, but doubtless both were necessary. And while the boys studied and played, read their Greek and Latin, and vomited from time to time, especially Anthony, what was going on at home and in the world outside the university?

Appalled by the Massacre of St Bartholomew in the August before his sons went up to Cambridge, when the Paris streets had run with Huguenot blood, the Lord Keeper had supported a bill in Parliament for the expulsion of all French residents in England. This made him the target of every Catholic living in the country or on the continent. Nevertheless the slaughter of four thousand Huguenots had roused universal horror throughout the whole of England. It was said that Queen Elizabeth went into mourning, and Sir Francis Walsingham, the ambassador to Paris, wished to give secret subsidies to the Huguenots. Lord Treasurer Burghley advised the Queen against so strong a measure, which would jeopardise the alliance with France.

Meanwhile, despite the massacre, there was speculation on Elizabeth's possible marriage to the duc d'Alençon (shortly to become the duc d'Anjou), the younger brother of King Charles IX of France, who was said to favour the Huguenots; and all the while the Queen kept her other favourites dangling, the Earl of Leicester and Sir Christopher Hatton, with Leicester having liaisons on the side.

No flirtations went on in the households of Lord Treasurer Burghley and Lord Bacon. Even had they been so inclined—and no such rumour was ever breathed about either of them—their wives Mildred and Ann would soon have stifled any rising flame of dubious passion. Burghley, who was by this time Master of the Court of Wards, kept what was virtually a school for the sons of noblemen under his roof, taking a personal interest in the curriculum. The young Earl of Oxford, who had married Burghley's daughter Anne, was proving a disaster as a son-in-law; he drank too much, had homosexual tendencies and admitted he was an atheist. Burghley's son Thomas, the only child of his first marriage, who as a youth had appeared inclined to dissipation, had now settled down to marriage and family life, and had taken part in the war with Scotland, but he was never to show any intellectual ability. This was reserved for Robert Cecil, Burghley's son by Mildred, who was already as keen-witted, if not so outwardly precocious, as his cousin Francis, son of the Lord Keeper and Ann Bacon. Already when the boys met, at Theobalds or at Gorhambury, there was little friendship between the cousins. A mutual antipathy grew which developed with maturity, and despite surface courtesy, doubtless assumed for their mothers' sakes, the rivalry was there, deep-seated if unspoken.

The relationship was easier between the Bacon brothers and their Hoby cousins, the two sons of their aunt Elizabeth. Edward Hoby was only a year younger than Anthony, light-weight but intelligent, amusing, and interested in the arts, while Thomas Posthumous, born after his father had died in Paris in 1566 (hence his name), was a few years Francis's junior, and, like his other cousin Robert Cecil, undersized, with one shoulder higher than the other. Their mother Elizabeth had married again, her second husband being Lord John Russell, heir to the Earl of Bedford: and when a daughter of this second marriage was born Queen Elizabeth was godmother. This was a triumph sisters Mildred and Ann had never achieved.

With the plague closing down the University of Cambridge for several months during 1574-75, Anthony and Francis returned to Gorhambury, to seek relief from boredom as they might, under their mother's watchful eye. No flaunting of mockado at home, no dining and supping with gay young gentlemen. Anthony must begin to take an active interest in the estate which would one day be his, instead of poring with his brother over old maps of the Roman city of Verulamium, as it had once been, and tracing the tribal areas where Cunobelin, or Cymbeline, had ruled before the Roman invasion. Nor was it tactful for Francis to mention, in the presence of their parents, the fact that the only Englishman ever to occupy the Papal chair, from 1154 to 1159, had been one Nicholas Breakspear, otherwise Adrian IV, born near St Albans. Instead, it was time to plan Anthony's marriage, and on December 16th 1574 the Lord Keeper signed an agreement with one James Paget of Grove Place, Southampton, the son of a wealthy London

merchant and alderman, who had also been sheriff of the
city of London. This James Paget had been married three
times, each wife being very well connected and an heiress
in her own right. The bride he offered to the Lord Keeper
for Anthony was Dowsabell, the only child of his second
wife. Anthony was sixteen, Dowsabell, a year or so younger.
The marriage would take place in five months' time, in May
of 1575. The young couple would have an allowance of
£75 for the next three years, and the Lord Keeper promised £100 a year, various leases, and a further £500.
James Paget offered an estate of £314 a year, after his
own death and that of his wife. James Paget was so certain
of his future son-in-law that he placed an heraldic shield,
combining the arms of Cooke of Gidea Hall and Bacon of
Redgrave, in the gallery of Grove Place, alongside the
shields of the other distinguished families to whom he was
allied.

However decorative the effect, the gesture was premature,
for in the event there was no marriage the following May.
The university opened again in March, and the Master of
Trinity was back at his ledgers once more. "For carriage
from London, and for mending of Anthonie his hat",
3s. 11d. Perhaps the lad flung it in the air with relief to be
out of range of the parental eye and of Miss Dowsabell
Paget. The attentions of the apothecary were not needed,
but the boys were beginning to think about their appearance. Two dozen "silk poyntes" for Anthony, the same for
Francis, pantofles and pumps, shoes and slippers, and as
summer passes and autumn sets in the glazing of Francis's
chamber windows, candles and coals, a dozen buttons for
Francis's doublet and for "setting them on"; and then on
December 4th Anthony must have kept his room again, for
he was "out of commons", and this continued until the 9th.

The ledger for the Bacon brothers closes on December
23rd 1575 with a note saying, "I have paid to D. Perne
[Doctor?] for bokes bowght for my L. keeper which he
bestowed upon the universitie, so all ys quit."

Anthony was now entering his eighteenth year, and
Francis, who would be fifteen on January 21st, already
showed proof of a sharp and brilliant intellect. He queried
everything he had been taught, from philosophy to science,
and perhaps this was the reason why there is no record of
his having taken a degree. Any similar failing on Anthony's

part was put down to his delicate health. The problem was, what was their future to be? The law, like their father? In any event, they must enter Gray's Inn as their half-brothers had done before them.

The Gray's Inn admission register states that Anthony and Francis Bacon were admitted on June 27th 1576, and being the sons of a judge had the honour of entering immediately into the Grand Company of Ancients. This status gave them an advantage over fellow-students of the law who had entered from grammar school or university without such privilege. Indeed, it was possible to be an Ancient without the intention of following the legal profession, but "for persons of distinction to form their manners and preserve them from the contagion of vice".

The Lord Keeper had his own set of chambers ready furnished for those of his sons who chose to occupy them. Nicholas and Nathaniel being by this time married, there was only Edward, the third son of his first marriage, who seems to have been at Gray's Inn when his half-brothers arrived. Edward was now twenty-eight, good-natured and well-liked by the two youngsters, but it was his intention to tour the continent like many of his contemporaries, and he was waiting a favourable occasion to do so.

The quadrangle at Gray's Inn was closed on the far side by buildings which lay adjacent to the hall. It was in these buildings, directly opposite the gateway, that the Bacon sons had their lodgings. There was a large library on the first floor. The great hall was both refectory and lecture-room, with a carved gallery at the lower end. The hearth was in the centre of the rush-strewn floor. The members met here for meals, for it was not permitted to eat in chambers. Discipline was stricter at Gray's Inn than at any of the other Inns of Court, and there were many rules about dress. Caps and gowns must be worn in commons, and boots, cloaks, hats, long hair, and for a time beards were excluded, like-wise spurs and swords. No mention of "silken pointes" or "mockado", and Anthony, who at a later date was spending a small fortune on beaver hats, must have found the restrictions trying.

When they were admitted, however, they would have been in mourning, for their grandfather, Sir Anthony Cooke, had died sixteen days earlier. He was buried in

great style at Romford in Essex, and a monument with
Latin and English verses upon it placed to his memory. His
loss was deeply felt by his surviving daughters, especially
Ann, whose religious fervour for the Protestant faith was
increasing rather than diminishing with the years. She inclined more and more to ministers with Puritan sympathies,
insisting that her husband should appoint them not only as
chaplains in her household but to those living in Hertfordshire that came within his gift.

The Lord Keeper was now sixty-five, his wife forty-eight,
and Sir Nicholas in particular was showing signs of approaching age. He had for some time been tormented by
gout, and, never one for exercise, had put on considerable
weight. A fine, upstanding man in middle years, he now
moved with difficulty, even his features becoming swollen,
and his massive head seemed shrunken into his shoulders.
He made a joke of this to his friends, and the Queen said
"that the Lord Keeper's soul lodged well", but it was no
joking matter in the privacy of his home, and his health
began to be a constant anxiety to his wife. She counselled
him not to drink between meals, or after supper, or at
bedward or in the night, and to "wash out his mouth with a
gargolyn glass". Almond milk brought relief, the same
remedy that Anthony had tried at Cambridge. The Lord
Keeper would also sit up to his loins in a bath filled with a
mixture of water, milk and herbs for as long as two hours.
The "stone" was an added complaint racking him with
pain from time to time.

He was a man of great courage, and seldom complained,
but he realised that his disability would increase, and he
wished to see the more brilliant of his two young sons
gain some experience in diplomatic circles, preferably
abroad, before his own health worsened. Francis could then
choose between a diplomatic career and the legal profession. So when Amias Paulet, son of Sir Hugh Paulet the
governor of Jersey, returned to the mainland after some
twelve years as lieutenant of the island under his father,
where as a convinced Puritan he had been engaged in re-
pressing those who upheld the Catholic faith, and in
August was knighted by the Queen and made ambassador
to the French court—replacing Sir Francis Walsingham,
who had been recalled to become Secretary of State—the

Lord Keeper deemed it an excellent opportunity to have young Francis join his retinue.

The Queen approved the plan, as did Sir Amias, and there was some idea that Francis's half-brother Edward should also be of the company. Edward himself was of a contrary opinion. At twenty-eight he had no desire to follow an ambassadorial train merely to keep a watchful eye on the precocious Francis, but preferred to travel on his own in more amusing company, and find his way to such places as Padua, Ravenna and Vienna. He slipped off before his father became too insistent. There seems to have been no question of Anthony accompanying either party. The Lord Keeper and his wife thought it advisable that the heir to Gorhambury and the various other manors in Hertfordshire should remain in England.

In the third week of September 1576 Sir Amias Paulet, his lady Margaret and a retinue of followers, including the fifteen-year-old Francis, departed for Calais, and Anthony, left behind as companion to his father and his increasingly dictatorial mother, uninterested in either his legal studies at Gray's Inn or the management of the Hertfordshire estates, wondered how much he was missing: whether the French court under the new King Henri III—who had recently succeeded to the throne on the death of his brother Charles IX—was really as brilliant, and as decadent, as people whispered; whether his own hero, the French King's brother-in-law, twenty-five-year-old Henri of Navarre, head of the Huguenots, who had made his escape from Paris six months previously to his own kingdom near the Pyrenees, was as great a leader and as fine a horseman as he was reputed to be by all who followed him; whether Francis at the French court would meet poets and painters as well as courtiers; and whether Edward in Padua and Ravenna might fare even better. Meanwhile, with a sigh, back to his studies, missing his lively young brother but too devoted to be envious, and very thankful for the friendship of a new companion, three years senior to him, one Edward Selwyn of Friston Place, West Dean, in Sussex, who had been admitted to Gray's Inn in 1573.

Francis might be learning the finer arts of diplomacy in Paris and Blois, watching Henri III, that most astute of monarchs, play off the various factions of his subjects one against the other, bow to the wishes of the Queen Mother one minute, lend an attentive ear to his powerful cousins the Guises the next, all the while surrounding himself with his band of frilled and perfumed followers, *"les mignons"*, whose influence in the royal bedchamber and out of it was the scandal of Court circles; but in Hertfordshire the great event of the year for Lord Keeper Sir Nicholas Bacon and his lady was the visit of Queen Elizabeth to Gorhambury on Saturday May 27th 1577, a visit which began before supper and lasted until after dinner the following Wednesday.

When the Queen had appeared at the Lord Keeper's country home before it had been for the day only, and even then he had written to his brother-in-law Burghley in a state of panic when he first heard rumours of the approaching visit. "If it be true, then I might understand your advice what you think to be the best way for me to deal in the matter, for in very deed, no man is more raw in such a matter than myself." He had learnt some wisdom in five years. The great gallery with its painted windows had been built for just such an occasion, 120 feet long by 18 feet wide, with a decorated vaulted ceiling. Beneath were the cloisters, with a life-sized statue of the Queen's father Henry VIII wearing gilt armour, placed in a semi-domed niche between the central columns. Here the Queen and her host could pace up and down with measured tread—it is to be hoped the Lord Keeper's gout was kept at bay during the ordeal—and, should she desire some lighter form of entertainment, there was a ballroom added where musicians could play and the retinue of accompanying courtiers, including their royal mistress, dance.

Lady Bacon presided over the kitchens before the company arrived, and the fare was generous. She knew that comparisons would be made between her establishment and that of her sister Mildred at Theobalds. "Beer and ale in the buttery, wine of all kinds in the cellar, beef, mutton, veal, lambs, kids, all kinds of fowl from capons, pullets, chickens and geese to mallards, teals, larks and curlews. Sea fish of all kinds, freshwater fish. Bacon, tongues, cows' udders and calves' feet. Rabbits, butter, eggs, cream, milk and fruit. Salcery, for vinegar and verges, spicery for spices of all sorts, confectionery, in banqueting stuff. Herbs, flowers and artichokes. Woodhouse and coalhouse necessities." Further items on the exhaustive list were "Presents for officers of the Queen. Their carriage from London to Gorhambury and back again. Money to them of the Revels. To the cooks of London. For loss of pewter and napery. A cup presented to the Queen besides 25 bucks and 2 stags."

The cost of the visit was between one-fifth and one-sixth of the original cost of building Gorhambury itself.

How Francis, who would by now have mastered the French custom of bowing so low at the monarch's approach that his forehead touched the ground, would have excelled himself on this occasion had he been in England and not in France; and how Anthony must have flung himself upon his bed with pills from the apothecary and a draught of almond milk when it was over! If, indeed, he was ever present. He could have pleaded sudden illness, as he was invariably to do in later years when warned of a possible summons to the Queen's presence.

The Queen herself was said to be "highly gratified" by her visit, and by way of expressing her thanks to have sent her picture to hang in the long gallery. If the bejewelled, red-wigged, hook-nosed lady in the portrait that hangs in Gorhambury today is really Queen Elizabeth—and it bears small resemblance to any of her other well-known portraits—then Her Majesty insulted her hosts by palming off on them an indifferent likeness that she evidently preferred to have out of the way.

Alas for the Lord Keeper. He had barely eighteen months left in which to dwell on the memory of that great occasion, and to pace up and down the long gallery at Gorhambury. The image of death had preoccupied him during the plague year when the boys were home, and when he was endeavouring to arrange a marriage for Anthony. He saw himself lying, not at St Michael's by St Albans, but in St Paul's Cathedral, and with the Dean's compliance sent workmen to start building his tomb as early as 1574. On September 11th 1577 he made his will, and followed it up with another on December 23rd a year later.

January came in bitterly cold, with heavy falls of snow continuing until the end of the month. This was followed by a sudden thaw in February. The third week, it being warmer than usual, the Lord Keeper, installed for the winter at York House, desired his barber, who was shaving him, to open wide the windows. The man obeyed, and presently left his master seated in a chair, dozing. Waking some time later he found a current of fresh air blowing in upon him, and himself sweaty cold.

"Why," said he to his servant, "did you suffer me to sleep thus exposed?"

"I durst not presume to disturb you," replied the barber.

"Then," answered the Lord Keeper, "by your civility I lose my life."

He was carried to his bedchamber, and within a few days, on February 20th, he was dead. The morning he was taken ill Francis, in Paris, awoke from a shattering dream that he was standing before his home in Gorhambury to find it plastered all over with black mortar. The sense of foreboding did not leave him, and when a messenger from England arrived to see the ambassador Sir Amias Paulet, he knew what dread news had been brought. Several days later he returned to London, bringing a dispatch from the ambassador to the Queen in which Sir Amias stated that Francis was "endued with many good and singular parts and if God gave him life, would prove a very able and sufficient subject to do her Highness good and acceptable service".

On the morning of March 9th 1579 a crowd assembled outside York House by Charing Cross. The house was swathed in black, the curtains were draped at the windows, and black bays were hanging all round the outer courtyard. Black valances covered the widowed Lady Bacon's bed, and perfumed rushes were strewn upon the floor. It was now seventeen days since the two physicians, the two surgeons and the Queen's chandler had performed the necessary services. Staff from Redgrave, where the eldest son Nicholas Bacon and his wife and family resided, were in attendance, as well as Nathaniel and his household from Stiffkey in Norfolk, and the staff from Gorhambury and the other properties in Hertfordshire. The bells from St Martin-in-the-Fields tolled throughout the day, and from St Paul's Cathedral likewise. The tomb wherein the Lord Keeper was to be laid was next to that of John of Gaunt, "time-honoured Lancaster", by the express desire of the dead man.

The chief mourners were his brother-in-law Lord Treasurer Burghley (for whom twelve yards of black cloth had been ordered in the will), Mr Secretary Walsingham (who received eight yards of cloth), the Master of the Rolls, the

Attorney-General, the Solicitor-General, the Master of the
Queen's Jewel House, Sir Thomas Gresham, and brothers-
in-law William Cooke and Henry Killigrew. Accompanying
these personages were the five sons of the Lord Keeper,
Nicholas, Nathaniel, Edward (only lately returned from the
continent), Anthony and Francis. His daughters-in-law, his
three daughters by his first marriage (all married by now),
and the gentlewoman in attendance upon the widow had all
been provided with mourning garments in the will. But they
did not form part of the funeral procession to St Paul's.
Only the widow, mounted upon a horse draped in black,
followed the cortège.

The Lord Keeper's household comprised some seventy
persons: the steward, the seal bearer, the sergeant-at-arms,
the treasurer, auditor, receiver, secretary—these were all
senior officers. There were yeomen officers in charge of
cellar, pantry, kitchen, wardrobe, chamber, hall and lodge.
Then came the lesser servants, cleaners, grooms, and so on.

The procession went by horse and foot up the Strand
and Fleet Street. At the head were sixteen beadles, whose
function was to clear the street. Then came sixty-eight
poor men, who had been given mourning cloth for the
purpose and a shilling each for dinner, their number being
the same as the Lord Keeper's age. The household followed, and then the mourning relatives and friends. The
Lord Keeper's helm and crest, sword and coat-of-arms
were carried before the hearse, escorted by four heralds.
Last came the sons, mounted, with the widow.

In St Paul's Cathedral all was draped in black, pulpit,
arches and communion table, while the tomb of John of
Gaunt, the Lord Keeper's companion in death, had been
boarded up for the ceremony to prevent damage.

So finally Nicholas Bacon, son of a yeoman sheep-
farmer in Suffolk, was laid to rest, having served under
four monarchs and given a lifetime of service to the
Crown. His widow knew that public life for her was finished. She must quit York House, dismiss her London staff
and retire to Gorhambury with her son Anthony, there to
watch over him and see that he managed his estate in the
way she desired. Francis, just eighteen, with two and a half
years' experience in diplomatic circles and a distaste for
the society he had encountered at the French court—apart
from the poets and painters he had met, and the his-

torical associations with places such as Blois, Tours and Poitiers—knew, as his father's bier was borne before him, that there had been little or no provision made for him in the will, which was so drawn up that he must depend financially on his mother and his brother Anthony; and he knew also, as certainly as he had seen his home covered with black mortar in his dream, that one day, many years hence, he too would become Lord Keeper, he would wear the robes of Lord Chancellor, he would live once again at York House where he had been born, his retinue surpassing even that of his father, and no obstruction, no jealousy or envy, should stand in his way when his moment of power came.

And Anthony . . . Soon to be twenty-one, heir to estates in Hertfordshire and Middlesex, inheritor of Gorhambury after his mother's death—though she was to enjoy it for her lifetime—harassed, preached at, cosseted through babyhood and boyhood, Anthony had no long-term vision of the future, no dream of fame or fortune in years to come. All that mattered was that finally, at last, he need listen no longer to duty, to filial conscience; he too would travel, he too would see the world, the present was his, to seize, to have and to hold.

Chapter 4

Anthony does not appear to have left England until the late autumn of 1579 at the earliest. He had to settle his mother at Gorhambury with a greatly reduced staff and visit his other properties, the manors that belonged to him and those he held on lease. He appointed his father's faithful elderly steward, Hugh Mantell, in charge of all rents, and one of the first difficulties was a disagreement between himself and his half-brother Nathaniel about the valuable leasehold property of Pinner Park, in Middlesex, which under their father's will had been left to Anthony. Nathaniel disputed this, and insisted that it should have been his by right of seniority. The tenant was one William Burbage, whose brother Robert had sold the manor of Theobalds to Lord Treasurer Burghley. Anthony had no desire to involve himself in litigation with Nathaniel, and before he left England he put matters in the hands of his uncle the Lord Treasurer.

It was to his uncle, too, that he had applied for permission to travel abroad, and to the Secretary of State, Sir Francis Walsingham, who had been a good friend of the Lord Keeper's, Walsingham, who had been ambassador in Paris prior to Paulet, was an ardent Puritan: indeed, it was said that he was a fanatical Calvinist, and a ruthless persecutor of all Catholics. He hoped to see the Protestant cause triumph everywhere in Europe. "I wish first God's glory, and next the Queen's safety," he would say, and soon after he became Secretary of State he began to organise an extremely efficient secret service on the continent, involving foreign agents in France, Italy, Spain and the Low Countries, as well as Englishmen travelling abroad. When Anthony Bacon expressed his wish to go overseas Walsingham was very satisfied that the young man, raw as he was to foreign travel, and without great

experience of the world outside Cambridge and Hertfordshire, would nevertheless, in due course, prove his mettle.

Farewells were said, Lady Bacon warning her son
against those Catholic influences which she insisted were
everywhere on the continent, and in Paris in particular.
There might be Jesuits concealed in his bed-curtains, for
he would not be lodged with the ambassador as Francis
had been. Francis, for his part, instructed his brother to be
cool and politic with both factions, to be intimate with
neither, and above all to watch his purse, with which
Anthony had ever been too ready, casting largesse about
him to all and sundry, whether in Cambridge, Hertfordshire or Gray's Inn.

Sir Amias Paulet had by now been recalled, and his
place had been taken by Sir Edward Stafford, whose marriage to the widowed Lady Sheffield had just taken place.
The new Lady Stafford was notorious as having been the
Earl of Leicester's mistress for a number of years—indeed, she had borne him a son whom he did not disown—
and here was further reason why Anthony was warned not
to stay close to diplomatic circles. Lady Stafford's hatred
for her former lover the Earl of Leicester—still close to
the Queen despite his amours with other ladies—was so
intense that unwary talk and gossip might filter back to the
English Court, and young Englishmen abroad for the
first time might find themselves implicated against their
better judgement. Lady Stafford was also said to have
strong leanings toward Catholicism.

So Anthony Bacon sailed for France, accompanied, it
would seem, by one or two attendants, their status something between that of an actual servant and an assistant
secretary. It was the custom, when touring the continent,
to surround oneself with a small retinue, and the son of
the late Lord Keeper would doubtless have lost face
amongst his fellow-countrymen if he had not travelled
with his own modest household.

The first intimation that the staff left behind at Gorhambury were missing their young master comes in a letter
from one of them, Thomas Cotheram, under-steward to
Hugh Mantell, written apparently in March 1580.

"My duty always remembered, most loving master.
I know you would gladly hear of your house Gorham-

bury, and I have written to you three or four times and never heard from you again. My Lady doth take to your house very well and hath great care to repair it where it is needful, and it doth lack nothing but you to come home and dwell there yourself and I would to God it might be so. My Lady doth think you will come home in debt and therefore you shall have the felling of the trees in your woods to set you out of debt. Your water-mill is well and when it is out of repair the plumber doth come presently to mend it. There is nobody here doth so much miss you as I do. Neither I nor my wife, and though I say it myself, never have broken your commandment and that was we should pray for your prosperous journey and your happy return again every night and every morning upon our knees, and I am persuaded that the Lord hath heard and shall hear our prayers still. I hope you do not nor need fear my Lady's marriage for truly she is as far of that as when you departed from her, nor never none came to her for that, as far as I can hear of, and if it do you shall hear of it by me as soon as I can send you word, but I hope to God there shall be no such action yet. I pray you sir, come home as soon as you can, it is good to doubt the worst ever. Mistress Tutes doth send you hearty conn [?], John Bruer your poor servant the like, Nicholas of the kitchen the like, and John Cotles the like.

* "Your poor servant to command as long as life doth last in all your affairs,

"Thomas Cotheram.
"I pray you, sir, to do my wife's conn and mine to Master Brigennes and to George."

(The latter was almost certainly George Jenkyll, whose name appears in a later letter.)

A fortune-seeker after his mother and the Gorhambury estate was not the least of Anthony's worries. He remembered his aunt Elizabeth Hoby and her subsequent marriage to Lord John Russell; and although Lady Bacon at fifty-two was hardly one to cast a coy eye on prospective suitors, she might fall prey to one of pronounced Puritan tendencies, perhaps even a preacher of slender means.

Meanwhile, trouble was brewing in Paris. Open-hearted and generous, as was his nature, and anxious to show himself friendly to Protestants and Catholics alike, Anthony had cultivated the acquaintance of a somewhat notorious Welsh Catholic, Dr. William Parry, who a few years previously had been involved in a theft, and possibly a murder, in the Inner Temple. Lord Treasurer Burghley had obtained Parry's pardon from the Queen and sent him to Europe as a secret agent. Anthony's half-brother Edward had been at Gray's Inn when Parry had made his break-in, and had been full of it at the time, so Anthony knew well with whom he was dealing when he struck up his acquaintance with the Welshman. Possibly he hoped to win his spurs as go-between in Walsingham's secret service, but if so this first attempt was unfortunate. The knowledge that he had lent Parry the considerable sum of £20 came to the ears of the Earl of Leicester, who had his own spies in Paris to sniff out what they could to the discredit of anyone employed there; not only because his ex-mistress was the wife of Edward Stafford, but because he had a personal dislike of the Lord Treasurer, Anthony's uncle Lord Burghley. Whispers of indiscretion spread, the Queen was informed, and it took all Burghley's tact and persuasion to reassure the monarch that his nephew was completely trustworthy and loyal, and a firm supporter of the Protestant faith. Indeed, many years later Anthony told his aunt Elizabeth that he had only been acting under Burghley's instructions.

The immediate sequel is intriguing, for Anthony was evidently summoned back to London to give an account of himself. On December 29th 1580 his uncle Sir Henry Killigrew wrote to a former secretary who was at that time on a mission abroad, "I received your packet when I had half-a-dozen couple of good fellows with me at dinner, among which were Mr Astley, Mr Randall, Master Henry Knowles, my nephew Anthony Bacon and my brother William Cooke, who were gladdened by your good news. Thanks for your friendly mention of my nephew. Pray use him in all things as a common servant; he should be kept with a hard hand." Anthony, however, managed to evade the supervision of his uncle's ex-secretary, and on

his return to France went straight to the university city
of Bourges, captial of the ancient province of Berry. Here
he wrote to his uncle Burghley, the Lord Treasurer, on
January 14th 1581.

"Right honourable very good Lord,
"Being arrived here the 15th of December, I
thought it my duty to certify your lordship thereof.
Two or three days ago it was my good hap to receive
divers letters from my friends in England, and few of
the letters failed to mention your Lordship's honourable and fatherly dealing with me. All joined in one,
that if ever poor gentleman had cause to honour and
esteem so fatherly a friend, I should be very unthank-
ful if I should not judge myself to be as much bound
to your Lordship as possibly I may be. There is nothing in me which is not yours, and I am unable to offer
your Lordship any other duty or service than plain
confession that your Lordship hath power to dispose
of me at your pleasure."

There is small doubt that the Lord Treasurer had saved
his nephew from what could have been an awkward scrape.
Anthony continued by thanking his uncle for his assistance in the thorny problem of the lease of Pinner Park,
which was still in dispute: William Burbage, the tenant,
who continued to occupy the premises and farm, was a
difficult man, forever engaged in litigation, and some few
years later he entered into a lawsuit about another house,
this time at Stratford-upon-Avon, with one John Shakespeare. Anthony ended his letter,

"With my hearty praise to God for your Lordship's
happiness and contentment, I most humbly take my
leave.
"Your Lordship's most humble to command,
"Anthony Bacon."

University life in Bourges was very different from the
more sheltered confines of Trinity, Cambridge, and
Anthony, despite his twenty-three years, was shocked. He
found the manners corrupt and the spirit of the people
irreligious, and wrote to Sir Francis Walsingham to tell

him so. At least, this was his excuse for wishing to move on elsewhere. Besides, the air did not agree with him. He felt ill.

Walsingham, with his vast experience of human nature, and knowing more about Anthony Bacon than Anthony Bacon realised, replied with words of excellent advice. "The number of evil-disposed in mind is greater than the number of sick in body; and as the mind is infinite, so is the infection that cometh from the mind. Many that are far off, are very much inflamed by the heat of that fire. Then they, that are nigh, cannot but burn unless they have some very extraordinary preservation, surpassing the nature of the salamander."

Anthony, disconcerted, pondered on his meaning. The words were obscure, but plainer ones were to follow.

"I have been informed you too easily and too often give yourself to the taking of physic, a thing which as I have by experience found hurtful in myself, when I was of your years, so you shall find in time many incommodities, if you do not break it off. Your years will better wear out any little indisposition, by good order of exercise and abstinence, with some other little moderation in diet, than abide to be corrected by physic, the use of which altereth nature much, yea, maketh a new nature, if it be without great cause used in younger years."

Avoid the flames of corruption, then, lest like the salamander he should be burnt. And away too with pills and potions, and take more exercise, instead of strumming upon his lute.

Anthony decided to follow the example of his half-brother Edward, who, when he travelled abroad, had sought sanctuary for some time in the more salubrious air of Geneva under the roof of the eminent theologian Théodore Beza, the greatest exponent of the Reformed faith since Calvin himself. Calvin, in fact, had died in Beza's arms. Beza was a Frenchman by birth, and had originally studied law. Conversion came to him after a severe illness, and his first act after seeing the light was to put his own house in order by marrying his mistress. Thereafter he became Calvin's adjutant, settled in Geneva in 1558, and after the great Reformer's death in 1564 became virtually his successor. A prolific writer, his Latin version of the New Testament was known in London, and young Anthony Bacon was doubly welcome in his household not only as half-brother to the likeable Edward but also as the son of the learned Lady Bacon, whose twenty-five sermons from the Italian had been read by all the faithful in Geneva.

Daily prayers, study and earnest conversation were the routine under this pious roof, but what was more interesting to Anthony was the chance of meeting Protestants from other countries who happened to be passing through—Huguenots who were in touch with the King of Navarre, for instance, or Dutchmen from the Low Countries, men who might give him information which he could pass on through some returning intermediary to Walsingham back in London. Letters were frequently lost, and his description of his journey and impressions travelling from Bourges to Geneva unfortunately never reached the hands of the Secretary of State. The most trustworthy emissary was Nicholas Faunt, one of Walsingham's secretaries, whom Anthony had met in Paris. Correspondence passed between the two when Faunt was in Frankfurt and later in Padua; and in November of 1581, when Anthony had been lodging with Théodore Beza for six months, they met again, Faunt staying in Geneva en route for Paris.

Anthony was becoming restive, and asked Faunt to use his influence to procure him a passport to cross the Alps: he too wanted to visit Padua, Verona, Venice, then pass into France again via the Mediterranean coast. But when Nicholas Faunt arrived in Paris he reported difficulties. The present ambassador, Sir Henry Cobham, was on poor terms with Walsingham, and in consequence was behaving very coldly to all the Secretary of State's friends and assistants.

"He is at odds," wrote Faunt, "with all the honest gentlemen my master favoureth, even to have chased them away; and for those that yet remain, he hath ever in suspicion. Therefore I am glad it was not your resolution to come hither in his time (though you might have matched him well enough) but I doubt not, before the end of your travel, you shall find a new, and I dare not say worse, in his place."

The New Year brought no passport for Anthony, and it was not until the end of February or the early part of March that his release came. Italy, though, was now out of the question. The King of Spain was preparing invasion, English travellers were said to be held prisoner, and some of them clapped into gaol. The Inquisition was set up in Venice, and Nicholas Faunt urged his young friend to return home before all Europe was set alight. He himself had been bidden back to London.

Anthony stayed unshaken in his resolve to remain abroad. If Italy was out of bounds, then he would cross the Massif Central into the Midi, and thence proceed to Marseilles and into Acquitaine. His mother and his brother might shake their heads and deem it imprudent, but he was resolute. Furthermore, his close friend from Gray's Inn, Ned Selwyn, had arrived to join him. Théodore Beza and his wife were embraced and thanked for all their care and trouble during the past twelve months, and the elderly divine was so much moved by Anthony's departure that he promised to dedicate his volume of Meditations to Lady Bacon as a tribute to her own great scholarship and piety, and to the devotion with which she had brought up her elder son.

So to Toulouse, to Lyons, to Montpellier, and finally to Marseilles, spending two or three months in each city before moving on, the retinue of these two young gentlemen growing larger all the time: a groom here, a page there, two or three personal servants and attendants made little difference to the ever-open purse of Anthony Bacon; besides, his good steward Hugh Mantell kept him supplied with funds from Hertfordshire and Middlesex. The mills were grinding corn at Gorhambury, the trees were being felled for timber, rents from Pinner Farm were being paid up by the reluctant William Burbage, hedging, ditching and shearing were all being entered into the faithful steward's ledger and the accounts brought to the master's hands by Ned Selwyn, including protestations of devotion from the writer.

"Your Worship shall so command me I will not stick to sell anything I have to raise money of and to disburse the same for your worship, so as I may have convenient time to do it." A gentle reminder, though, that it was not always easy. "I am verily persuaded that if you did enter into a reckoning and consideration of the great charge you have been at since your going over and the troublings of her Ladyship and other of your worship's friends, you would surely have greater desire to return to England than you hitherto seem to have."

Nicholas Faunt touched on the same theme, having called on Francis at Gray's Inn, and found Anthony's younger brother unwilling at first to see him. "I was answered by his servant," he wrote, "that he was not at leisure to speak with me, and therefore you must excuse me if I cannot tell you how your mother and other friends do at this present: only I perceive by your brother's boy that he was but newly come from St Albans, where I take it my Lady is now, and well. I was asked where you were and what I heard lately from you, but I could say little that he knew not, neither was I so simple to say all to a boy at the door, his master being within."

That Francis should have been wary of Nicholas Faunt, Walsingham's personal secretary and Anthony's friend, is strange, unless, being "newly arrived from St Albans", he was irritated by the unexpected visit. However, he relented and later admitted the caller, who continued his letter by saying, "Yet by the way, in a word or two, he hath showed his earnest desire to have you return, wishing me to be a persuader thereof, and saying that he marvelled how those that keep abroad more than that time [of their licence] could live to their contentment, seeing that himself was more than weary of his being forth, and that the home life is to be thought upon as of the end of due season."

It must be remembered that Francis had been under the eye of Sir Amias Paulet when he had travelled in France. To wander through the Midi, as Anthony was doing, with Ned Selwyn, who was such excellent company, enjoying the wine and the food and the hospitality of the friendly French people, was a vastly different matter from standing on ceremony in ambassadorial circles. It is possible, too, that the younger brother's shrug at life abroad masked unconscious envy. He was now a barrister at Gray's Inn, but had little to show for it. Courteous requests to his uncle, Lord Treasurer Burghley, and to his aunt Mildred to recommend a suit to the Queen had brought small response. Unlike Anthony he had no estate to fall back upon, and young men like himself with great ambition seldom rose to high office except through influence and royal favour, as he knew very well.

The plums of legal success were still far beyond his reach, but there were other fruits to be picked. He may have despised the French Court but he did not scorn French literature, and the group of poets who formed the Pleiades, naming themselves thus after their Greek predecessors, and desiring to break with all the traditions of the age in which they lived and return to classical grace, had been an inspiration to him since boyhood. Who better to foster the English equivalent of the Pleiades than her Majesty, scattering largesse to young writers and philosophers who would then dedicate themselves to the pursuit of knowledge in all its forms? Francis, who some few years later was to write to his uncle Burghley with superb arrogance, "I have taken all knowledge for my province," found his suit unsuccessful. Her Majesty was not interested. Though the precocious son of her late Lord Keeper may have amused her when he was a small boy, with his gallant reference to her happy reign, his professions of service were not now opportune.

Jean de la Jessé, personal secretary to the duc d'Anjou, himself a poet and an ardent admirer of his native Pleiades, assured the impatient Francis that he would act as intermediary between French and English writers. But all that came of the suggestion was an impassioned sonnet from la Jessé to "Monsieur Francoys Baccon" which began,

> Ce qui inspire du ciel, et plein d'affection,
> Je comble si souvent ma bouche, et ma poitrine,
> Du sacre nom fameux de ta royne divine,
> Ses valeurs en sont cause et sa perfection.

He continued by asserting that his own Muse had been inspired by "Bacon's Pallas", "bien que votre Pallas me rende mieux instruit". So back to Gray's Inn, to his books and legal papers, his long-term plans for literature, science and philosophy, but also to the overseeing of brother Anthony's affairs, who had granted him power of attorney to buy, sell, or raise money on his lands should the necessity arise.

Anthony, now in Marseilles, staunch Ned Selwyn temporarily absent while acting as courier to England, inevitably fell ill. It was possibly malaria, endemic on the Mediterranean coast at that period, but through the winter and spring of 1583 he endured "a long and severe sickness", and Nicholas Faunt, writing from the Court at Richmond with Selwyn acting as his letter-bearer, told Anthony that, "I hope, upon Mr. Selwyn's return, you will be cured in body, mind and purse." The shoe was beginning to pinch, and part of Ned Selwyn's mission to England was to replenish the coffers, provided that faithful Hugh Mantell at Gorhambury was able to oblige.

Anthony when sick was never idle, but scribbled endlessly. Science and philosophy were not his forte, as with Francis, but people were: how they acted, what they thought, whether in Bourges, Montpellier or Marseilles. His brother and his mother were the recipients of many letters, none of them now extant, and Nicholas Faunt, whose replies were filed and docketed by the careful Anthony, mentions descriptions of the people of Marseilles just received in a letter dated May 31st. More tantalising still, he thanks Anthony for his "enclosed sonnets". So Anthony Bacon, now twenty-five, was a poet. Did Nicholas Faunt show the sonnets to his friends at Court? Did brother Francis know of them? Were they printed anonymously? If so, no copies exist amongst Anthony's papers.

Sonnets, however, were for leisure hours only, for Anthony Bacon had been instructed by Secretary of State Walsingham to send particulars of European affairs back to England. Notes on the state of Christendom, discovered a century and a half later amongst Francis's papers, were almost certainly compiled by Faunt and Anthony between them. None other than Nicholas Faunt can have provided the information, no one but Anthony Bacon could have assembled the notes. The duchies of Italy and the dukes who ruled them are all described—Tuscany, Ferrara, Mantua, Urbino, Parma, Savoy; the cities of Lucca, Genoa and Venice. The Austrian Empire, the many princes of Germany, the kingdoms of Poland, Denmark, Spain, and of course England's nearest neighbour and ally, the kingdom of France. A brief portrait of the French King gives some example of the writer's style.

"Henri III, of thirty years of age, of a very weak constitution, and full of infirmities; yet extremely given over to his wanton pleasures, having only delight in dancing, feasting and entertaining ladies, and chamber-pleasures. No great wit, yet a comely behaviour and goodly personage. Abhorring wars and all action; yet daily worketh the ruin of those he hateth, as all of the religion and the house of Bourbon [Henry of Navarre was a Bourbon]. Doting fondly on some he chooseth to favour extremely, without any virtue or cause of desert in them, to whom he giveth prodigally. The Queen Mother ruleth him rather by policy and fear he hath of her, than by his good will; yet he always doth show great reverence towards her."

The description of the King's brother, the duc d'Anjou, who still had a lingering hope he might win the hand of Queen Elizabeth, is, perhaps for diplomatic reasons, in a kinder vein.

"Francis, Duke of Anjou and of Brabant. There is noted in the disposition of this prince a quiet mildness, giving satisfaction to all men; facilty of access and natural courtesy; understanding and speech great and eloquent; secrecy more than is commonly in the French; from his youth always desirous of action, the which thing hath made him always followed and respected. And although hitherto he hath brought to pass no great purpose, having suffered great wants and resistance both at home and abroad, yet by the intermeddling is grown to good experience, readiness, and judgement, the better thereby to guide and govern his affairs, both in practice, in treaty, and in action."

The allusions to the various princes, dukes and states prove that the notes were written during the months of 1582, when letters were passing all the while between Anthony and Nicholas Faunt, and Anthony himself was moving around France from Montpellier to Marseilles. He left Marseilles during the summer or early autumn of 1583, and certainly by September had installed himself at Bordeaux. The change of climate did little for his health, and letters began to reach him from home urging his return.

"I can no longer abstain from telling you," wrote Nicholas Faunt on December 17th, "that the injury is great you do to yourself, and your best friends, in this your voluntary banishment (for so it is already termed) wherein you incur many inconveniences . . . They are not the best thought of that take any delight to absent themselves in foreign parts, especially such as are of quality, and known to have no other cause than their own private contentment."

And from the faithful old steward Hugh Mantell, on

December 23rd, "Her Ladyship hath very earnestly affirmed that she will from henceforth receive all your worship's revenues and convert the same to her proper use, until such time as her Ladyship shall be fully satisfied of all such money as she hath at any time, since your going over, disbursed for you, very often adding with all these speeches, that she is utterly unable to pay these great sums out of her Ladyship's so small a revenue . . . Thus craving pardon of your worship for my over boldness in my rude writing to you, may the Almighty ever preserve you, and grant you safe and speedy return."

The old man had only briefly mentioned his own sickness, "the black and yellow jaunders" and "a dropsye that hath continuance in my legs"; nevertheless, his letter has written upon it "Mantell's last letter", proving that he died at Gorhambury shortly afterwards, faithful to the end.

No one now to send Anthony funds from the estate. Francis, with power of attorney, would not do so; and as for Lady Bacon, she was adamant. It was well past time her elder son returned to England. There were too many Jesuits in Bordeaux, too many Spanish spies. She would not forward any of the Gorhambury rents to fill Catholic coffers.

If his mother was obdurate, so was her son. Anthony, despite his sick stomach, found French living on the western seaboard greatly to his liking. A letter in February 1584 to one of his half-brothers—most probably Edward, who was now married—says, "Being upon the place where the best wine groweth I have presumed to send you two hogsheads, which indeed would have been more in number, if the bearer could have afforded me more room in his ship." He was tasting, furthermore, the sweet fruits of success in high places. The duc de Montmorency had shown him favour, and entrusted to his care letters to the Queen and to the Earl of Leicester. They reached their destination by courier, and brother Francis, always glad of an opportunity to appear at Court, himself delivered them to the Earl. The Queen, it appears, was gratified, and told the Earl of Leicester "she was glad to have found so good a man as Mr Anthony Bacon to send and to receive letters". Walsingham also wrote that her Majesty had observed that "Mr Bacon's care and diligence showeth whose son he is". Which was pleasing to a young man whose relatives and friends complained that he stayed abroad for amusement only.

On June 10th 1584 two events took place which were to have a profound effect on European affairs. Prince William of Orange, a Protestant, and the heroic leader of the Netherlands in their struggle for freedom against their hated Spanish masters, was assassinated; and the duc d'Anjou, brother to the French King and one-time wooer of Queen Elizabeth, died suddenly of a fever. King Henri of Navarre, leader of the French Huguenots, was now the heir to the throne of France.

Anthony Bacon, who had followed Navarre's career since early boyhood, decided to pay him a visit. He left for the kingdom of Béarn in early July.

Chapter 5

The future King Henri IV of France had been born in the château of Pau between two and three on the morning of December 13th 1553. His grandfather Henri d'Albret, King of Navarre, had married the talented and artistic Marguerite de Valois, sister of François I. Their daughter Jeanne was wedded to Antoine, head of the younger branch of the Bourbons; and it was she who gave birth to the young Henri that December morning. The King of Navarre, triumphant with joy, entered his daughter's bedroom, placed his own golden chain round her neck, and put into her hands a box containing his will.

"This is yours, my daughter," he told her, "but this"—reaching for the new-born infant—"is mine." The young prince had entered the world without a cry. The King of Navarre then rubbed the child's lips with garlic and poured wine down his throat, which he swallowed thirstily. "You are a true Béarnais," he declared. He turned to the attendants standing by and told them, "When my daughter Jeanne was born, the Spaniards said my consort Queen Marguerite was a cow who had given birth to a ewe. Well, look you upon this. My ewe has brought forth a lion."

The lion-cub's father died of wounds in 1562 in the religious war between Catholics and Huguenots, and Henri was nine years old when he succeeded to the throne of Navarre through his mother. Queen Jeanne was an ardent Calvinist, as her own mother Marguerite had been, and during the continuing wars she and her children, Henri and his younger sister Catherine, were often driven from their châteaux in Pau and Nérac to take shelter in the fortress of Navarrenx. The boy grew up with a cool head and a courageous spirit. There was much of his grandfather in him. From the earliest age it was impressed upon him that he would be the leader of all the Protestants in

France, and his openhearted ways, his ready laughter and his swiftly developing appreciation of the proverbial wine, women and song masked tremendous energy and an indomitable will.

His testing-time came almost immediately after his mother's death. Jeanne, for reasons of policy, had arranged a marriage between her son and the Princess Marguerite of Valois, sister to the French King Charles IX. The coincidence in names was striking—a second Henri of Navarre to marry a second Marguerite de Valois—but with the names any resemblance ended. No deeply religious, brilliant, strong-minded Marguerite in 1572, as in 1527, but a spoilt, talented, amorous young woman who flitted from lover to lover despite the watchful eye of her mother Catherine de Medici.

The wedding took place in Paris on August 18th, and six days later the infamous Massacre of St Bartholomew, which shocked public opinion in England, struck down the many hundreds of Huguenots who had come to Paris not only as wedding-guests but as followers and supporters of their nineteen-year-old leader, King Henri of Navarre. Henri and his sister Catherine were virtually prisoners at the French Court, and only saved themselves from death by agreeing to abandon the Reformed faith. Young Henri played for time, negotiating secretly with his friends in Normandy and the south-west, while outwardly conforming to life in Paris; and it was not until February 1576 that he made his escape, under the pretext of joining a hunting party. Soon after Catherine joined him, and almost immediately brother and sister, at the Huguenot stronghold of La Rochelle, renewed their profession of faith to the Reformed Church.

Henri had left his wife Marguerite behind in Paris without a qualm, nor had she ever pretended any affection for him; but when peace between Catholics and Huguenots was signed at Bergerac a year later it was considered politic that they should come together again. But not for long. Provincial life seemed tedious and rural to the spoilt Marguerite de Valois after the sophisticated pleasures of Paris. Henri was always in the saddle, and her sister-in-law Catherine de Bourbon, though hardly beautiful and therefore not a rival to her own charms, surpassed her in artistic talent. The soldier-poet d'Aubigné wrote songs which

Princess Catherine set to music and sang upon her lute,
she taught dancing to the future statesman Sully—in short,
the Queen of Navarre felt herself outfaced, and returned
to Paris in 1582.

When Anthony Bacon visited the principality of Béarn
in the summer of 1584, Henri was thirty-two years old and
his sister Princess Catherine twenty-five. They were strik-
ingly alike, both with expressive eyes and strongly marked
features, and Catherine, who resembled in so many ways
her famous grandmother the first Marguerite de Valois,
was devoted to her brother just as that Marguerite had
been to François. She helped him in the administration of
Béarn, which at that time extended over the extreme south-
western portion of France, comprising what is today the
provinces of Lot-et-Garonne, Tarn-et-Garonne, and the
Hautes et Basses Pyrénées. The Court was sometimes at
Pau, the capital, at other times at Nérac or Agen, or less
frequently at Montauban.

The position of the King of Navarre, now he had become heir to the throne of France, was extremely delicate.
The Catholics wooed him, hoping to convert him back to
Rome, the Huguenots watched him, fearful that he might
comply. "No man," protested Henri, "can be expected to
change his religion as often as he changes his shirt." The
assassination of the Prince of Orange had been a tremendous blow to the Protestant cause; and, worse still, the
unity of the old Huguenot party seemed to have vanished.
Rivalry had crept in between the leaders, Navarre did not
always agree with his Bourbon cousin the prince de
Condé, and at the same time, as heir-presumptive to the
throne of France, he must remain on good terms with his
brother-in-law, Henri III, who had succeeded to the throne
in 1574.

This was the state of affairs when Anthony arrived in
Béarn, his visit coinciding with that of the duc d'Epernon
—Henri III's latest *"mignon"*, with whom he was said to be
besotted. The Duke had been sent by his master with a
magnificent train to lure the King of Navarre back into
the Catholic fold—and what a contrast between the high
protocol of the Parisian courtiers, for all their licentious
habits, and the free and easy atmosphere of Nérac, with
Henri and his sister Catherine welcoming all comers with
open arms!

Anthony was enchanted. Henri was no intellectual, and he had his mistresses, but what of that? He greeted the Englishman as he would a friend and an equal, showed him his stables with his thirty hunters, his hounds with their leather collars, armed thus to chase the wild boar, his greyhounds, spaniels, falcons, while near at hand were the tennis courts and bowling grounds. And Princess Catherine, so like her brother but small and slight, ready to discuss any subject from Greek literature to French history, gracious, kindly, yet from time to time with something hesitant in her manner, something melancholy, a legacy of the terrible days of childhood when she had been a witness to the Massacre of St Bartholomew.

It was without reluctance, therefore, that Anthony, after wrenching his foot accidentally—either at tennis or dismounting from a ride—was persuaded by his royal host and hostess to prolong his visit. It was with genuine sadness that he finally left the Court of Navarre and returned to Bordeaux, only to fall victim, in his own words, "to a quartan ague" (a recurrence, surely, of malaria). What was more, his lengthy stay with the Protestant leader had brought him under the suspicion of the Catholics in Bordeaux, and complaints were made to Marshal Matignon, the provincial governor, via "an old mass-monger named Wenden, penned and subscribed by two English Jesuits [Anthony's own words], that my lodging was charged to be the receptacle of all rebellious Huguenots. My pen their intelligence, and the director of their commotions, my personal presence and assistance at their assemblies and communions no small countenance and encouragement to them. In such sort, as some of the Court of Parliament, believing this information, pronounced me worthy of the rack. But the Marshal Matignon very honourably and kindly drew the matter into his own hand, and protected me in all kindness and safety."

The information was very probably laced with truth. Anthony had by now many friends amongst the French Protestants. He had been close on five years in France, and he spoke and wrote French fluently. Throughout this time he had been feeding intelligence back to the English Secretary of State Walsingham. So if Bordeaux was becoming too hot for comfort, his Protestant friends in Béarn would be delighted to receive him. In January 1585 he travelled south to Montauban.

This gracious city, superbly set on the banks of the river Tarn, had been one of the capitals of French Protestantism since 1562. Two centuries earlier, under English occupation, it had known all the rigours of the Hundred Years' War, and the Black Prince himself had occupied the fortress. Now a Huguenot stronghold and a favourite resting-place for Henri and Princess Catherine as they travelled round Navarre, it seemed the ideal centre from which Anthony Bacon could make more contacts and continue to send information to London.

Ned Selwyn was no longer with him. Family affairs in Sussex had recalled him home, and he was to marry a few years later. A new friend had taken his place, one Tom Lawson. A Catholic of no very great persuasion—he made light of the fact—he had no sooner entered Anthony Bacon's household than he became the dominant feature of it. Like Ned Selwyn he was good company, but he had little of Selwyn's steadiness of purpose, and in a very short while his influence upon the warm-hearted and easy-going Anthony was considerable. He could do what he liked with him, make him laugh, make him sigh, make him mock even at some of the customs of the Reformed church; and he encouraged his employer—for he was, after all, acting in a secretarial capacity—to spoil his pages, his groom, his lackey, the little group of hangers-on who came and went at will in Anthony Bacon's lodging close by the bridge that crossed the river Tarn.

The most influential Huguenot in Montauban was Philippe de Mornay, sieur du Plessis-Marly, chief Councillor to the King of Navarre. It was partly through his encouragement that Anthony had come to Montauban. His wife, the Councillor said, would be pleased to welcome him in their house at any time; and when he himself was absent on the affairs of his master the King, who was never in one place for long, she would be able to entertain the Englishman whenever he so desired. Indeed, he could escort her and her daughter by a previous marriage, Mlle Suzanne de Paz, to church.

The arrangement sounded harmless enough but trouble was almost immediate. Madame du Plessis, as she was generally known, was a cultured woman of high principles

—she was later to write her memoirs—and an equally high opinion of herself as wife of the chief Councillor to the King. She had travelled widely and was accustomed to moving in the best circles, and she found Montauban somewhat provincial and the resident minister of the Reformed church, Monsieur Berault, narrow in his ideas. He had issued a decree that none of the women in his congregation should wear wigs, or nets of gold thread in their hair, which were symbols of vanity, and that anyone who disregarded this decree should be forbidden the Sacrament. Madame du Plessis was outraged. Ladies of fashion should be allowed to dress as they pleased; no complaint had ever been made against her in all the fifteen years she and Monsieur du Plessis had attended a large number of Reformed churches, and to suggest that by dressing her hair in a certain way she was lacking in modesty was an insult to her position.

Many other ladies in Montauban, equally disturbed, came to her for advice as to whether they could wear wigs or must discard them, and Madame du Plessis did her best to reassure them that they should do as they pleased. But this was an error. Those members of the congregation at Montauban who wished to take Communion on Sacrament Sunday were given tokens, some days previously, to admit them to the church; and when Monsieur du Plessis applied to the minister for tokens for his household the minister declined. Shortly afterwards a deputation arrived from the local Senate, Monsieur du Plessis being absent at the time, to inform his wife that she must discard her false hair, or else . . .

She appealed to the minister who conducted the church services at Court, but he excused himself with many apologies; the Senate had forbidden him to issue Communion tokens to any member of her household. Immediately the news spread throughout Montauban that Monsieur du Plessis and his family had been excommunicated, and when the Councillor appeared at the King's levée on the Saturday morning he found himself the laughing-stock at Court.

It was in this mêlée that Anthony Bacon found himself involved. Nothing could have been more awkward. Like any other young man of his age he inwardly mocked at the whole absurd business, and did so in private to Tom Lawson. Indeed, he could imagine what the King of Navarre himself was saying to his immediate circle, everyone splitting their sides with amusement. But not in Madame du Plessis's household, with the lady pouring forth her indignation into his ears, demanding his support, not only for her own sake but for her daughter's, who by design was placed next to him every time he called at their house, the implication being that if Mille de Paz could only marry an Englishman things would be very different. No one would dare to insult her. Especially if her daughter's husband was allied to someone in a high position at Queen Elizabeth's Court.

This was too much for Anthony Bacon. He had nearly been trapped once before, with Miss Dowsabell Paget. Never again. He made his excuses—was feeling a little unwell, a touch of the ague—and at the first opportunity sought out the offending minister Berault and told him how right he was in his judgement that wigs and gold-threaded nets were abhorrent and should never be worn in the precincts of a Reformed church. The minister was delighted.

It was many months before the great scandal died down. Whenever Madame du Plessis ventured forth into the streets of Montauban she muffled up her hair with a black kerchief so as to give no offence, and once she attended church with a night-cap on top of the kerchief. "In this question of false hair," she declared, "I see quarrels arise and flourish to the great scandal of all men, caused solely by the fact that Monsieur Berault has not correctly interpreted the decision reached by the General Synod on the wearing of quinquelets, which he takes to mean the use of brass wire in the hair."

As for Monsieur du Plessis, his greatest concern was neither with wigs nor with brass wire, but "that the story would spread from Montauban all over France, where, by God's grace, his name was tolerably well-known."

The truth was, in Anthony's own words, that *"Madame du Plessis porte la briggaine"* ("wears the cod-piece"), an expression conveying a familiarity with the French slang of his day which his mother would not have appreciated. Indeed, she could not understand why her son persisted in staying abroad despite all her wishes to the contrary, forever asking for money which she could ill afford to send. Nor did she care for the sound of this man Lawson, with

Catholic connections, who was reputed to be lodging with him.

Madame du Plessis's head-dress was forgotten in the turmoil that was to sweep through France during the summer of 1585. Since the duc d'Anjou's death the preceding year, when Henri of Navarre became heir apparent, his claim to the throne of France had been opposed by the powerful duc de Guise, cousin to Henri III. As leader of the Holy Catholic League, the Duke threatened his cousin with civil war unless he agreed to debar the King of Navarre from the succession and condemn all Huguenots throughout the realm. This put the King of France in an impossible position, and with great reluctance he signed the Treaty of Nemours on June 20th. Amongst its chief provisions was an order that every heretic was to be banished from the kingdom within six months, all heretics were to be dismissed from office unless they recanted, and the officers of the Holy League were to remain in undisputed possession of the various cities which they had seized during the dispute, including Rheims, Soissons and Tours.

The severity of the treaty shocked all France. Henri of Navarre, against whom it was mainly directed, was appalled; it was said that his hair turned white within an hour. War was inevitable between himself, as leader of the Reformed church, and his brother-in-law the French King, between Huguenots and Catholics. Once again the countryside of France would be fought over, trampled, ravaged, as it had been so often during centuries of bloody history, both factions claiming that God was on their side. Light-hearted levées at Montauban and Nérac became a thing of the past, and the King of Navarre must be amongst his troops and his supporters, raising regiments, fortifying the stronghold at La Rochelle, throwing up defences on the banks of the Loire.

The position of England was embarrassing. It was one thing to assist the Dutch Protestants in the Netherlands by sending an army led by the Earl of Leicester, for there the enemy was Spain. It was quite another to interfere in France engaged in civil war, and the ambassador in Paris must act with prudence. As for Englishmen who whiled away their time in Montauban, it was surely better to recall them.

"Considering the troubled state of the country," Walsingham wrote to Anthony in September, "your friends wish

you at home." Lady Bacon, writing either in person or
through her brother-in-law the Lord Treasurer, implored
her Majesty Queen Elizabeth to send someone to recall her
son from abroad.

Anthony ignored the latest missive from the Secretary
of State. He chose to remember the letter he had received
from him the previous year, in which Walsingham had
said, "Touching the matter by you advertised, her Majesty
conceiveth thereby your rightness of judgement, and findeth
that you have better intelligence in that corner than hath
been received from any others in those parts; whereby it is
seen that your credit is good with the evil affected of that
nation remaining there. I shall heartily pray you by all the
best means you may devise to continue your intelligence
with the parties with whom it seemeth you can prevail;
very much the rather for that the same may greatly import
her Majesty's service."

Living without means, however, was becoming increasingly difficult. Anthony wrote to his brother Francis asking
for £500 and for certain jewels that were his by right of
inheritance—"Which I know will give occasion to my
mother and you of marvel, perhaps of suspicion. How I
mean to employ them you shall understand hereafter, and
neither you nor any able to dislike, no more than the
rest of mine expenses; if you knew as well as myself, as by
God's grace one day you shall, the times, places, manner,
and end of their spending."

These lines are significant. Was Anthony already in touch
with Catholic agents in Spain, from across the Pyrenees,
who were keeping him informed of the King of Spain's de-
signs? Were merchants in Bordeaux, their ships plying
between that port and Spain, carrying news of Spanish
affairs? This could be the intelligence to which Walsingham had referred in his letter, but it was a dangerous game
for the Englishman who played it. French Catholics, and
French Huguenots too, would dearly love more precise information about the Queen of England's intentions. An
Englishman whose uncle was Lord Treasurer to Queen
Elizabeth might be vulnerable to pressure, while the oldest
trick in the world of espionage, then as today, was to take
advantage of any compromising incidents in a man's personal life, and threaten exposure when the moment seemed
opportune.

Anthony, when he declined to pay court to Mademoiselle de Paz and eased his way out of greater intimacy with her family, had not realised the extreme offence he had given to her mother. Nor did it occur to him that, with the King of Navarre away at La Rochelle making preparations for war against the de Guises and the King of France, society at Montauban would lose many of its pleasanter members, and that those who remained, forming a close circle around the unforgiving Madame du Plessis, would be glad of an excuse to spread gossip about the young man who had caused her so much displeasure. How did he manage to live in comparative comfort, they asked themselves? Who was this Monsieur Lawson, said to be a Catholic and forever in his company, and what actually took place in his lodging by the bridge, whence came the sound of music and song, and the laughter of young boys? Anthony, always an indulgent master, and more so since he had known Tom Lawson, never imagined, as he fondled the curls of one young page and sat him upon his knee, or gave another money to play cards and tennis, that a third would turn spy and blacken his reputation, and a fourth quit his service and go blabbing indiscretions to a lawyer in the town. He believed himself on the high road to success. Walsingham was pleased with the information he continued to send him; no trained diplomat could be better. Indeed, brother Francis when he toured France under the wing of Sir Amias Paulet had never boasted similar achievements. Life was good in Montauban. Even his health had improved.

Then the blow fell. He was arrested on a charge of sodomy.

Chapter 6

It is remarkable that, amongst the state documents of Queen Elizabeth for the years 1586–87, there is not a single one referring to the charge brought against Anthony Bacon. If any ever existed it must have been destroyed. The only records extant today repose in the *Archives Départementales* at Montauban. Even here the dates are confusing. Certainly the original charge must have been made in the summer of 1586, for on September 23rd Henri of Navarre intervened personally from La Rochelle. The law in France was extremely severe: anyone proved to have committed sodomy was condemned to death by *"le bûcher"*. One Benoist Grealou, a priest, found guilty of this crime at Moissac, not far from Montauban, was *"brûlé tout vif"* at Cahors in 1563. It is significant that no letters to or from Anthony Bacon exist for this particular period. In later years the charge is never mentioned, and other reasons are given for his unhappiness at this period of his life.

The chief offender in his household appears to have been his favourite page Isaac Burgades, who used to chase a younger lad David Boysson up to the garret in the roof of Anthony's lodging, there threaten him with a whip, and then proceed to "mount him" (details of the assault are given unsparingly in the document), so that the unfortunate child cried out in distress. A lackey, Michel Fortier, came to the rescue, and was bribed with a smart black hat to say nothing of what he had seen and heard. David subsequently left Anthony Bacon's service and his place was taken by another page, Paul de la Fontayne, who admitted before the Council for the Prosecution at Montauban that the English gentleman frequently caressed his page Isaac Burgades, and that they remained together in Monsieur Bacon's room for hours at a time, in broad daylight and at night, and that Isaac Burgades had told him there was nothing wrong in the practice of sodomy. Indeed, Monsieur Théodore Beza of Geneva approved of it, as did the minister Monsieur Constans at Montauban.

This was a shocking affirmation! And the statement was confirmed by another lackey, Barthélémy Sore, who had also left Anthony Bacon's service, and declared that his former master frequently "abused" his pages, then bribed them with sweetmeats and money to keep them silent, and that he, Barthélémy, would rather die than return to his service, for all the world knew that Monsieur Bacon was a bugger. The name of Thomas Lawson is not mentioned in the documents: it is Monsieur Anthony Bacon who is the offender.

True or false? In general terms, very probably true. In the particulars, certainly false. Tenderness was part of his nature, and he had craved affection from his childhood onward. The little sisters had been preferred to him, even if they lived in his mother's memory only. Her teaching had made the sexual act taboo, even abhorrent to him, as between man and woman. The example of his half-brother Edward, his friends Ned Selwyn and Nicholas Faunt had convinced him otherwise, and in France he had seen that the love of a man for a woman could be beneficial, even pleasurable. Yet he held back. He stretched out his arms to the boys who sang with him, and played the lute, and wheedled money from his purse, and who perhaps had inspired those sonnets written from his bed of sickness in Marseilles and sent to Faunt. But cruelty, no. Force was not in his nature. It took a man who made love to women throughout his life, Henri of Navarre, to come to his rescue.

"To Monsieur de Scorbiac, King's Councillor, Château de Verlhaguet, Montauban.

"I hear that Monsieur Bacon is appealing to my Council against a sentence given against him by the Seneschal of Quercy at the bench in Montauban. I write now desiring you to bring his right of appeal promptly before the judge and have it granted as expeditiously as possible. The merit of those to whom he belongs is great. We owe many obligations to the Queen, his sovereign; he is also himself strongly to be recommended. He will know how to repay us in kind for mercy shown to him, and we ourselves are told by God to have care for the strangers in our midst, to safeguard their rights, and to see they win justice, and furthermore in the situation in which we find ourselves at present it is as well to show leniency, nor is it reasonable to use all the formalities and harshness of French justice towards them. I am assured of your prudence, good judgement, and fairness in these matters and that you will bring reason to bear upon them. It is not my intention to say more on the subject, except to assure you of my good wishes and to pray the Creator to hold you, Monsieur de Scorbiac, in His Holy care.

"From La Rochelle, this twenty-third of September, 1586,

"Your entire good and affectionate friend,

"Henri."

There the matter rested for a twelvemonth at least. According to the documents, on November 17th 1587 the evidence against Anthony Bacon was heard again; after which silence. No other references to the case have been traced in the archives of Montauban.

One thing is clear. Anthony escaped the death sentence but remained in his lodging, possibly on parole for good behaviour. His brother Francis was now a bencher at Gray's Inn, and had been returned as MP for Taunton in the Parliament of 1586–87, that same which condemned the Queen of Scotland to death. There is no record of his having made a speech on that occasion, and if he wrote to Anthony urging his return the letter is lost. The King of Navarre remained the only friend and ally of Anthony Bacon, languishing in Montauban; and shortly before the appeal was heard in November Monsieur du Plessis (this must have gone against the grain) was ordered by his royal master to send the Englishman 1,500 écus through a Monsieur Buzanvel.

"I desire to gratify Monsieur Bacon for his own sake, and for those to whom he belongs," wrote the King of Navarre amidst his wars, "and I will say no more except that I shall be easy in mind if Monsieur Bacon is content." The money, however, seems not to have arrived, for in December the King of Navarre wrote direct to Anthony Bacon:

"Monsieur de Bacon,

"I am very distressed Buzanvel has not yet paid the sum he had received for you, as he knows how much I esteem those to whom you belong, and how fond I am of you myself. I have told Monsieur de Plessis to look after your needs, and to take care of any great necessity. I wish your health had permitted you to be beside me, or you would never have fallen into such difficulties.

"I pray you, always appeal to me, and I remain your affectionate and certain friend,

"Henri."

The King of Navarre had put an end to the accusations brought against Anthony, but his troubles were not yet over. The 1,500 écus had been spent, and there were those in the town to whom he owed money. He had shifted his lodging, and merchants and others, who knew only too well the accusation which had been brought against him, were pressing for payment. Possibly they were not above blackmail. In February 1588 Monsieur du Pin, one of the King of Navarre's councillors, took it upon himself to write to Walsingham.

"Monsieur, I am very worried that Monsieur Bacon stays so long at Montauban. He has never come to see me and he has entered into a lawsuit with some people with whom he lodges about grievous matters and against unworthy people who are in such contrast with himself. I have given him all the service that I could and given him all the counsel that I would wish for myself or perhaps for my son. He would have been better advised to follow the advice of men of principle than of those wrong ones who possess him, and of whom the King my master is not satisfied. I have given him passports to go away and to send these men towards you. It would be good, Monsieur, to take him away from there. I honour extremely all that belongs to you."

The line "the wrong ones who possess him" was surely an oblique reference to Thomas Lawson. The "lawsuit" concerned debts owing to merchants in Montauban and Bordeaux, dating back to May of 1586, which Anthony insisted had been cancelled. Now, desperate for further financial assistance, he turned to the Catholic Bishop of Cahors, who advanced him a thousand crowns. There was, very naturally, a condition attached. Would Monsieur Bacon write to Secretary Walsingham in London and ask for the release of two Welsh Jesuit priests imprisoned in Westminster? Monsieur Bacon could do no other but agree; his mistake, though, was to send his friend Tom Lawson as the courier. Anthony, despite his talent for diplomacy, was still naïve. It had not occurred to him that du Plessis would already have been in touch with the Secretary of State.

March 24th 1588, Anthony to Walsingham. "I beg to recommend to you Monsieur Lawson, who has been of great service to me and others, and I hope you will see him soon after he arrives. Now that I am convalescent, I hope soon to be with you. I feel sure that by your help and that of the Lord Treasurer, the King will make no difficulty in granting me ample passports, for the ambassador wrote to me that he would do it when asked, and I know not why the King should be offended with me." (The reference here surely is to Henri III of France, not Anthony's friend Henri of Navarre.)

Illness had, therefore, been his excuse for remaining so long in Montauban. No mention of the action brought against him, nor the pending lawsuits brought by the irate merchants. A further letter, dated April, says, "Ingratitude is the basest of sins, and I have received so many kindnesses from M. de Cahors, without having seen him, that I cannot lose this opportunity of pleasing him in begging favour for Powel and Jonas Merideth of Wales, prisoners only for religion. I entreat you to enlarge them, on account of the signal services I have received from M. Cahors, and other very honourable Catholics."

Anthony sealed his letters and bade farewell to his friend, wishing him God speed and a quick return after their safe delivery, little knowing that it would be many months before he would see him again. For Thomas Lawson was arrested as soon as he arrived in London and was thrown into prison. No reason given. Some eight years later, discussing this unhappy period of his life with his aunt Lady Russell, and writing about it to the Earl of Essex, Anthony said, "The Lord Treasurer imprisoned and kept him [Lawson] in durance ten months, giving way, without any resistance by his grave authority and wisdom, to my mother's passionate importunity, grounded upon false suggestions and surmises, authorised by du Plessis and his wife, out of mere envy against Lawson's merit and credit with me."

A Catholic friend of evil principles and influence, possibly even an agent of the King of Spain, was sufficient to put both Burghley and Walsingham on their guard, and so throw the unfortunate Lawson into prison. After all, it was not the first time Anthony Bacon had been over-friendly with Catholic contacts. The affair of Dr Parry was still on the records (he had been executed for high treason, and for a plot against her Majesty, on returning to London from Paris in 1585). As for Lady Bacon, she was almost out of her mind with anxiety. Her son under Papist influence? Therefore a traitor to God and to his country. She could not bear to hear of him, he was cursed of God in all his actions.

Meanwhile Anthony remained in Montauban, and both the Secretary of State and the Lord Treasurer had their minds too full of other matters to concern themselves with the doubtful friendships or the financial difficulties of one solitary Englishman. In July the Spanish Armada was on the high seas, then observed off the coast of Dorset, and Queen Elizabeth rode to Tilbury to rally her troops. The Earl of Leicester became Lieutenant-General for the defence of the realm, and his stepson, the twenty-two-year-old Robert Devereux, Earl of Essex, joined him with a company of his own light horse, wearing the Devereux livery.

The defeat of the Armada by Lord High Admiral Howard of Effingham, with Hawkins, Drake and Frobisher under his orders, and the subsequent loss of most the finest vessels of the Spanish fleet in gales off the English coast, meant that the King of Spain had forfeited his mastery of the seas. It was a triumphant moment, and the exiled Englishman, still pressed for money by his creditors in Montauban, was unable to take part in the great rejoicing.

He had found a new friend, a Captain Francis Allen, who promised to act as courier to London, and being of unblemished reputation could travel to England without risking arrest on arrival.

Anthony's letter to the Lord Treasurer is dated September 28th 1588.

"After having waited for about seven months for the return of Mr Lawson without having any news of him, I have been constrained to make use of the good will of the present bearer, Mr Allen, who has kindly offered to hazard his life for the relief of my great and present necessity, and to prevent the dangers by which I am threatened on all sides, if I should remain longer in this uncertainty. I beg you to believe, that all the hardships and misery I have undergone during my most unfortunate sojourn are supportable compared with my regrets at not having been able better to perform my humble duty.

"I remit it, however, to your Lordship's wisdom to consider, whether certain notable events which have occurred since my last letter have not justified a part of my statement." (This last line suggests that Anthony had continued to send information concerning the religious war in France to his masters in Westminster.) "Messieurs du Plessis and du Pin have at any rate got wind of it and are both sweating into their doublets to find themselves known on both sides for other than they pretend to be, and this through my information. That is to say, as being more careful and attentive to their own welfare than well affected to the public good, or to the advantage of their master, the King of Navarre, who, worthy and valiant prince that he is, will only advance in God's good time and without having gained much from the advice and counsel of the two above-named gentlemen."

It is evident that the stigma put upon him by the charges in 1586, and never mentioned by himself, had left an indelible mark on Anthony Bacon's character.

But his financial and other troubles were of small account compared with what was happening elsewhere in France in December 1588. Henri III was holding court at

Blois, Paris being in the hands of the Catholic rebels, and great pressure was being put on him to declare Henri of Navarre, as a Protestant, unfit for succession to the crown. The powerful duc de Guise, head of the Holy Catholic League, supported this move, becoming ever more impatient and insolent, seeing the crown within his own grasp, so great was his popularity with the people. On the evening of December 22nd Henri came to the decision which had been brewing in his mind for many months. His cousin de Guise must die. He summoned his forty-five guardsmen, his personal bodyguard, and gave them their secret orders. Early on the morning of December 23rd de Guise was told that the King desired to see him. He passed into the ante-room, where the guardsmen were waiting. Then, as they saluted him with respect, he turned to look at them. Suddenly a dagger was in his breast, then a second, then a third. He dragged himself to the King's bedroom, and imploring God's mercy fell dead at the King's feet.

"C'est fait?" asked the King, and one of the guardsmen came forward and covered the Duke with a piece of tapestry. *"Enfin . . . je suis roi,"* said the King, and measuring the length of his cousin upon the floor he added, *"Je ne savais pas qu'il était si grand."*

Eight months later he too would die by an assassin's hand. Henri of Bourbon, King of Navarre, would become Henri IV of France, one of the greatest kings that country would ever know. And Anthony Bacon, an obscure young Englishman just turned thirty-one, would never forget the monarch who had shown him friendship and compassion, and had saved him from the criminal's death of burning at the stake.

Chapter 7

The assassination of the duc de Guise, and of his brother the Cardinal of Lorraine the next day, created confusion throughout France, and when on January 5th 1589 the King's mother Catherine de Madici also died, Henri III was free to attempt a reconciliation with Henri of Navarre. He trusted that this alliance with the Huguenots would bolster him from the ever-increasing enmity of the Holy Catholic League and the vast number of his Catholic subjects, with whom the murdered Duke had been immensely popular.

The last of the Valois and the first of the Bourbon monarchs met at Plessis-les-Tours on April 30th. Henri III of France was thirty-eight, his brother-in-law thirty-six. The King of France, no longer the painted monarch of earlier days surrounded by his *mignons,* was pale and troubled; he was said to be forever on his knees these days, haunted by his conscience, the Pope having refused to grant him absolution after de Guise's murder. Henri of Navarre, only two years younger, was in the prime of manhood, still the "lion" that his grandfather and namesake had predicted he would be.

Here in the park of the château at Plessis-les-Tours, where their joint ancestor Louis XI had died just over a hundred years before—that same king who, fearing death, was coaxed into smiling by the sight of four little piglets dressed in skirts dancing before him—the two Henris shook hands and made a pact to march on Paris.

"The world is marvellously changed," Lord Treasurer Burghley wrote to the Earl of Shrewsbury in May, "when we true Englishmen have cause, for our own quietness, to wish good success to a French king. . . . At this time the French King's party, by the true subjects of his crown, both Catholic and Protestant, doth prosper in every place."

The Lord Treasurer's personal life was not so happy. His beloved wife Mildred had died on April 4th. They had been married for forty-two years. She was buried at Westminster Abbey, and five days later Burghley wrote a meditation on her death. This meditation pays a moving tribute not only to her scholarship—she was renowned as the most learned woman of her day—but to her great generosity and kindness of heart. "She did also four times in the year secretly send to all the prisons in London, money to buy bread, cheese and drink for four hundred persons, and many times more, without knowledge from whom the same come. She did likewise sundry times in the year send shirts and smocks to the poor people both in London, and in Cheshunt. Not long before her death, she caused secretly to be bought a large quantity of wheat and rye, to be disposed amongst the poor in time of dearth."

Mildred Burghley had undoubtedly a sweeter nature than her sister Ann Bacon, who, when her son's friend Captain Allen visited her during that summer, gave vent to her feelings, as Allen reported to Anthony on August 17th.

"When I did my duty to the Rt. Hon. Lord Treasurer he demanded the cause of your not coming home, and said you spent like a prince being but a squire, yet for your spending and not coming home, he would not condemn you before he heard you speak. He said you must hereafter find men with deeds and not with words.

"Upon my arrival at Gorhambury my Lady used me courteously until such time when I began to move her for Mr Lawson and to say the truth for yourself, being so much transported with your abode there you seek her death. She is resolute to procure her Majesty's letter for to force you to return, and when that shall be, if her Majesty give you your right desert she should clap you in prison. She cannot abide to hear of you, nor of the other. . . . She saith you are hated of all the chiefest on that side and curst of God in all your actions since Mr Lawson's being with you. I am sorry to write it, considering his deserts and your love towards him, but the truth will be known at the last, and better late than never. It is in vain to look for his return. No, no, saith she, and although you should never come home, he shall be hindered from coming to you.

"My Lady saith it is not in your power to sell any part of your living about Gorhambury. Mr Lawson is in great necessity, and your brother dare not help him in respect of my Lady's displeasure. My Lady said she had rather you made the wars with the King of Navarre than to have stayed so long idle in Montauban, and with great earnestness also tears she wished that when she heard of Mr Selwyn's imprisonment you had been fairly buried, providing you had died in the Lord. By my simple judgement she spoke it in her passion and repented immediately her words. I must confess unto you I have never seen or never shall see a lady and an honourable woman a mother more perplexed for her son's absence than I have that honourable dame for yours. Therefore lay your hand on your heart, look not for Mr Lawson, he hath, as a man may say, heaven and earth against him.

"Francis Allen."

So Ned Selwyn, Anthony's faithful travelling companion, had also been imprisoned. But where, and for what fault? No word of him at all in the documents at Montauban, nor in the State Papers, but the implication is that a round-up had been made of anyone connected with Anthony Bacon during his residence in France, for earlier in the year a Mr Richard Gest was examined in Chester about his travels in Spain and Portugal and his correspondence with Mr Anthony Bacon over a period of two years.

On August 1st Henri III, who had arrived at St Cloud with his own army and that of Henri of Navarre to lay siege to Paris, was stabbed to death by a mad Dominican monk, and with his dying breath told Henri of Navarre that the crown was his.

The whole of France was in uproar, torn apart by divided loyalties. Some Catholics, faithful to the King's dying words, stood firm for the Bourbon succession, on condition that he maintained the Catholic faith throughout the kingdom. Others declared for war. The Huguenots too were at a loss. If their leader Henri of Navarre, now King of France, favoured the Catholics, how would they fare themselves? Would it not be best to disband their armies and go home? Henri, deserted by some of his friends and with half his army left, marched into Normandy, knowing in his heart and mind, despite his present setback, that one day Paris and the whole of France would be entirely his.

His sister, Princess Catherine, was still unmarried, but deeply in love with her cousin the comte de Soissons and hoping to marry him, a match of which her brother did not approve. Now that he was King of France and still actively engaged in civil war, he left her to govern his province of Béarn. Monsieur du Plessis, kept on as councillor to the new King, had been made governor of the château-fortress at Saumur, commanding a strategic position on the banks of the Loire. He was not amongst those of the King's advisers—and they were many—who were urging him to change his faith, if not his private convictions, thereby winning the allegiance of his Catholic subjects. Among them was Marshal Matignon, governor of Bordeaux, who had befriended Anthony Bacon during his sojourn there. The King agreed that, if this matter of his religion could be settled, many other matters could be settled too, but first he must crush his enemies, and bring peace to his shattered country.

Anthony's debts had been cancelled in July, so he was now safe from his creditors. Whether he was still being harassed in some way, or whether the continued presence of Marshal Matignon in Bordeaux appeared to afford a better asylum, is not made clear in his correspondence. Whatever the reason, some time during the year 1590 he crossed the Tarn for the last time, leaving behind him for ever the city of Montauban, which he had first entered with such anticipation, and travelled to Bordeaux. His master, Secretary of State Walsingham, had died on April 6th, and no one had been as yet appointed to succeed him. It could have been this uncertainty, and wondering to whom his secret correspondence should now be directed, that was foremost in Anthony's mind as he rode west.

Sir Francis Walsingham had been in wretched health for some months. He had lived to see his daughter Frances, the widow of Sir Philip Sidney, take for her second husband Robert Devereux, Earl of Essex, who was by now the established favourite of Queen Elizabeth. His stepfather, the Earl of Leicester, had died in 1588, soon after the rout of the Spanish Armada, and Essex had been ap-

pointed to many of his honours and privileges. Walsingham, who had spent a lifetime in the service of his Queen,
died in poverty. He had been forced to sell The Papey,
his house in Bishopsgate, and move to a house in Seething
Lane, and he was buried secretly in St Paul's by night in
case his creditors should come to tear open his coffin. The
Queen, for all her sagacity, or perhaps because of it, expected her statesmen to pay for information about foreign
affairs out of their own pockets, and Walsingham, who
had recruited more agents than any other of her ministers
or those of Henry VIII before her, was a victim of her
closed fist. Where Walsingham had failed, smaller fry such
as Anthony Bacon would hardly do better from the Privy
Purse, but his disapproving uncle Burghley was, after all,
still Lord Treasurer, and Anthony must continue to keep
in touch with him.

Anthony was ill when he arrived in Bordeaux, and remained so for at least five months. The foot he had
wrenched in Béarn four years previously had been giving
him trouble for some time, and a tendency to gout, which
had so irked his father the Lord Keeper, now showed
signs of becoming chronic. Reliance upon pills and potions,
laced with the wine of Bordeaux, played havoc with his
digestion. Nevertheless, it was at this period of his life,
during the years 1590 to 1592, that he formed a new
friendship which was to mean a great deal to him. Through
a Bordeaux poet, Pierre de Brach, he came to know the
writer Michel de Montaigne, the publication of whose essays, between 1580 and 1588, had made him famous
throughout France.

Montaigne was by now in his late fifties, had twice been
mayor of Bordeaux, and was a close friend of Henri IV,
who had stayed with him when he was still King of Navarre. He had been born and bred a Catholic, but Chris-
tianity played a small part in his philosophical thought;
he was an individualist in thought and action. The theo-
logians of the past, and the learned saints such as Augus-
tine and Thomas Aquinas, he discounted; it was to the
Greeks and the Romans that he went for guidance: He-
rodotus, Tacitus, Caesar, Cicero, Plutarch and Seneca were
his bedside reading. His curiosity, his search for truth, were
ceaseless. Both sceptic and humanist, Montaigne believed
that the greatest force within man was his own will. Death

had no terrors, it was man who made a terror of death. Again, man must come to know and understand himself, for without this knowledge, how could he come to understand his fellows? Violence, cruelty, torture, which figured so much in his own time, Montaigne abhorred; and in a century torn apart by religious wars he was careful to guard his liberty of judgement and his independence. For Montaigne, observation of his fellow human-beings was his primary task and his absorbing interest, and with it the discovery of the riches that dwelt within.

"Nous sommes chacun plus riches que nous ne pensons," he said. *"Sachons donc être à nous."*

This philosophy, so entirely different from, and indeed alien to, anything he had absorbed at Gorhambury at his mother's knee or in Théodore Beza's study in Geneva, awakened within Anthony Bacon a response that nipped firmly, for the time being at any rate, his budding self-pity and hypochondria. Here was a man approaching sixty, who did not judge, who did not condemn, to whom he could pour out all his own doubts and fears and be understood, who discussed the great literature of the past with him as with an intellectual equal, and whose ideas on friendship, when writing of his dead friend la Boétie, were summed up in a single phrase: *"Si on me presse de dire pourquoi je l'aimais, je sens que cela ne se peut exprimer qu'en répondant 'Parce que c'était lui: parce que c'était moi'."*

During the two years that Anthony remained at Bordeaux Montaigne was preparing yet a fourth edition of his essays, which he did not live to see published. They appeared posthumously, prepared by his friends Pierre de Brach and Mlle de Gournay. The last letter he ever received was from Anthony Bacon.

This, though, is to anticipate. Friendship with Montaigne did not interfere with Anthony's more pressing business in Bordeaux. On April 8th 1591 he received a letter from a man signing himself Andrew Sandal, smuggled from the fortress in Bordeaux where political spies were imprisoned. Anthony visited the man, and discovered him to be a Scotsman and a Catholic, who, despite the fact that he had at one time been in the service of Mary Queen of Scots, had later become one of Walsingham's secret agents and had toured both Italy and Spain, whence he had sent back information to England. His real name was Anthony Standen. On arrival in Bordeaux the preceding August he had been arrested and committed to prison, under suspicion of being an agent of the King of Spain and therefore a spy on French affairs. Aged between forty-five and fifty, intelligent, witty, and of considerable experience in the field of foreign affairs, Standen made an immediate impression upon Anthony Bacon. This man must not be allowed to languish in a Bordeaux prison; he was too valuable an agent to be lost to the English cause.

Anthony approached both the Lord Treasurer at home and Marshal de Matignon, and in October managed to obtain Standen's release, the arrangement being that Standen should return to Spain secretly in order to discover further Spanish intelligence which he would then send, via agents in Italy, to the Lord Treasurer in London. This was the method he had used when forwarding information to Walsingham.

Anthony was well pleased with his latest stroke of diplomacy. Standen was a useful ally, with his Catholic connections in Spain and Italy, and promised to keep him as fully informed as he did the Lord Treasurer himself. Anthony's own contacts amongst French Catholics were also increasing since he had come to Bordeaux, and he knew they would become of vital importance once Henri IV succeeded in uniting the whole of France, when Catholic as well as Protestant envoys would arrive at the Court of Queen Elizabeth to discuss pacts and treaties.

His mother was not so satisfied. Hints from certain English sources in Bordeaux alarmed her, perhaps even an ill-judged word dropped at random by her brother-in-law Burghley. Was it true, she wrote, that Anthony had manoeuvred the release of some Catholic prisoner, had given him money, and was even thinking of travelling with him to Rome, there to be converted by the Pope himself? Anthony handed the letter to Standen with a lifted eyebrow and a Gallic shrug. This, he implied, was the sort of thing that awaited him when he finally decided to return home. He would ignore the letter.

"Write back to her," advised Standen. "I know well my Lady, your mother, is without comparison amongst her sex. But a woman is a woman, frail and variable as every wavering wind. I mind what the Queen of Scots once said to me: 'Never tell a woman she is learned and wise, only that she is less foolish than the rest; for all women tend to folly'."

Standen left Bordeaux in December and wrote to Anthony from St Jean de Luz, close to the Spanish border. "I stayed an afternoon in Bayonne," he said, "and lighting in a lodging where were some English, passed amongst them for a Frenchman, and great entertainment and courtesy they used to me. But when they cackled amongst themselves, it was a pastime nonpareil to hear what they said of me. I was much in their good grace, which had been the contrary, if that they had known my quality. This night I am to set my doubtful steps on Spanish soil."

If his health had only permitted, what sights, and scenes, and adventures too, Anthony and his new friend might have known together!

Events in France, however, and in England too, were proceeding apace. In June of that year, 1591, Queen Elizabeth had sent troops to France to help Henri IV in his siege of Rouen. The Earl of Essex, much against her will, had persuaded her to give him the command, and he landed in Dieppe on August 10th. Unfortunately the siege started poorly. The Duke of Parma, ally of the King of Spain and the Holy Catholic League, entered France to relieve Rouen. King Henri IV asked for further help from England. The Queen, who had already sent some seven hundred men from the Netherlands to replace those who had been killed, flatly refused, and ordered the Earl of Essex to return home. Relations between England and France became extremely strained. The English ambassador to France had the unenviable task of explaining to Henri IV that the Queen had suggested he was exposing her troops to greater risk than his own, and that this was something she refused to accept.

Henri IV, realising that he must send an envoy to England who was not only a Protestant but skilled in diplomacy, summoned du Plessis from Saumur and entrusted him with the mission. Du Plessis left Dieppe on December 31st and arrived in London on January 4th. News travelled fast, and when Anthony Bacon heard that his one-time enemy was on his way across the Channel to discuss the current situation not only with his uncle the Lord Treasurer but with the Queen herself, he gathered his possessions together and made his farewells to Bordeaux. If—and, although it seemed unlikely, Anthony was sensitive enough to believe it possible—du Plessis should mention past events in Montauban and the ill-conduct of one of her Majesty's subjects, that subject must be at home to defend his character.

Du Plessis was granted an audience of the Queen on January 6th. He had hoped for a favourable reception, but on entering the audience chamber the first thing the Queen did was to lose, or perhaps pretend to lose, her temper. She hurled reproaches at du Plessis's royal master, and against the Earl of Essex for staying by his side in France, despite her express commands. He makes the King of France believe that he, Essex, governs here in England, she told du Plessis, but she would soon prove him wrong. She had every intention of calling all her troops home, she added, and then, without hearing any explanation from du Plessis, she cut short the audience and retired.

Du Plessis repaired forthwith to the Lord Treasurer and gave him a very clear and concise account of the military operations to date. This Burghley promised to transmit to the Queen, and at the second audience, on January 8th, her Majesty appeared slightly more gracious. She was still firm, however, that the King of France should have no further aid from her, but must use those troops that were about him at present.

The following day du Plessis produced a second memoir for the attention of the Lord Treasurer. "Surely," he argued, "it would suit her Majesty better if our common enemy Spain was fought on the soil of some other country than her own. If her Majesty would send but 4,000 troops into France the Duke of Parma would instantly retreat. Without such aid battles will be lost, even kingdoms may be lost, and in consequence every Christian state be placed in peril."

Grudgingly the Queen consented to the levy of two thousand pikemen and a thousand musketeers from Kent, Sussex and the Isle of Wight. Then, exactly two hours later, she changed her mind. She told her councillors that she knew very well they had come to some private agreement with the French envoys to send more troops, and that she would prefer the Earl of Essex to be killed in action rather than give him any further aid.

Three days later, on January 12th, du Plessis having put

the French case yet again, the Queen informed him that further aid was out of the question. "My subjects reproach me," she said, "for sending so many of them to perish uselessly. I am beset with conspiracy and menace on all sides, and this is proven by the depositions of certain prisoners. My troops have no place in which to retreat in France, should some setback strike the King. He digs no trenches, he seems to take pleasure in losing a battle, the English alone are sent into attack. The Earl of Essex is the least suitable of men to be thus employed."

Du Plessis replied to every one of her Majesty's reproaches, but nothing he said could move her. On January 14th he received his passports. He was delayed at Dover for three weeks by contrary winds and high seas, the same ill weather that kept Anthony Bacon confined to port on the French side of the Channel. The two vessels must have crossed, for on February 4th 1592, as du Plessis landed in Dieppe, Anthony Bacon set foot on English soil for the first time in over twelve years. Seasick, apprehensive and exhausted, he stumbled ashore, to be greeted by Thomas Lawson and Nicholas Faunt, who told him that a room had been prepared for him at Gray's Inn by his brother Francis.

PART TWO

Chapter 8

Anthony's first enquiry of his friends upon landing was not
about family news, but whether du Plessis was still at
Court. No, Nicholas Faunt was able to tell him, Monsieur
du Plessis and his suite had sailed from Dover on the 2nd,
and must by now have reached Dieppe. What, Anthony
asked next, had transpired between him and her Majesty?
Faunt had not been informed, but rumour had it that the
visit had been unsuccessful, and her Majesty had shown
him the rough side of her tongue. Nor did he know what
matters, other than the political situation, had been discussed between the King of France's envoy and the Lord
Treasurer. In any event, Anthony appeared ill and distressed, and the sooner he allowed himself to be put to bed
at Gray's Inn the better. Faunt then handed him, reluctantly, a long letter from her ladyship his mother.

Anthony allowed his eye to travel over the scrawled
words, the sense of which brought little consolation to his
weary brain.

"... That you are returned at length I am right
glad. God bless it to us both. But when I heard withal
that Lawson, whom I fore-suspected, stole hence unto
you, to serve his own turn as heretofore; how welcome
that could be to your long-grieved mother, judge you.
I can hardly say whether your gout or his company
are the worse tidings. I have entertained this gentleman, Mr Faunt, to do so much kindness for me as to
journey towards you, because your brother is preparing your lodging at Gray's Inn very carefully for you.
An honest gentleman, but one that feareth God indeed, and wise withal. ...

"This one counsel your Christian and natural
mother doth give you before the Lord, that above

all worldly respects you carry yourself ever at your
first coming as one that doth unfeignedly profess the
true religion, and are not afraid to testify to the
same by hearing and delighting in those religious exercises of the sincerer sort, be they French or English." (Oh, dear God, Anthony surely thought, for
the untroubled equanimity of Michel de Montaigne.)
"Courtesy is necessary," his mother continued after
half a page of Greek and Latin intermixed, "but too
common familiarity in talking and words is very unprofitable, and not without hurt-taking, *ut nunc sunt
tempora*. Remember you have no father. And you
have little enough, if not too little, regarded your kind
and simple mother's wholesome advice from time to
time. . . .

"Let not Lawson, that fox, be acquainted with my
letters. . . . He commonly opened underminingly all
letters sent to you from Council or friends. I know
it, and you may too much, if God open your eyes as
I trust he will. Send it back, to be sure, by Mr Faunt
sealed; but he will pry and prattle. So fare you well,
and the Lord bless you and keep you forever.

"Your mother, A. Bacon.
"I trust you, with your servants, use prayer twice
a day, having been where reformation is. Omit not
for any. Your brother is too negligent herein."

For which heaven be praised, and let there be some
measure of peace and a well-warmed bed to greet him in
that chamber at Gray's Inn.

So much had changed during those twelve years of absence, and the nineteen-year-old beardless youth with curl-
ing hair that had been his brother Francis, of whom the
artist Hilliard had said on painting his likeness, "If only
I could paint his mind", had now turned one-and-thirty.
He had filled out and grown to middle height, and the
expression in his eyes was more lively and penetrating than
ever. One curious weakness that had been his from childhood, which he was never to overcome, was a sudden fit
of fainting when the moon was in eclipse; the eclipse
ended, he was himself again. His health was never robust,
although he was not to be crippled by gout or to suffer

from nervous anxiety like his brother Anthony. His powers of concentration were formidable; he could work long hours day and night without sleep, and turn with the greatest facility from drafting a speech, which he would throw off with consummate ease in Parliament, to composing a masque or some nonsensical trifle for his juniors in Gray's Inn.

If Francis had matured, so twelve years abroad had left their stamp upon the elder brother. Here was a man of thirty-three who looked nearer forty, pale of complexion, heavier of build, who, because of his lameness, walked with a cane, while the cut of his hair, the trim of his beard, his intonation, even the accent, proclaimed him a Frenchman. His gestures were foreign, the shrug and the smile were Gallic, and, like all expatriates returning to their own shores, he seemed more interested in the affairs of France than in those of his mother country.

However, he must adapt and learn. And his younger brother Francis had much to tell him. Their mother was more irascible than ever, she must not be crossed. Gorhambury needed its master, farms and manors were in a sad state, debts were piling up. Tenants were at odds with one another. Servants were one day dismissed and the next day reinstated. Their mother was more tight-fisted than her Majesty, if such a thing were possible, and Francis himself did not know where to turn for money. As for their uncle Burghley, the Lord Treasurer, he had been singularly unhelpful both financially and in advancing the younger brother's affairs. Francis must make his own way in the world. No, his uncle would not further this or that suit to her Majesty.

And yet—and here was the rub—uncle Burghley had taken great care to advance his own son, their cousin Robert Cecil, to a place of great authority, namely, to take over much of the work and many of the duties of the late Secretary of State Walsingham. There was Robert, creeping about at Court with bundles of paper under his arm, full of self-importance. A visit by the Queen to the Burghley home at Theobalds had doubled his conceit; she had called him "Elf" and been extremely gracious, and then topped it all by knighting him three months later. Their cousin, that sneaking hunchback who used to go running with tales to their aunt Mildred, was now Sir

Robert. Yes, indeed, it was only a matter of time before he was raised to the full position of Secretary of State, his father the Lord Treasurer would see to that. But the Lord Treasurer's nephews, Anthony and Francis Bacon? No honours had come their way or were likely to, unless they found a patron. Anthony, Francis considered, had at least earned some reward for all his years in foreign service. The sooner he appeared at Court the better.

Their other cousin Edward Hoby, son of aunt Elizabeth, Lady Russell, was of the same opinion. "It will be best if you repair to Court as soon as you come to London," he urged in a letter of welcome. Anthony took to his bed instantly. His leg was too painful, he could not walk. He had a touch of ague into the bargain. Edward Hoby came to visit him, and shook his head in sympathy. Unlike cousin Robert, he promised to see her Majesty on his cousin's account, and was as good as his word.

"It pleased her sacred Majesty much upon the stroke of eleven tonight (he told Anthony on February 19th) to call me unto her, and among other things, questioned me if I had seen you since your return. I told her Highness that I had, and that as I had found an infirm body of you, so a much more grieved mind to have had that unhappiness, as through your own infirmities, not to have been able to behold her, which your heart so much coveted to serve. I added further, that her Majesty should find you *un homme arresté*, much more stayed and advised than others of us your kinsmen. She concluded, that she was sorry you were in so evil a plight, earnestly affirming, how that you had been greatly and from good hands recommended to her. And this I thought good to give you, as a taste of her Majesty's grace towards you. I humbly thanked her for her great care and princely regard had of you in her absence, wherewith you as yet relieved yourself. And so, praying God to send you perfect health, and you to command me, I end, very late,

"Your poor kinsman to serve you,
"Edward Hoby."

So du Plessis had not blabbed, at least to the Queen. Unless, Anthony wondered, her Majesty had been playing cousin Hoby with her customary finesse? The gout, which had eased, returned twofold. He was certainly not well enough to go to Court. The lodging in Gray's Inn would serve for the time being, with his faithful companions Tom Lawson and George Jenkyll at his side, all the French books he had brought with him to unpack, correspondence to sort from France, Italy and Spain, and, when Francis could spare a moment, conversations between them lasting far into the night. Because Francis had a plan for their joint future, which was to cease importuning their uncle Burghley and cousin Robert for advancement and offer their services instead to the one man in the whole of England who, by natural charm and personality, had stepped as if by magic into his later stepfather's shoes as favourite to the Queen, namely, Robert Devereux, Earl of Essex.

Francis, not invariably a shrewd judge of character, felt instinctively that Essex, though not yet twenty-five, had the potentiality of a great leader. The Queen of England, now middle-aged, had no heir. It was possible, indeed probable, that she would turn increasingly to the Earl of Essex during the years to come, and Essex needed behind him men with brains, who could supply him with information from every European source. Who better to do that than Anthony? His contacts were wide, and indifferent health was no barrier to the receiving and forwarding of intelligence. If necessary he could do it from his bed! While Francis himself, acting in an advisory capacity to Essex, would also be well-placed to advance in the legal field. As those in high positions grew older and had to be replaced by younger men, one who was close to the young Earl would not be overlooked.

Anthony saw the force of his brother's arguments. As he was to say some years later, "On the one side, coming over, I found nothing but fair words, which make fools vain, and yet even in those no offer, or hopeful assurance of real kindness, which I thought I might justly expect at the Lord Treasurer's hands, who had inned my ten years' harvest into his own barn, without any halfpenny charge. And on the other side, having understood the Earl of Essex's rare virtues and perfections, and the interest he had worthily in my sovereign's favour, together with his special noble kindness to my germain brother, whereby he was no less bound and in deep arrearages to the Earl, than I knew

myself to be free and beforehand with my Lord Treasurer,
I did extremely long to meet with some opportunity to
make the honourable Earl know, how much I honoured
and esteemed his excellent gifts, and how earnestly I desired to deserve his good opinion and love, and to acknowledge thankfully my brother's debt."

Why Francis should have been indebted to the Earl, in
1952, is not clear. Possibly some financial assistance had
been given in return for legal advice or letters written in
the Earl's name—Francis had the natural ability to turn
his hand to anything—and while Essex was in France at
King Henri's side from August 1591 Francis, from Gray's
Inn, would seem to have been already in his service.

Anthony indebted to the King of France; Francis indebted to the Earl of Essex; Henri IV and Essex
brothers-in-arms on the field of battle, and with a good
understanding of each other. Intelligence could be a two-
way measure. Information passed to the Earl of Essex
could also be fed to the King of France, who had saved
Anthony's life in Montauban and still expected some return. Anthony had little choice. If he could serve two
masters without dishonour, and at the same time help his
younger brother towards higher things than the wearing
of a bencher's gown, he was prepared to do so.

He was perhaps less well prepared, despite all Francis
had said, for the tremendous effect that Robert Devereux,
Earl of Essex, would have upon him, turning natural
courtesy and diplomatic self-effacement into instant admiration and enthusiasm. Here was someone more worthy of
devotion than even Henri IV had been while still King of
Navarre, and less coarse-grained, less robust, than that
monarch, who, with his broad jesting and his garlic breath,
had sometimes seemed larger than life itself. Robert Devereux was sensitive, aware; he came into the room and looked
about him as though uncertain of what he should find, and
his eye, meeting Anthony's, held a light of recognition,
showing interest and pleasure, and understanding too, as if
to say, "Ours shall not be the relationship of master and
man but that of friends". True, Henri of Navarre had
shown familiarity from the first encounter, familiarity in
a hearty fashion, let us all be fellows of a kind and so to
the stables, or to tennis. Not Robert Devereux. Tall,
stooping a little, head thrust forward to enquire, complexion

pale, and his manner first eager, then of a sudden hesitant, withdrawn. The ruddy hair he had inherited from his mother, Lettice Knollys, hung to his shoulders. He wore as yet no beard, and a small moustache brushed his upper lip. Almost at once he fell to discussing not the French wars, not the plight of Europe, but literature. Mr Bacon had known Montaigne? He had read the Essays? Anthony was won. Francis had no further qualms about his brother's possible diffidence. He smiled to himself, and then withdrew and left them.

Robert Devereux had been nine years old when his father, Walter Devereux the first Earl of Essex, had died in Ireland in 1576 of dysentery. His illness had seized him suddenly, and there were those who said later that he had been poisoned. He wrote a touching farewell letter to the Queen from his sick bed, asking her to be a mother to his children. Those same gossips who murmured poison said that even as her husband lay dying his wife Lettice, the Queen's cousin and the daughter of Sir Francis Knollys, Controller to the royal household, was mistress to the Earl of Leicester, their liaison kept secret from the Queen. Their marriage was performed in private two years later.

Young Robert had for some months been educated in the establishment which Lord Burghley kept for sons of noblemen, before going to Cambridge. He had inherited estates in Wales, at Lanfey, and had hoped to remain there, leading a studious life and farming. He had no desire to come up to London and present himself to the Queen. Finally, at the age of seventeen, he had been persuaded by his mother and his stepfather, the Earl of Leicester, to do so, and was at once received into the royal favour. Active both in body and in mind, he had found life at Court too slow, and when his stepfather was appointed in command of the expedition to the Low Countries in 1585 Robert Devereux had gone with him. It was in this campaign that Philip Sidney, the flower of English chivalry, had lost his life, bequeathing his sword to his young friend Robert for sentiment's sake. Sidney had loved Robert's sister Penelope when she was barely fourteen, and she had been the inspiration for his poem *Astrophel and Stella*. But Penelope had married Lord Rich, whom she did not love, and Philip Sidney had wed

Sir Francis Walsingham's daughter. When Robert Devereux inherited his dead friend's sword he vowed to look after the widowed Frances, and did so for good measure, for he married her four years later.

Romantic, moody, impulsive, yet hesitant, these were the qualities that Anthony Bacon savoured most in his new employer-to-be. The fact that he had the ear of his middle-aged sovereign, who frankly spoilt him as she might a wayward child, was no great matter, except that Anthony would be able to warn him against du Plessis as a scandal-monger and a teller of tales. And if the Earl of Essex were to learn the truth about what had happened at Montauban? Somehow, with sure instinct, Anthony knew he would understand.

When, in early January 1592, du Plessis had been negotiating with the Queen, and she had told him she would send no further troops to succour the King of France, the Earl of Essex was actually at Dieppe preparing to return to England. He had lost his younger brother Walter in the siege of Rouen, and was accompanied by many sick and wounded men. What remained of his army he had left in charge of his bluff and devoted companion-in-arms, the Welshman Sir Roger Williams. It was soon after his return to England that the meeting between the Earl and the two brothers took place.

Anthony kept to his quarters at Gray's Inn during the first six months after his return. If he had not the strength to present himself to the Queen, neither could he brace himself for a long encounter with his mother. Friends must act as go-betweens. And anyway the weather made a good excuse.

"I pray you be careful to keep good diet and order," she warned him at the end of February. "It is here marvellous cold and sharp: too sharp yet for you, I think . . . I would gladly you had well seen her Majesty; but be in some good state of health first. . . . Look well to your servants and your things." And in March, "Believe not everyone that speaks fair to you at your first coming. It is to serve their turn."

Lady Bacon could still not hear Lawson's name mentioned, nor would she have approved of Anthony lending George Jenkyll, with him at Gray's Inn, works by Plato and Hippias, the great astronomer of antiquity. As for

Francis, he surrounded himself with thieving Welshmen, one after the other, and her greatest hate was reserved for one Henry Percy (surely a scion of the Earl of Northumberland's on the wrong side of the blanket), about whom she said, "I pity your brother yet as long as he pities not himself but keepeth that bloody Percy as I told him then, yea, as a coach companion and bed companion, a proud profane costly fellow, whose being about him I verily perceive the Lord God doth mislike, and doth less bless your brother in credit and otherwise in his health." Despite her disapproval, Henry Percy was to remain with Francis until his death.

The truth was that Anthony and Francis, after twelve years' separation, found one another's company congenial, and that of their joint attendants too. There were merriment and feasting in their chambers; the more favoured of the law-students were welcome guests; and when the Earl of Essex himself could be spared from Court and snatch an evening at Walsingham House in Seething Lane, which his wife had inherited from her father, it was only a short drive thence to Gray's Inn.

"My man said he heard you rose at three of the clock," Lady Bacon scolded. "I thought that was not well. So suddenly from bedding much to rise so early; newly out of your diet. Be wise and godly too, and discern what is good and what not for your health. I like not your lending your coach yet to any lord or lady. If you once begin, you shall hardly end. . . ."

The letter arrived only a few days after a previous warning. "Be wary of suppers late or full. Procure rest in convenient time. It helpeth much to digestion. I verily think your brother's weak stomach to digest hath been much caused and confirmed by untimely going to bed, and then musing *nescio quid* when he should sleep, and then in consequent by late rising and long lying in bed; whereby his men are made slothful and himself continueth sickly. But my sons haste not to hearken to their mother's good counsel in time to prevent."

But bed was the best place for writing, whether correspondence or other matters. Both Anthony and Francis found it so. By now they had grown so strong in renewed fraternal friendship that they could exchange ideas on all subjects, literary and political, and if gout attacked An-

thony's right hand then one of his attendants took over, or
some willing law-student skilled in penmanship.

The Inn of Glaucus became a code word for Gray's Inn
and all who dwelt therein—a classical allusion to Glaucus,
who was devoured by his horses for having spurned the
power of Venus. Lady Bacon, for all her scholarship,
might not have grasped the significance of such a term;
but she would have been aghast had she known that one
of Anthony's contacts in Bordeaux, a certain John Blagge,
had written to warn him that an ex-debtor of Mr Bacon's
was speaking evil of him both in Bordeaux and in La
Rochelle, calling him a bastard and a sodomite, and was
even now on his way to London to spread mischief. Mr
Blagge had threatened to pull the fellow's ugly nose from
his drunken face, but to no avail. "Let your worship," the
writer continued, "beware of the viper, and chastise him
for his villainy if he appears in Fenchurch Street, where
he is like to lodge. It spited him to the guts that your bills
were so honourably and speedily paid. Truly I bewail the
time that ever I knew him."

Whether the "viper" ever appeared in the city of London
does not appear from Anthony's correspondence. Perhaps,
if he did, the roaring boys of the Inns of Court knew how
to deal with him when darkness fell.

Summer had arrived, and the brothers were demanding
strawberries from Gorhambury. Their mother obliged, one
fair day towards the end of June. "I have sent I think all
there be, and this day gathered," she told them. "I send
them by my boy of the kitchen [his name was Peter],
a shrewd-witted boy and prettily catechized, but yet an
untoward crafty boy . . . I look for him again at night.
I pray you stay him not. He is able enough to do it, God
willing; do not pity, it will make him worse. If you give
him 6d of your own self, it is too much . . . It is here
very hot indeed. Let not your men drink wine this hot
weather; nor your brother's neither, tell him."

Lady Bacon, now sixty-four, fanning herself in the heat
as the strawberries were gathered, and dispatching the boy
Peter with his laden basket. Jottings for the storehouse of
the mind, as the brothers smiled and scanned her letter.

"Peter?"
"Anon."

"Peter, pree-thee give me my fan."

Words that would raise a laugh in the playhouse a few years later.

The strawberries were eaten, and some half-dozen young pigeons too, also carried on foot by "Peter my kitchen boy", but soon afterwards, in early August, Anthony received a shock. Her Majesty the Queen was expected at his aunt Elizabeth's house at Bisham, and Lady Russell, through her son Thomas Posthumous Hoby, invited both him and Francis to be present. Here at last, aunt Elizabeth insisted, was the opportunity for her nephew to wait upon her Majesty.

Anthony was immediately attacked with severe gout. Indeed, he felt so ill that he was obliged to order his coach and go forthwith to Gorhambury. On August 15th George Jenkyll, writing from Gray's Inn to the invalid in Hertfordshire, reported, "Mr Francis had appointed one Mr Field a scholar to be my bedfellow [Richard Field later a famous preacher, or Richard Field the printer of *Venus and Adonis?*], but he suddenly changed his determination in dislodging both himself and Mr Field for the Saturday morning after your departure from hence, himself with the company of Mr Dunch, Mr Cecil [Richard, son of Sir Thomas Cecil, the Lord Treasurer's eldest son by his first marriage] and Mr Copnall abandoned Gray's Inn and went post to Twickenham, where he meaneth to continue for some four days only, upon a flying rumour spread through the town of the sickness."

Whether, after four days, Francis left his friends and went on to Bisham is not clear, but her Majesty certainly graced his aunt's house with her presence, and a charming pastoral play was performed on the hills above the river to entertain her.

George Jenkyll, in a postscript to his letter, added, "I have sent by Mr Smith to Gorhambury your worship's virginals and the lute, and have desired him to have special care of the carriage thereof."

If Lady Bacon thought it was to be all sermonizing and sobriety under her roof, she was mistaken.

Chapter 9

There were practical, as well as personal, reasons for Anthony's flight to Gorhambury and his brother's to Twickenham, where he had borrowed his half-brother Edward's
house. The sickness mentioned by George Jenkyll was in
fact the plague, which raged through mid-summer into the
autumn of that year of 1592, and was to recur the following year. Anyone who had the means to quit the city and
go to the country did so at the earliest opportunity. Nevertheless, Anthony realised that week after week passed
under his mother's roof would prove disastrous; she would
give him no peace, question his every action, and find
fault with each and every one of his entourage until, in
despair, they asked to be dismissed.

He had already taken care that she should not encounter
Tom Lawson. As soon as he had moved to Gorhambury
Anthony had dispatched Lawson into France, to St Jean
de Luz, bearing letters to his secret agent in Spain, Anthony Standen. Standen had travelled extensively since
leaving Bordeaux, and had made several exceedingly useful contacts in Turkey, Italy, Portugal and Spain; it was
the intelligence from Spain that mostly concerned Anthony,
who would then pass it by messenger to the Earl of Essex.

The King of Spain, it seemed from Standen's information, was rebuilding his fleet, with the intention of attacking the coast of Brittany and thence advancing on England.
An eye should be kept to the defences of Guernsey and
Jersey, Standen warned. He also advised that great care
should be taken with the handling of her Majesty's
Catholic subjects. Rigorous dealings against them would
only prejudice their loyalty—the Lord Treasurer was already as disliked by Catholics as the Earl of Leicester and
Walsingham had been in the past—and every effort should

be made to bind all the Catholic subjects of Christendom to the Earl of Essex.

Standen, being Catholic himself, was possibly biased. Nevertheless the advice was sound, and only confirmed what Anthony had known from his own experience in France. If Henri IV had taken severe measures against all his Catholic subjects he would not have held his crown for six months. In any case, rumours increased daily—and this Standen had direct from contacts in Bordeaux—that it was only a matter of time before the King of France abjured his Protestant faith and was received once more into the Catholic Church.

Messengers riding to and fro between Gorhambury and London caused comment, and ceaseless enquiry from his mother. Anthony knew that he must shift his quarters to another roof, and it was about this time, in the autumn of the year, that he installed some of his staff, if not immediately himself, in one of his leasehold properties at Redbourne, a village about five miles distant from Gorhambury. The house—at that time Place House, on the site of the one-time priory—was bounded by the village street on one side and the large expanse of village green on the other; there was stabling and a barn; and the whole dwelling was indeed suitable for a bachelor who might wish to entertain his friends from London, and whose male staff could amuse themselves by riding, roaming and drinking in the village taverns, of which there were at least five, a large number for a small village with a single narrow street.

Anthony might conceivably have risked the plague in London during the autumn but for the presence there, from September until after Christmas, of one of du Plessis's closest associates, who had been sent on yet another mission to the Court of Queen Elizabeth. This young man, Benjamin Aubéry du Maurier, had curiously enough lived for thirteen months under the roof of Théodore Beza in Geneva, arriving there only a short while after Anthony had left. Recalled at his father's death to the family château near La Flèche, du Maurier later joined the forces of the King of Navarre, and was certainly in Montauban at some period between 1587 and 1588, when Anthony was still in trouble and awaiting the results of his appeal. He was employed by Monsieur du Plessis in the capacity of secretary, and went with him to Saumur. He may not have met Anthony Bacon, but he would certainly know all about him, and what he would have heard would hardly reflect to Anthony's credit.

Aubéry du Maurier arrived in London on September 6th 1592, bearing with him the ratification of the treaty in which the Queen had promised to send troops to aid the forces of the King of France, and certain very private letters from the King to the English monarch, informing her that in order to trick his enemies he was sending Cardinal de Gondy to the Pope to negotiate his conversion to the Church of Rome. This was, Henri IV explained, merely a ruse; naturally he would remain true to his Protestant beliefs. The King of France was playing a double game, but he seems to have succeeded in duping the Queen. In any event his letters had the desired effect, for in the spring of the following year English troops were dispatched to Dieppe.

It may be wondered why a young man of twenty-six was sent on such an important mission rather than du Plessis in person, who had seen the Queen the year before. The explanation came from du Maurier himself in later years. "It became known," he said, "that the person of Monsieur du Plessis was disagreeable to her Majesty. She had received certain ill reports of him." It appeared that Monsieur du Plessis had permitted certain of his entourage to mock at "the bizarre and ridiculous accent with which Queen Elizabeth spoke the French language". This was intolerable! The Queen of England could never permit such an affront to her dignity. Young du Maurier, during the four months he remained in London, was careful to respect her Majesty's pronunciation. And Anthony Bacon remained at Gorhambury, equally careful to keep out of trouble.

It was in October that he learnt of the death of Michel de Montaigne in a letter from the poet Pierre de Brach.

> "I have been so deeply moved by the death of Monsieur de Montaigne that I am not my true self. I have lost the best of friends, and France the most complete and the most forceful personality she ever had, in the whole world the purest mirror of philosophy; to all of which his writings testify. The last letter he ever

received was from you, which I sent to him, and which he could not reply to because death claimed him first. His name and his memory will never die until all things perish, and will remain within me always.

"Your very humble and affectionate servant,
"de Brach.
"Bordeaux, October 10th, 1592."

Pierre de Brach wrote again to Anthony before Christmas, and here he gives some indication of the impression which the Englishman had produced upon him and the little circle around Montaigne. He began by telling him that Princess Catherine of Navarre had been in Bordeaux for three weeks, on the way to see her brother the King, and had been very sorry to see de Brach only the day she left. Verses were exchanged between them, which de Brach now ventured to send Anthony. "They are worth little," he says, "you need only spare a few minutes upon them, for I know that you are capable of far better things, nevertheless I would value your opinion." Capable of far better things . . . Had Anthony, then, continued to write verse, both at Montauban and in Bordeaux?

Another of his former friends was the painter and engraver Gaultier, who had sent him an engraving of Princess Catherine. He had done it from memory, but the sitter had been recognised by several people; and he was delighted to know through "Monsieur Lawson, whom I met in Bordeaux, that you had received the portraits of Monsieur the little Prince and Mlle his sister, which my son sent you from St Jean, while he was in their service, and that you were well pleased with the work." (The reference must be to the King of France's heir apparent, the three-year-old Prince de Condé, and his sister.) Anthony therefore possessed a small collection of French royal portraits which possibly, at that time, adorned the long gallery at Gorhambury. Gaultier added in a postscript, "Please to engage the good services of Monsieur Hilliard, the Queen's painter, should he live near you, and ask him to send me samples of his colour, as I do not care for my own."

Christmas came and went, the plague had eased with the cold weather, and once Aubéry du Maurier had sailed

for Dieppe Anthony could return to his brother's chambers
in Gray's Inn. Parliament met on February 19th 1593,
and both Bacon brothers were returned, Francis for the
county of Middlesex, Anthony for Wallingford in Berk-
shire. Anthony can hardly have put in an appearance, or
her Majesty would have come to hear of it, and demanded
why the gouty Mr Bacon could sit in Westminster and yet
not pay his respects at Court after being a twelvemonth in
England. Francis, on the other hand, did take his seat, and
found himself in considerable trouble in consequence.

Briefly, the matter before Parliament was the question
of supply. The country was still in danger from attack by
Spain. The Crown was in debt from assisting the King of
France and sending troops to the Netherlands also. Money
must be levied to pay for all the vast expenses incurred in
the previous year and for the year to come. A committee
was set up, comprising members of both Houses, to consider these questions. The Lords demanded a triple subsidy,
to be payable in three years instead of the normal six.
Francis, a member of the select committee, listened to a
speech from a fellow Commoner who spoke in favour of
a still larger grant than the one proposed, insisting that the
country could well afford it, then rose in opposition. It was
said of Francis Bacon as a speaker that "he commanded
the attention of his hearers, and had their affections wholly
in his power. As he accompanied what he spoke with all
the expression and grace of action, his pleadings never
failed to awaken in his audience the several passions he
intended they should feel." On this occasion he was alone.
Peers and Commons were alike in favouring a larger grant,
only the Member for Middlesex was obdurate.

"The poor men's rent is such as they are not able to
yield it," he declared with passion, "and the general com-
monalty is not able to pay so much upon the present. The
gentlemen must sell their plate and the farmers their brass
pots ere this will be paid. And as for us, we are here to
search the wounds of the realm and not to skim them
over; wherefore we are not to persuade ourselves of their
wealth more than it is. The danger is this, we shall breed
discontentment in the people. And in a cause of jeopardy,
her Majesty's safety must consist more in the love of her
people than in their wealth. In granting these subsidies thus
we run into two perils. The first is, that putting two pay-

ments into one year we make it a double subsidy; for it maketh four shillings in the pound a payment. The second is, that this being granted in this sort, other princes hereafter will look for the like; so we shall put an ill precedent upon ourselves and our posterity; and in histories it is to be observed that of all nations the English care not to be subject, base, and taxable."

He sat down amid silence. The committee voted for the grant, and the resolution of the Commons was passed to the Lords. The Bill went through its regular stages and was presented to the Queen, who signified her gracious acceptance, but she knew very well that thirty-two-year-old Mr Francis Bacon, son of her loyal old servant the Lord Keeper, had opposed, in the name of the people, a grant to the Crown. Her Majesty was seriously displeased. Mr Bacon might in future press some suit upon her a dozen times, seek a position, hope for advancement, she would close her ears to all requests. She would not even suffer him to appear at Court.

"I was sorry to find," Francis told his uncle the Lord Treasurer, "that my last speech in Parliament, delivered in discharge of my conscience and duty to God, Her Majesty, and my country, has given offence." But he did not retract what he had said. He did not apologise for his opposition to the subsidy, only expressed his regret that his motives had been misunderstood. All hopes of preferment were instantly blighted. Even the Earl of Essex, who on Shrove Tuesday had been sworn in for the first time as a member of the privy council, could do no more at this moment than bid Francis have patience and bide his time; the Earl would make it his business to satisfy the Queen that Mr Bacon had intended no insult to the Crown.

The trouble was, as Francis confessed to his brother when Anthony arrived at Gray's Inn, that he owed money in every quarter. When he spoke of the plight of the English people in face of threatened taxation he knew only too well, from personal experience, what it meant to have creditors on the doorstep. He was in debt to a Mr Harvey, in greater debt still to a friend and fellow barrister at Gray's Inn, a Mr Nicholas Trott—indeed, he had been borrowing from the latter freely most of the time his brother had been overseas. What could Anthony do?

Would it be any use approaching their mother? Anthony
tried, once Easter was behind them.

"My duty most humbly remembered, I assure myself
that your Ladyship, as a wise and kind mother to us both,
will find it neither strange nor amiss, which, tendering
first my brother's health, which I know by experience to
depend not a little upon a free mind, and then his credit,
I presume to put your Ladyship in remembrance of your
motherly offer to him the same day you departed; which
was to help him out of debt. . . ."

The suggestion was that the sole property which Francis
had inherited from the Lord Keeper, a farm near Wool-
wich called Marks, should be sold to pay off Harvey. Lady
Bacon, as the widow, had to give consent and forfeit her
claim to the proceeds.

Her ladyship, predictably, replied with a torrent of reproach. "I have been too ready for you both till nothing
is left. The state of you both doth much disquiet me." All
his brother's ills had been brought about by bloody Percy,
Jones, Ennis—a filthy, wasteful knave—and his Welshmen
one after the other ("for take one, and they will all swarm
ill-favouredly"). "If your brother desire a release to Mr
Harvey, let him so require it himself, that is, that he make
and give me a true account of all his debts, and leave to
me the whole order and receipt of all his money for his
land, to Harvey, and the just payment of his debts thereby.
For I will not have his cormorant seducers and instruments
of Satan to him committing foul sin by his countenance, to
the displeasing of God and his godly true fear. Otherwise
I will not *pro certo*."

She had not finished, though. A second letter arrived
the following day. A further tirade against Welsh wiles,
and a prayer to God to sanctify her son's heart, and that
he might rightly use his good gifts of natural wit and
understanding.

"He [Francis] perceives my good meaning by this, and
before too. But Percy had winded him. God bless my son.
What he would have me do and when, for his own good,
let him return plain answer. I send the first flight of my
doves to you both, and God bless you in Christ."

Alas, poor Ann Bacon. Did she pass sleepless nights
alone at Gorhambury, regretting past times when the Lord

Keeper was at her side to give wise counsel, and her father would send guidance from Gidea Hall?

Harvey was settled. But Nicholas Trott remained unpaid. There was nothing for it but that Anthony must sell one of his own properties to help his younger brother, and the fine manor of Barley in Hertfordshire came up for consideration. Alderman Spencer of the City, likely to become Lord Mayor of London, showed interest, but negotiations were to take several months, and the sale of this property would also displease their mother. Nor was the noble Earl of Essex, himself continually hard-pressed for ready cash, able to assist financially. He could barely find the necessary sums to pay his foreign agents. Anthony must find ways and means to keep them quiet, though never, naturally enough, by suggesting they withheld intelligence. Standen, that most assiduous of Anthony's correspondents, was shortly due in England out of Spain brimful of information, and would expect good recompense, while Captain Goade, another under-cover agent now stationed in France, complained of an empty purse.

It was hardly an easy summer that the brothers Bacon could look forward to at the Inn of Glaucus, the younger still harried by his creditors, and the elder sifting his intelligence as best as he could and emptying his own pockets at the same time. They were running short of linen and must needs write to Gorhambury for replenishments, but this request, though granted, brought a furious outburst from her ladyship, not because of the linen, but because young Edward Burbage, son of the William Burbage who had caused lawsuits over Pinner Farm, employed by her son out of the kindness of his heart as a courier, had not only spoilt one of her best horses but had shown insolence to her very face.

"He lied and wrangled disdainfully with me," she exploded, "so I bade him get out of my sight like a lying proud varlet. Whereupon, glad belike, he went immediately to the stable and put on his cloak and sword, and jetted away like a jack. I write this to tell you the truth, howsoever he lieth . . ."

Familiar words. "And a speake any thing against me, Ile take him downe, and a were lustier then he is, and twentie such Jacks: and if I cannot, Ile find those that shall: scurvie knave, I am none of his flurtgils, I am none of his skaines mates." Thus Juliet's nurse. The Lord Keeper's widow wouldn't be put upon either.

Anthony summoned George Jenkyll and dispatched him forthwith with a message to the offending Edward.

"Burbage,

"Although your unthankfulness, and unfaithful dealing, would weary any master's patience in England, how liberal and kind soever he were, yet for charity's sake I am content to forebear just rigour till I receive by my man, this bearer George Jenkyll, your answer, which if it be not effectuate, then blame none but yourself if I make you feel what it is to incur wilfully the displeasure of so good a master, as the world knows, and your self cannot deny, I have been unto you. Therefore advise yourself thoroughly in the name of God.

"From Gray's Inn, this 21st of May, 1593."

Nothing but trouble with these Burbages. Anthony would dismiss young Edward. . . . But the boy turned up the next day and acknowledged his faults, and Anthony had not the heart to send him away. The whole affair had precipitated an attack of gout, however. He felt ill. He must get away to Bath and take the waters. How to afford it, though? Then, suddenly, Standen arrived in London, and all thought of Bath was at an end.

Chapter 10

Standen had not set foot in England for twenty-eight years. Banished for his services to Mary Queen of Scots, he now returned to the country as a secret agent of Queen Elizabeth, but uncertain whether his information should be passed to her Majesty through the Lord Treasurer or the Earl of Essex. He was greeted with open arms by his friend and correspondent Anthony Bacon, who then threw a chain around his neck with a medallion of the Earl of Essex upon it.

Standen had been expected since early May. It was now June 13th, and Anthony, with his plans for Bath, had given up hope of his ever arriving. Standen had an exhausting tale to tell. He had been held up at Calais, he had been robbed, letters had been stolen, he had expected some assistance from the Lord Treasurer—with whom, in duty bound, he had been in correspondence—and none had been forthcoming. Was the Lord Treasurer, then, not interested in his arrival? Did he not value the intelligence which Standen brought?

Anthony calmed him down. Standen would indeed see his uncle Burghley, and the Earl of Essex too. The intelligence would be very welcome to them both. The Lord Treasurer was at present at his country estate at Theobalds, and Anthony promised that Standen should have his own coach and drive there the following day, or the day after, when he was rested. The truth was, as Anthony knew very well, and to his own cost, that his uncle was full of promises but very short on performance, and Standen would very likely find that, once his intelligence had been submitted, he would then be conveniently forgotten. Hence the gold chain from the Earl of Essex.

However, it did not do to offend the Lord Treasurer, and Anthony had always taken care to make copies of the various letters which Standen had sent him from the continent, the originals going to his uncle and the copies kept to pass to the Earl of Essex. As he told his brother, "The world stands and goes upon punctos. The best is, my gout has made me wakery, and my long living and conversing with the French hath taught me to look about me in such ticklish matters." He was not surprised, therefore, when word came from the Lord Treasurer at Theobalds that his son Sir Robert Cecil had that day arrived from Court, and could not as yet signify what her Majesty's pleasure was concerning Mr Standen, and it would be best if he remained at Gray's Inn for the present.

First rebuff. The coach that had set forth for Theobalds with its passenger returned, and Standen sat down and wrote a long letter to the Earl of Essex with the latest intelligence, mentioning how certain Irishmen had been in touch with the King of Spain and had offered him the town of Galway on the coast. More Irishmen had arrived in Madrid. There was talk of rigging ships and sending Spanish forces to Ireland. Standen concluded, "I am persuaded that I myself have been forgotten by the Lord Treasurer, since I have heard no more of him; in the meantime I live idle, and her Majesty's service sleeps."

Be that as it may, the gentlemen at the Inn of Glaucus did not sleep. Francis, who had been sick of a tertian ague at Twickenham, returned, and Anthony was obliged to write to their mother for some assistance in the entertaining of "a gentleman from beyond seas". "Since my brother's return hither whose chiefest ease and comfort during his sickness is by company . . . I am so bold as to desire your Ladyship to spare me if you can one hogshead of the same beer I had last, and three others of a later brewing, and also the Standing Cup doubly gilt which my father left me."

It was hardly surprising that in Mr Standen's next letter to the Earl of Essex he said, "Mr Bacon, by the change of the weather, is assaulted with his familiar infirmity, and his grief is the more, for it hath seized his left elbow and hand, likewise the right thumb, in such sort as he hath not been able to write to your Lordship, and that which is worse, unapt to stir abroad and take his wonted exercises. . . ."

The hogshead of beer had arrived, but with a caution

from Lady Bacon. "Be not too frank with that papist. Such have seducing spirits to snare the godly."

Snares and wiles aside, there was small sense in staying at the Inn of Glaucus with the plague increasing daily, people dying in the streets, the epidemic threatening to be as bad as it had been the preceding summer. Far better to take the visitor and the usual retinue of attendants to Twickenham, where half-brother Edward's house was always vacant for them. Edward Bacon, happily married since 1581, with a growing brood of sons and daughters, had installed himself at Shrubland Hall near Ipswich, and had no further use for the secondary residence that her Majesty had leased him for twenty-two years, until 1595.

Twickenham Park, named also, rather aptly, "Ferie Meade", consisted of some eighty-seven acres of parkland, meadows, orchards, woodlands, all spreading most pleasantly on the Middlesex side of the river Thames. The house itself, said to have been built originally as a hunting-lodge for Edward III, was on rising ground fronting the river. The windows looked across to Richmond Palace on the Surrey bank, a feature that was likely to appeal more to Francis than to Anthony; but the secluded walks about the grounds, and the lake in the midst of them, meant that the elder brother could take "his wonted exercises" without fearing that her Majesty, when at Richmond, might peer down at him from some high turret of her palace on the opposite side of the river.

On the other hand, the Earl of Essex could be ferried across with the greatest of ease, meet Mr Standen, and reassure Francis that he was doing everything possible in his power to move the Queen to receive him back in favour and, what was more, have his name placed high on the list for the vacant place of Attorney-General. The trouble was that Mr Edward Coke, the Solicitor-General, who aspired to the post, already had a high reputation and was greatly favoured by the government. He was forty-two, nine years senior to Francis, and had vast experience in the Law Courts (Francis had very little), his only fault being that in argument he was very apt to lose his temper and become offensive, a defect which could never be attributed to Francis.

On July 18th Anthony wrote to his mother, "Our most honourable and kind friend the Earl of Essex was here

yesterday three hours, and hath most friendly and freely
promised to set up, as they say, his whole rest of favour
and credit for my brother's preferment before Mr Coke's.
. . . His Lordship told me likewise he had already moved
the Queen for my brother, and that she took no exceptions
to him, but said that she must first dispatch the French and
Scotch ambassadors and her business abroad, before she
thinks of such home matters."

Meanwhile, the summer months by the Thames were
not passed idly by either brother. The Earl had handed
over to Anthony some private correspondence which he
had been having with Sir Robert Bowes, the ambassador
to Scotland, and Anthony, besides his numerous contacts in
Europe, found himself dealing with agents north of the
border, chief of whom was a Mr Morrison, to whom he
sent £30 by way of encouragement. It seemed that certain
Scots noblemen, like their counterparts in Ireland, were in
secret treaty with the King of Spain, and there were plans
afoot for an army of 30,000 men to land in Scotland, of
whom 1,500 would remain there, while the rest of the
Spanish army invaded England. Thus King James VI of
Scotland had the makings of a full-scale war on his hands,
besides a rebellion by some of his own subjects, a situation
which was rendered all the more dangerous by the fact
that his wife, Queen Anne, was said to have Catholic
sympathies.

Then, on July 25th, affairs in Scotland were temporarily
forgotten in the news from France. Henri IV had re-
nounced the Protestant faith and had been received into
the Catholic church.

Those were some who, like Anthony Bacon, had long
expected it and were not surprised; but to many Huguenots,
who had so loyally and faithfully served the King through
the years of civil war, it seemed like treachery. They could
not understand that the change of faith was politic, that
the useless slaughter of brother by brother would soon be
ended, and before very long the gates of Paris would open
and the citizens of the capital welcome their crowned
King. *"Je veux tout pardonner, tout oublier,"* Henri IV
was to say, and it was true that he forgave his enemies,
and also forgot his friends. Du Plessis wrote in his memoirs: "At the end of twenty-five years (and what years!)
for the most part I have retired without gain, without a

home, without position or privilege, this is my reward for service. Despair to those who serve only men. But I serve God and I shall not lose His reward."

Young Aubéry du Maurier was more fortunate. By the time he had turned forty he was ambassador to Holland.

The conversion of Henri IV was received in England with mixed feelings. Appreciation that he had taken the only possible step to prevent the complete disintegration of his kingdom was qualified by the feeling that there was surely loss of face and much humiliation in publicly disavowing the cause for which he had fought. Besides, how would he now stand with Spain? If he made peace, then England would find herself alone.

So discussion and argument between the brothers and their guest went on at Twickenham Park, with Standen, "that papist", firmly supporting the King of France, who knew so well what he was about, and Anthony somewhat discomfited, despite his agreement, by a letter from good Théodore Beza, who had just written some sermons on the ascent and descent of the Holy Ghost, and professed himself aghast at what had so suddenly and unexpectedly happened in France.

On July 26th one of the Lord Treasurer's secretaries, Michael Hicks, arrived at Twickenham Park to inform Mr Standen that her Majesty would be graciously pleased to grant him access to her, and he was commanded to appear at Windsor, where the Court now was, within four days. Once Hicks had taken his leave Standen, at Anthony's direction, wrote to the Earl of Essex, telling him of the visit and the summons to Court, and saying that he would wait upon the Earl to receive his directions and commands as soon as he arrived at Windsor. By so acting, he would be primed by the Earl of Essex before seeing the Lord Treasurer.

Essex, who was presumably at Barn Elms, his house in Putney, another Walsingham inheritance, sent his reply by return of messenger. "It is folly in me to give you any direction. For your good I cannot, for I know your sufficiency, and mine own weakness. For mine, I need not, for I know you are of yourself careful of your friends. Only this caution I will send, that your affection to me breed not too much jealousy in the other parties, or offence against you. I hope this first access will make so good an impression, as they, that shall labour to effect any thing for your good with the Queen afterwards, shall find the mark easy."

Standen left Twickenham at once in company with Tom Lawson—the pair had become close friends since Lawson had acted as courier between England and Spain—and en route to Windsor Standen dined with contacts at East Molesey, who brought him the latest news from France: that the King had sung his first Mass and had met with the Catholic nobility, and the Paris gates were open. Standen sent word of this back to the brothers at Twickenham, and bade them watch for the effects of this French encounter, combined with the blazing star above their heads; a reference to the great comet that streaked through the sky for five weeks during July and August, something that had all the soothsayers and prophets of doom foretelling woes to come.

Standen arrived at Court on August 1st and made his bow to her Majesty, presented by the Lord Treasurer's son, Sir Robert Cecil. Francis was also at Windsor, but not in evidence. He kept himself well in the background, seeing all, forgetting nothing.

The audience was brief, and Standen was commanded to write down all he had done abroad since he had quitted England in 1565, after which her Majesty might take thought of him again. And that was that. Shaken but undaunted, Standen returned to Twickenham Park hoping that his friend would help him in the appalling labour awaiting him—twenty-eight years to be condensed into a few pages; but Anthony's right hand was so crippled with gout that there could be no active assistance: the pens of others, those young men forever hovering within call, must be pressed into service.

The work was accomplished, doubtless relieved by feasting, more beer and pigeons from Gorhambury, and possibly some strumming upon the virginals and lute. The effect upon Standen's liver was detrimental; he had barely returned to Windsor when he was seized with ague, which, as he wrote to his host Anthony, "was thro' the large diet twice a day at your table". Anthony himself was in little better shape, nor was his condition improved by a lecture from his mother on August 14th.

"You must be tender with keeping in your bed so continually," she told him. "The gout is named *pulmonarius morbus* because it liketh softness and ease. Good son, call upon God to take patiently his correction, and using ordinary good means have comfort and hope yet of better, and endure it as you may with some travel of body more than heretofore. You eat late and sleep little and very late, both enemies to a sound and short recovery. Make not your body by violent and incessant putting in physics, and by practices unmeet, unable to serve God, your prince and country. Make not night day, and day night, by disorder, discoursing and watching, to greater undoing both mind and body."

He was also threatened with a visit from her Puritan chaplain, Mr Wyborn, a prospect so alarming that despite the crippled right hand Anthony scribbled a note at once to dissuade the good man from making the journey.

"I pray you, Mr Wyborn, however moved you may be by kind affection towards me, not to suffer for me in my sickness. God has strengthened me with a continual patience, and I would not exchange bodily health for the inner blessings He has given me. I assure you of my continued friendship . . ." etc., etc.

Standen returned and took instantly to his bed, and a few days later Anthony told Francis that, "My coachman yesterday arrived almost as sick, though not of an ague, as Mr Standen, and hath complained much all this day, and therefore I have given him respite of rest till tomorrow morning, when, God willing, he shall wait upon you with two horses. . . . God be thanked Mr Standen hath found some little ease since his coming by the help of company and attendance to his liking, and will soon recover from his violent sickness."

No respite for Anthony, though. He had to translate into French the Earl of Essex's instructions to the Scottish agent Morrison, then into cipher, all within one hour, only to discover that the Earl had changed his mind, and the work had to be done all over again. The continual patience he had spoken about to chaplain Wyborn was sorely tried, as well as the inner blessing; bodily health was not to be despised. If only he could get to Bath he might find relief from pain. Both his friends and a physician urged it, he told his mother in September, but he had been warned that "the way thither is very ill for a coach, and I beseech your

Ladyship to spare me if you may your litter. As for horses
and guides the Earl of Essex hath promised to furnish me.
I have likewise special need for a cook, if your Ladyship
could conveniently spare Richard, but if you should in any
way be incommoded I will take the other." (Peter, the
crafty boy?)

His mother replied that she herself was sick. Anthony's
conscience pricked him. Should he go to Gorhambury instead of to Bath? Would his presence be of any service to
her ladyship? He had made mention of the cook before he
knew of her ladyship's sickness, so he wrote in deep contrition. No, came the answer, let him go to Bath. She
would send her cook. In that case—there apparently being
some difficulty with the Earl of Essex's coach—Anthony
paused for thought, and wrote again. "One hindrance only
remaineth of my journey, I am to crave, if it standeth with
your liking, to wit a couple of your Ladyship's geldings,
which upon my credit shall be so well used and service-
able, God willing, at their return, as if they had stood all
the while in the stable, and so with remembrance of my
humble duty, and offer of my presence and service, either
now or hereafter, whensoever it shall please your Ladyship
to command the same."

Alas, poor Anthony. The journey to Bath was postponed
for the second time. Gout seized the sole of his foot and
reached his ankle. It was impossible to stand. Francis, who
was still at Windsor hoping to have news as to whether or
not he might be chosen as Attorney-General, pressed his
brother to forget about Bath and come to Court; it might
be that his presence there would move her Majesty.
Anthony, "to his unspeakable grief", was instantly seized
by a long fit of ague and the stone. He was certainly in
pain, but there can be no doubt that the very prospect of
paying his duty to the Queen, so long overdue, had produced once again some profound psychological distur-
bance.

Was it that he feared she would put some question about
Montauban? But no one had done so, not even the Lord
Treasurer, for the simple reason that nobody appeared to
know the truth. Did his fear of an encounter with the
Queen date back to boyhood days, when possibly he had
committed some gaffe before her on the visit to Gorhambury? It could hardly be so. A man of thirty-five could

not be blamed for a childish mishap, if indeed any such mishap had ever occurred. Was he self-conscious about his appearance? Had gout so affected his bearing that, like his father before him, he had swollen in size and was ashamed of the fact? Yet the Lord Keeper had made a jest of his own unwieldy girth. No known portrait exists of Anthony Bacon; no description of his person has survived the centuries. One portrait, said to be the likeness of the Earl of Essex but doubted by all experts and unlike the authentic portraits of the Earl, hangs today at Gorhambury. It may well be Anthony Bacon. If so, he had no reason to fear mockery or averted eyes. But the fact remains that he could not face the Queen, and for this there is still no explanation.

On Saturday October 13th he made a supreme effort, for his brother's sake, to go to Windsor. He got as far as Colnbrook, when he was seized by what he afterwards described as "a sharp fit of the stone", and he told his coachman to drive to Eton, where he rested awhile under the roof of an old friend Dr Paman, presumably a master at the college. To proceed to Windsor Castle was out of the question, and it was imperative to send a message to the Earl of Essex, who awaited him there, and explain what had happened, his attendance upon her Majesty being expected that evening.

Word must have reached the castle quickly, for his aunt Lady Russell, who was herself at Court, came to see how he was doing some time on Saturday afternoon. Fortunately for Anthony, she could see plainly that her nephew was in no fit state to attend the Queen. She was able to relieve his anxiety by telling him that she had been walking with her Majesty in Windsor Park only a week before, and that the Queen, without any prompting and in front of several other persons, had protested with an oath that if her nephew Mr Anthony Bacon had half as much health as he had honesty, she knew nowhere throughout her realm where to find a better servant or one who was more to her liking.

This news was a great solace, but not enough to induce Anthony to prolong his visit under Dr Paman's roof. He was supported into his coach—though whether that same evening or not until the Sunday morning is not known— and so back to Twickenham Park, passing midroute his uncle the Lord Treasurer's coach, who, observing him from the window, descended into the road to enquire what had happened. He too, like his sister-in-law Lady Russell, expressed his concern, and promised to make additional excuses to her Majesty.

Once Anthony was safely installed again at Twickenham he received the following message from the Earl of Essex, obviously himself laid low by some kind of sickness.

"I have broken promise by necessity and not for negligence. I spake largely with the Queen on Saturday in the evening, and forced myself to get up this morning (Sunday) because the Queen on Saturday told me she would resolve this today." (The Earl alludes to the question of Francis becoming Attorney-General.) "But ere I could get from the Queen to my chamber, pain so possessed my head and stomach, as I was sent to my bed, where I have remained ever since.

"On Saturday the Queen kindly accepted your promise to come to her, and as she said herself, sorrowed for your sickness which arrested you on the way. She used many words which showed her opinion of your worth and desire to know you better. She was content to hear me plead for your brother, but condemned my judgement in thinking him fittest to be Attorney whom his own uncle did name but to a second place; and said that the sole exception against Mr Coke was stronger against your brother, which was youth . . . Your offers [perhaps Anthony had intimated he would ask no payment for his services abroad if his brother could become Attorney?] and my mingling of arguments of merit with affection moved somewhat . . . but she referred me over till today. Today I found her stiff in her opinion that she would have her own way. Whereupon I grew more earnest than ever I did before, insomuch as she told me that she would be advised by those that had more judgement in these things than myself. I replied so she might be, and yet it would be more for her service to hear me than to hear them; for my speech had truth and zeal to her without private ends.

"I am full of pain and can write no more. I wish to
you as to myself, and am your most assured friend,
                                          "Essex.

"Burn this."

So no preferment yet for brother Francis. No recompense for himself. Gracious words from her Majesty the
Queen but nothing more. Debts piling up as usual, and
even the noble Earl, who had promised the agent Morrison
in Scotland £100, had only sent 100 crowns, so the difference had to be made up out of Anthony's own pocket.
Nor had Standen, with his twenty-eight years of secret
service on the continent, received one penny yet from the
Lord Treasurer.

No matter. What was it Montaigne had said? *"Il gît en
votre volonté, non au nombre des ans, que vous ayez
assez vécu".* Whether you find solace in life depends not
on your tale of years, but on your will.

Chapter 11

The plague, or the sickness as it was generally called, continued without abatement through the autumn of 1593. Playhouses remained closed, the Law Courts also, and it was decided to hold Michaelmas term at St Albans. This meant that the present Lord Keeper, Sir John Puckering, and all his legal retinue would be living in the neighbourhood of Gorhambury until Christmas. Francis, with his expectations of becoming Attorney-General, must be on hand to see that his rival, Edward Coke, did not steal a march on him; yet at the same time he did not want to be far from the Earl of Essex, who was in constant attendance on the Queen, since her decision in the matter would be final. The Court, because of the sickness, moved between Hampton Court and Windsor.

Anthony wrote to his mother on November 2nd, "The soonest I can do my duty to your Ladyship will be tomorrow or next Monday come sen'night. My brother, I think, will go to St Albans sooner with my Lord Keeper, who hath kindly offered him room in his lodgings there, as he hath already resigned unto him the use of his chamber in the Court. God forbid that your Ladyship should trouble yourself with extraordinary care in respect of our presence, which, if we thought the least cause of your discontentment, we would rather absent ourselves than occasion any way your Ladyship disquietness."

Lady Bacon, who was still unwell herself, was much upset by the death of one of her most faithful retainers, "goodman Fynch", who had been a victim of the plague, and whose want, she told Anthony, she would have cause to lament daily. "His careful, and skilful, and very trusty husbanding my special rural businesses every way procured me, and that even to the very last, much quiet of mind and leisure to spend my time in godly exercises, both public and private. I cannot choose but mourn my great loss thereby, now in my weakish sickly age."

Anthony could foresee a difficult time ahead for himself and his brother, and it was providential that Francis could use the Lord Keeper's lodging in St Albans, and he himself could move a few miles off to his house at Redbourne if his mother became too exacting. As it was, she could not finish her letter without a few scolding phrases about his attendants.

"Be not readily carried either to believe or do upon unthrifts' pleasing and boasting speeches, and but mockeries, in order to make their profit of you and bear out their, unknown to you, disordered unruliness. Among their preadventure pot-fellowship companions there will be craving of you, and I wot not what. Promise not rashly, be *hic juris:* you shall be better esteemed both of wise and unwise before that punitive experience shall teach you to your cost."

It was indeed a great relief that Lawson, and one or two others, could be housed at Redbourne; and when they bore messages to Gorhambury they would have discretion enough to keep well away from her ladyship's own quarters. Anthony himself left Twickenham Park for Gorhambury on November 14th and endured it for a month, but by mid-December he had removed himself to Redbourne, with what excuses and regrets the records do not state. Pressure of work, perhaps, too many messengers coming and going, her ladyship must not be disturbed; but the relief can be imagined in the change of atmosphere from Gorhambury, with prayers and sermons at stated times throughout the day and Mr Wyborn the chaplain forever hovering, and much clicking and clacking to and fro of his mother up and down the long gallery and across the court to see what was afoot amongst the servants.

To his own domain, then, the free-and-easy—slack, if you will—bachelor establishment at Redbourne, the laughter of Tom Lawson and the others, though Tom was not always there, for he had become an invaluable go-between, bearing letters to the Earl of Essex. Above all to be his own master, his movements not questioned. He could, if so he willed, lie abed all day, not to be idle, but to read the latest intelligences from Scotland, or hear what friend Standen was doing at Court, still unpaid, but making

merry with some of Anthony's friends of former days also
now at Windsor: Captain Francis Allen, who had carried
messages for Anthony while he was still at Montauban,
and that doughty Welsh warrior Sir Roger Williams, who,
having fought valiantly for Henri IV, both as King of
Navarre and as King of France, swore undying fealty now
to the Earl of Essex. Good Sir Roger, who loved to boast
of his prowess in the field and of how he had challenged
the enemy to single combat, unhorsing the leader of the
Spanish troopers, and nearly cutting off the head of an
Albanian chief with a blow of his sword.

> "I am eight times thrust through the Doublet, foure
> through the Hose, my Buckler cut through and
> through, my Sword hackt like a Handsaw, *ecee
> signum!* I never dealt better since I was a man: all
> would not doe. . . ."
> "What, fought yee with them all?"
> "All! I know not what yee call all; but if I fought
> not with fifty of them, I am a bunch of Raddish: if
> there were not two or three and fifty upon poor old
> Jack, then am I no two-legged creature."

Thus Falstaff.

Anthony received reports almost daily of everything
that passed at Windsor. The Lord Treasurer sick at his
lodging, and Standen, refused entrance by the servant,
being suddenly passed by the Queen on the back stairs.
The three roysterers, he said, "most commonly together
de camerade, where we discourse of all, and where I wish
you sometimes to hear Sir Roger in his satirical humour,
which *malgré* your greatest pain would make you heartily
to laugh." The company, though, not always male, for,
"most of these ladies of the chamber of mine old familiar
acquaintance have very courteously welcomed me home;
and thereby many, to whom I was unknown, do know
me." Ladies of the Court, and ladies of the Windsor
taverns too.

Unlike Anthony, who feared access to the Queen, bluff
Sir Roger never ceased, between spells of fighting in her
service, to "importune" her Majesty, and it was said that
once, observing a new pair of boots on his legs, she clapped
her hands to her nose and said, "Fah, Williams, I prythee

begone, thy boots stink", to which the warrior replied, "Tut, tut, madam, 'tis my suit that stinks".

So Anthony, cut off in Hertfordshire partly by ill-health, partly by choice, shared in the merriment of his friends, but at a distance, wondering how Sir Roger—to whom he sent salutations—would fare in mid-December at Barn Elms, where the Earl of Essex had invited both him and Standen. There was much laughter, much carousing, but serious matters also, for a certain Antonio Perez, one-time Secretary of State to the King of Spain, had fallen into disgrace with his royal master and had "defected" across the border into Béarn and thence to England, and was now, it seemed, ready to divulge all the Spanish information in his possession. Morrison in Scotland must be instructed too, once more in cipher and in French, and this Anthony could do from Redbourne. The agent was told to report back how King James behaved towards his Catholic subjects and towards those of the Reformed faith, to whom did he show favour, what intelligence was there between him and the King of France, what practices did he carry on with the Irish, was he pleased, or did he complain of the actions of the Queen of England, etc., etc.

Anthony spent Christmas at Redbourne, still crippled by his gout, penning a letter to his uncle the Lord Treasurer begging him to do something in payment for his friend Standen, while Standen himself wrote to Anthony on Twelfth Night saying he had danced all night, and that "the Queen appeared there in a high throne, richly adorned, and as beautiful, to my old sight, as ever I saw her, and next to her the Earl, to whom she often devised in sweet and favourable manner." Francis also spent Christmas at Court, ignored by his uncle and his cousin Robert, but the Lord Treasurer's eldest son, Sir Thomas Cecil, was more kindly disposed, and had already written earlier in the year to his father on Francis's behalf.

There was a good relationship between this branch of the Cecil family and the Bacon brothers; young Richard, Sir Thomas's son, was a frequent visitor to Twickenham Park, and his sister, the provocative, sparkling Elizabeth Cecil, although still in her teens, was ever ready to display her charms and her wit before "cousin" Francis, and he to reply in kind. It was rumoured that she was promised to Sir William Hatton, a widower, who had inherited the title and the estates of his uncle Sir Christopher Hatton, faithful servant and admirer of her Majesty for so many years. Meanwhile it did no harm, and passed the time pleasantly enough, for Francis to pay gallant attention to one of the liveliest young women ever to appear at Court.

Moreover, finances were looking up. Brother Anthony had finally sold his manor of Barley to Alderman Spencer for £3,500. He had asked £4,000; but one of the richest men in the City, who had just become Lord Mayor of London and had bought the old palace of Crosby Hall in Bishopsgate, must be expected to strike a bargain when he saw one. No hard feelings between purchaser and vendor either, for Alderman Spencer's nephew Edward bcame one of brother Anthony's numerous attendants.

The position of Attorney-General was still vacant, and Francis made another bid for attention by pleading his first case in the King's Bench on January 25th 1594, and his second and his third in February, with so much success that he received the congratulations of the Lord Treasurer. Still it did not please her Majesty to reward him with promotion, and Essex warned him that nothing would be done before Easter. What was more, the Earl himself was heavily engaged in matters of greater moment, no less than a discovery of a hideous plot against the Queen's life, and the chief instigator no other than her Majesty's own physician, the Portuguese Doctor Lopez.

The Queen refused to credit it. Doctor Lopez poison her? Impossible. "Rash and temerarious youth," she stormed, "to enter into a matter against the poor man which you cannot prove, and whose innocence we know well enough."

The Lord Treasurer and Sir Robert Cecil also protested the physician's innocence. The Earl insisted: Doctor Lopez was in the pay of the King of Spain. He did have proof. There were letters, witnesses, Lopez must go to the Tower and be shown "the manacles". In high excitement he dashed off a letter to Anthony at Redbourne:

"I have discovered a most dangerous and desperate treason. The point of conspiracy was her Majesty's death. The executioner should have been Dr Lopez; the manner poison. This I have so followed, as I will

make it clear as noon-day. I wish to you all health
and happiness, and will ever be,

"Your most assured and affectionate friend,

"Essex."

Consternation at Court. Rumours and counter-rumours.
The Earl was so angry the Queen did not credit his story
that he shut himself up in his room and did not appear
for two days. When Anthony heard this he was seized with
a sharp fit of the stone. How could her Majesty possibly
disbelieve the noble Earl? Francis listened carefully to all
the Earl had to say, then drew up a paper, "A True Report
of the Detestable Treason intended by Doctor Roderigo
Lopez", which would serve the Earl as a guide, should the
conspiracy come to trial.

Come to trial it did. Lopez confessed, retracted, then
confessed again. Her Majesty, her confidence shaken, forbade all access to her, except for her counsellors and her
nearest ladies. Lopez was tried at Guildhall and found
guilty of high treason. He remained under sentence of
death for three months, and was then hanged. The Earl of
Essex had proved his case and made all as "clear as noon-
day", helped doubtless by the "Report" written by Francis
Bacon, though it was not used in evidence or published in
his lifetime.

The Lopez *cause célèbre*, which had seized the public
interest for three weeks, was soon forgotten, though
security was tightened up about the Queen's person. Life
at Court continued much as before, and access to her
Majesty was still denied Mr Francis Bacon because of his
speech in the Commons twelve months previously. By mid-
March it became generally known that Edward Coke was
to be the new Attorney-General, and his predecessor in
office, Sir Thomas Egerton, was now Master of the Rolls.

One place remained to be filled, that of Solicitor-
General, and Francis, whose tenacity of purpose was remarkable in the face of disappointment, made those in
authority, and above all his patron the Earl of Essex,
aware that he was available for the post. If this final
request was denied then, so he told the Earl, "I cannot
but conclude with myself that no man ever received a
more exquisite disgrace. My nature can take no evil ply;
but I will, with God's assistance, with this disgrace of my

fortune, and yet with that comfort of the good opinion of
so many honourable and worthy persons, retire myself with
a couple of men to Cambridge, and there spend my life
in my studies and contemplation, without looking back."

Meanwhile the Earl of Essex, with intelligence coming
to his hands every day from Scotland, Italy and Spain,
was finding it impossible to deal with every agent himself,
and it caused too much delay to send messengers backwards and forwards to Redbourne. Could not Anthony
come to London? Find quarters somewhere in the city not
far from Walsingham House, where meetings between
them could take place more frequently? Then, even if the
Earl was in attendance at Court, at least communication
would be easier than it was at present. "There are things
which I dare not commit to paper," the Earl said, and it
was two or three hours' journey to Redbourne. In a further letter he added, "I wish I could lend you strength,
and borrow pain of you to free you from this ill companion, which keeps you from all your friends but those
that are able to go to you."

It would seem that Anthony was now attacked by pain
in both this legs, and while this was inevitably put down to
"the gout" it does suggest that possibly the root cause was
arthritis, that crippling disease affecting young and old
alike, for which there was no medical term in the sixteenth
century. His right hand, his feet and his breathing were
at times affected, and his handicap, combined with his already highly sensitive disposition, makes it all the more
remarkable that he was able to overcome natural weakness
and deal with the Earl's secret correspondence as compe-
tently as he did.

He decided there was nothing for it but to leave Redbourne and move to London, as the Earl wished. Half-
brother Edward wrote offering him his own house in London for £560, to include garden and stable, but not to
take it if he could find better elsewhere, which seems to
have been the case, for on March 19th his old friend Nicholas Faunt, who was now married, told Anthony that he
had reviewed the house he had taken for him in Bishopsgate. Whether this was the same house—and it is the only
one—described amongst Anthony's papers as in need of
much repair cannot be proved, but it does not sound very
enticing for a semi-invalid. "The doors which stand to the

weather partly rotten with rain. . . . Somewhat melancholy being of brick stepping down to the entrance. . . . The coming to it with draining cock unpleasant. . . . The boarding of great chamber much in decay."

Lady Bacon disapproved of the whole venture, which would mean the establishment at Redbourne being left in the care of servants. "Take good order how you leave your house in your absence. They will make havoc and revel abroad when you are gone." But worse was to come. "Having some speech with Mr Henshaw after you went hence touching your house taken in Bishopsgate Street, and asking him what ministry there, he answered it was very mean. The minister there but ignorant. And he thought you should find the people there given to voluptuousness and the more to make them so, having but mean or no edifying instructions, and the Bull Inn there with continual interludes had even infected the inhabitants with corrupt and lewd dispositions. I marvel you did not first consider of the ministry as most of all needful, and then to live so near a place haunted with such pernicious and obscene plays and theatres able to poison the very godly. And do what you can, your servants shall be incited and spoiled. Good Lord, thought I, how ill follows it out for the choice. No ministry at Twickenham either. Surely I am very sorry you went from Gray's Inn where there was good Christian company in comparison. But your men always overrule you."

Her scolding had no effect. By the middle of April or early in May Anthony was installed in Bishopsgate Street, almost next door to the Bull Inn, where plays were performed, and within easy reach of Shoreditch, where James Burbage had built his two playhouses, the Theatre and the Curtain, over fifteen years before, with the Earl of Leicester's men the first performers. Closed during 1592 and 1593 because of plague, these places of entertainment were now opened once more, and although James Burbage was to die this year, 1594, his son Cuthbert continued as manager and his son Richard as leading actor of the company, with the Lord Chamberlain himself as patron. Were these Burbages kinsmen to young Edward, who had been employed by Anthony Bacon? One suggestive link. When Cuthbert Burbage applied for a coat-of-arms he said he came from a Hertfordshire family. After Edward had

"jetted it like a jack" in May 1593, the next day showing
contrition, the name of Burbage does not appear again
amongst Anthony's papers, neither does that of his father,
William Burbage of Pinner Park, who had been engaged
in a dispute with Mr John Shakespeare over a house in
Stratford-upon-Avon.

Mr John Shakespeare's son William, aged thirty, was
one of the actors in the Burbage company, and, like his
fellow-players and the brothers Burbage, was lodging in
Bishopsgate when Anthony Bacon came to live next door
to the Bull Inn. It is not unreasonable to suppose that the
young actor-playwright, patronised as he was by Essex's
friend the Earl of Southampton, became acquainted with
the Earl of Essex's director of intelligence, Anthony Bacon;
and that the plays produced by Burbage's company in this
district of theatre-land, at Court, and elsewhere, with the
wealth of topical allusion which they contained, may from
time to time have owed something to themes suggested by
the two Earls and their companions, who watched and
applauded and sometimes, perhaps, even contributed to
the versification. Anthony, after twelve years in France,
widely read in French and Italian, and with information
coming in daily from his continental agents, could well
have been a valuable source of ideas to the budding dra-
matist—who, incidentally, a few years later became a
lodger in Silver Street, where Sir Nicholas Bacon had
owned tenements. Lady Bacon's fears that her eldest son,
and doubtless his brother too, would become involved with
theatre-folk were probably well founded.

If Anthony hobbled to one or other of the playhouses
for relaxation, or sat watching the clowns at the Bull Inn,
his hours otherwise were fully occupied in sifting through
intelligence from Scotland. Besides Dr Morrison there
were a James Hudson and a David Foulis, both of them
Scottish gentlemen about the Court of King James, and
both capable of carrying on their correspondence in
French. David Foulis, in particular, mentioned Anthony's
name to the King of Scotland, who thereafter had a good
opinion of him.

Certain of the Catholic Scots noblemen, Earl Bothwell
in particular, were in a state of rebellion against their
King, and James himself was desirous of financial aid from
Queen Elizabeth. He suspected the Queen's ambassador,

now Lord Zouche, of carrying on a clandestine correspondence with the rebel Bothwell. Relations between the
two kingdoms were sensitive, therefore, and must be
handled with care. The King of Scotland found the Earl of
Essex, via his agent Mr Anthony Bacon, more sympathetic
than the Lord Treasurer or the Secretary of State, both
of whom acted with extreme caution whenever loans were
in question, but matters were becoming urgent; the rebel
Earls had several hundred men in the field, and were
expecting reinforcements from Spain at any time.

David Foulis suggested that not all those in the immediate vicinity of King James were always to be trusted, and
thought that someone should be sent to reconnoitre, and
that someone a person well known to the Earl of Essex.
Whether this was the mission on which Francis Bacon
started forth for Scotland in July is uncertain, but the timing is significant. Unfortunately, sudden ill-health, the
family failing—in his case "a flux of the blood"—
overtook him when he had got as far as Cambridge, and
the mission was abandoned. So once more he was unable
to prove his worth to her Majesty.

Lady Bacon was again giving trouble, and Edward
Spencer, Alderman Spencer's nephew and newly one of
Anthony Bacon's attendants, was at his wit's end throughout the summer keeping the peace between Gorhambury
and Redbourne, reporting every few days to his master in
Bishopsgate. Tom Lawson had been sent a greyhound
bitch at Redbourne, and, not wanting her, had passed the
animal on to Spencer at Gorhambury. Lady Bacon was
furious and bade Spencer hang the poor bitch, which he
did reluctantly, and was then scolded for the deed. The
dialogue between her ladyship and the alderman's nephew
was good enough for the playhouse. Perhaps it found its
way there in altered form, but the original goes as follows:

Lady Bacon Go home to your master, and make a
fool out of him. You shall make none of me. I marvel
where he picked you out. There is Mr Lawson, who
hath gotten away my brewer and your master together, but he shall hear of it one day.
Spencer My Lady, Mr Bacon is minded to send to
the fair to buy some horses, and hath sent me and
Mr Lawson some money for the same.

Lady Bacon Let him do as he will, he shall have none of me.

Spencer My Lady, Mr Bacon hath got great experience and great worship both within this land and without.

Lady Bacon I know how vainly his money hath been spent. But I am sure he hath gotten a weak body of his own and is diseased in the meantime.

Spencer My Lady, he would have written to you, but the Scottish gentleman is come.

Lady Bacon How many horses does he mean to buy?

Spencer Four or five.

Lady Bacon My sons they be vainglorious, but they will hear of it one day . . . What hast thou there? A brace of partridges killed by your sparrowhawk? You shall keep no hawk here.

Spencer My Lady, shall I pull off her head?

Lady Bacon (stamping) Aye, as you did the greyhound bitch. As for that Lawson, he is a villain and a whoremaster, and the doctor in Redbourne is little better, being both Papist and sorcerer. Now to bed with you, and without your supper.

There was not one in the house, Spencer told Anthony, but she fell out with. She had taken away Winter's cloak, she had quarrelled with both brothers Knight, and she made Spencer buy his own starch and soap to wash his linen. Verily, there was no pleasing her. Anthony took pen in hand and addressed his mother.

"Madam,

"For answer on my part to your Ladyship's letter, I found myself emboldened with warrant of a good conscience, and by the force of truth, to remonstrate unto your Ladyship with a most dutiful mind, and tender care of your Ladyship's soul and reputation, that howsoever your Ladyship doth pretend and allege for reason your motherly affection towards us, in that which corcerneth Lawson. Yet any man of judgement and indifference must needs take it for a mere passion, springing either from presumption, that your Ladyship can only judge and see that in the man, which never any man yet hath seen; or from a sovereign desire to over-rule your sons in all things, how little soever you may understand either the ground or the circumstances of their proceedings; or else from want of civility, abandoning your mind continually to most strange and wrongful suspicions, notwithstanding all most humble submissions and endeavours possible on his part to procure your Ladyship's satisfaction and contentment. Whereupon, entirely reposing myself on infallible grounds, I remain more ready to receive and endure your blame for performing with free filial respect this my bounden duty, than your thanks, or liking for soothing or allowing by silence so dangerous humours and uncharitable misconceits.

"And so I most humbly take my leave.
"Anthony."

And less humbly, he might have added, turn to pursuits which gave more cause for concern, for the flow of documents between Bishopsgate and Scotland sometimes threatened to overwhelm him. Moreover, a messenger had arrived from brother Francis to say that one of their Cooke relatives was to travel abroad and needed £150 for the journey. . . . He must turn to Montaigne. *"Ce n'est pas assez de lui roidir l'âme; il lui faut aussi roidir les muscles."*

Chapter 12

Summer had come and gone, Anthony was in Bishopsgate Street and Francis at Twickenham Park. The appointment of Solicitor-General was still unfilled. Nevertheless, Francis was never idle; he had been engaged in some investigation into a criminal matter during September which had come to nothing, and in October he wrote to his brother from Twickenham that, "One day draweth upon another, and I am well pleased in my being here; for methinks solitariness collecteth the mind, as shutting the eyes doth the sight." At Twickenham he could turn to writing, his mind forever teeming with ideas, but before settling in the December recess to *Promus of Formularies and Elegancies* there was the usual trifle to be got out of the way for the students of Gray's Inn, a device for the Christmas revels in the Inn of Glaucus, in which Francis always took part.

It was customary for the students to elect a Prince of Purpoole—the word deriving from Portpool Lane, east of Gray's Inn Road—who held court for the twelve days of Christmas, with officers of state and all about him, in mock imitation of the Court of Westminster. The revel gave amusement not only to law-students, benchers, readers and all concerned, but to the real-life dignitaries of State also, who were invited for the occasion.

This time the play, *The Misfortunes of Arthur*, was written by a Welshman, Thomas Hughes, but there were also "speeches penned by others". The dumb show before the acts was devised by Christopher Yelverton, Francis Bacon, John Lancaster and Francis Flower. The Queen graciously supplied "cloth of gold and other stuff" for the handsome young Prince of Purpoole and his companions. Besides the performance in Gray's Inn and later at Court, the Prince and his retinue were invited to dine with the Lord Mayor of London, riding through the city in state, watched by the gaping crowds, a forerunner, perhaps, of the Lord Mayor's Show in later times.

The performance at Gray's Inn was on Innocents Day, December 28th 1594, and the guests were gentlemen and dignitaries from the rival establishment of the Inner Temple. Lady Bacon had earlier warned Anthony, "I trust they will not mum nor mask nor sinfully revel at Gray's Inn. Who were sometime counted first, God grant they wane not daily and deserve to be named last."

Her fears were justified. On the first of the grand nights, with the guests from the Inner Temple about to take their seats, the crowd in the hall at Gray's Inn became so great that there was no room for the actors. People were pressing on all sides to see the fun, and instead of an orderly and scholarly display a vulgar play, *A Comedy of Errors*, was performed before the shocked audience and the evening broke up in general disorder. A post mortem was held the following day. Such a thing must never be permitted again. A "graver conceit" must be produced on January 3rd when the Lord Keeper, the Lord Treasurer, the Vice-Chamberlain and others were invited. The post mortem was, of course, a pretence, as had been the uproar of the preceding evening. It was all part of *Gesta Grayorum*, and the lively students had performed many a light-hearted entertainment in other years.

After the gaiety of the Night of Errors, as it came to be called, a more sober production was performed on January 3rd, this time a playful satire on the contemporary scene, the whole obviously thought out by Mr Francis Bacon, with the Prince addressing his Privy Council and the Councillors replying, one advising the Study of Philosophy, another Fame, Buildings and Foundations, a third the Absoluteness of State and Treasure, and the last Virtue and a gracious Government. The Prince of Purpoole's reign lasted, as usual, until Shrove Tuesday, when he and his Knights of the Helmet performed *Proteus and the Rock Adamantine* before the Queen at Greenwich. Then the brief and glorious reign came to an end, and the Prince became a law student once more.

But Francis was still without the hoped-for position of Solicitor-General. It was a repetition of the preceding year and his attempt to become Attorney-General: the Earl of Essex pleaded with the Queen, the Queen replied that she had not made up her mind. Now Lady Bacon began to take a part in it, surely a fatal intervention, and early in January went herself to discuss the matter with her nephew Sir Robert Cecil. She was received with courtesy, very naturally, and the following dialogue took place.

Sir Robert   Your sons are well, I trust, madam?

Lady Bacon   I visited the elder yesterday. It would be much more to my comfort if his health would let him be, God having ennobled his mind.

Sir Robert   That is true, madam, he hath good parts, but gout and stone be too naturally drawn from parents.

Lady Bacon   Well . . . the eldest of my but two in all sons is visited by God and the other, methinks, is but strangely used by men's dealings, God knows who and why. I think he is the very first young gentleman of some account and yet nothing done for him. It is enough to throw a young and studious man, as he is given indeed, wise both for years and understanding. The world marvels in respect of his friends and his own towardness. Experience teacheth that her Majesty's nature is not to resolve but to delay.

Sir Robert   I dare say, madam, my Lord [his father, the Lord Treasurer] would gladly have had my cousin placed ere this.

Lady Bacon   I hope so myself . . . But some think if my Lord had been earnest it would have been done.

Sir Robert   Surely, my Lord even on last Tuesday moved the Queen that the term day was near and required a solicitor for her service, and she straightway answered it was a shame the place was so long unfurnished, and was there no one but Francis Bacon fitted for the place? I know not, said my Lord, but the judges and others have and do take him sufficient with your favour and it is expected of all this term. Whereto she gave no grant.

Lady Bacon   As for that, nephew, you yourself are Secretary, but were never nominated.

Sir Robert   I wait still, and think myself as hardly used as my cousin. I tell you plainly, madam, I disdain to seem to be thought that I doubted of the place, and so would I wish my cousin Francis do, as long as the room vacant, and to bear the delay. Let him not be discouraged, but carry himself wisely. It may be said her Majesty was too much pressed at the first which she liketh not, and at last will come of herself.

Lady Bacon reported the encounter to her sons, and certainly the dialogue between aunt and nephew bore fruit, for within a day Sir Robert Cecil spoke with the Queen, but the move was premature and irritated her Majesty.

"Why," stormed the Queen, "I have made no solicitor? Hath anybody carried a solicitor with him in his pocket? But it seems Francis Bacon must have it in his own time or else I am to be thought to cast him away. If he continues in this manner, I shall seek all England for a solicitor rather than take him."

So Lady Bacon might have done better to stay at home, or else sought an audience of the Queen herself. It would surely have proved a meeting worth recording.

Francis, at Twickenham, was short of money as usual, and had asked brother Anthony to write to their uncle Sir Henry Killigrew for a loan of £2,000. Uncle Killigrew excused himself. "To be plain," Francis told Anthony on January 25th 1595, "I mean to make the best of those small things I have, with as much expedition as may be without loss, and so I sing a mass of requiem, I hope abroad. For I know her Majesty's nature, that she neither careth tho' the whole surname of the Bacons travelled, nor of the Cecils neither." Then, a tantalising footnote to his letter, "I have here an idle pen or two, specially one, that was cozened, thinking to have got some money this term. I pray send me somewhat else for them to write out besides your Irish collection, which is almost done. There is a collection of King James, of foreign states, largeliest of Flanders; which though it be no great matter, yet I would be glad to have it."

Anthony had no idle pens in Bishopsgate, for the Earl had need of his services night and day. An agent recommended by his friend Standen, a Catholic named Anthony Rolston, was sending intelligence weekly from Spain, and confirmed reports that the rebel Scots noblemen were in secret treaty with the Spanish King. Several new ships were being built, all destined, so they said, for Scotland.

Another new correspondent was Sir Thomas Bodley, who was the Queen's resident Minister at The Hague, and it was part of Anthony's business to wean Sir Thomas from his dependence hitherto upon the Lord Treasurer and divert it to the Earl of Essex. Naturally, the Minister would continue to keep the Lord Treasurer informed of all that happened at The Hague, but the Earl of Essex would be privy to the same intelligence. For this was the object of all Anthony Bacon's undertakings, both in Scotland and in Europe: that Essex should have secret information before such matters came to the ear of the Lord Treasurer, or, if this were impossible, that at least Essex should not be left in ignorance.

Another contact who was becoming increasingly important was the King of Spain's former Secretary of State, now living in London, who had offered intelligence to Essex in December—the flamboyant and frequently indiscreet Antonio Perez. The Queen disapproved of him, saying that anyone who had betrayed his own sovereign would have little compunction in betraying another. Essex believed otherwise, and that he could be valuable. So Anthony became go-between, and Perez *persona grata* in Bishopsgate Street. Besides, he was amusing company, his speech full of flowery affectation that Anthony delighted in repeating to Francis. One recommendation to Anthony personally was the fact that Perez professed himself devoted to King Henri IV of France and even more so to the King's sister, the Princess Catherine, who—as he was fond of telling everyone—chose to confide in him. Meanwhile, awaiting some remuneration from the royal purse, Perez hovered about Queen Elizabeth's Court.

Another point in Perez's favour, so far as Anthony and Francis were concerned, was his dislike of their cousin Sir Robert Cecil, whom he nicknamed "Roberto il diavolo", which immediately became one of the family code-words. It was not only that dislike was mutual between the cousins, and had been so since boyhood, but there was mutual mistrust between the Lord Treasurer and his son Robert on the one hand and the Earl of Essex on the other. The Cecils, father and son, understood probably better than anyone that the Queen, being neither wife nor mother, must bestow her affection upon someone. The Earl of Leicester had possessed her heart for many years, and there was nothing unnatural that his stepson should appeal to her emotionally almost as if he were indeed the son she had never borne. Her indulgence of the young man was on a very personal footing, quite different from the mocking, challenging attitude she had adopted throughout her reign towards other favourites, Sir Christopher Hatton, for instance, and later Sir Walter Raleigh. Her godson, the witty John Harington, was also a young man who amused her and who was permitted much free speech that she would have denied another. But Robert Devereux, "Robin", was in a very special category, and had he been content to remain at her side as a courtier, on easy, even submissive, terms, with her chief counsellors the two Cecils, they would have accepted it. What they feared was his growing interference in matters of State. Sometimes he acted almost as an heir apparent would have done, and this was dangerous.

As their mistrust of Essex grew, so Anthony Bacon's affection and devotion to him deepened. The quality which the Cecils deemed headstrong Anthony called *volonté* or will, the desire to gain his own way not through some youthful pettiness but because he believed himself in the right. Impulsive? No, courageous. Haughty? No, proud. Lavish? No, generous. The Earl's personality was such that a man either looked askance at him and felt inferior, or was willing to lay down his life for him. There was nothing in between. Francis had judged him rightly from the first. Robert Devereux had all the qualities of leadership that could make him foremost in the land next to her Majesty, and because of this he must be guided.

Francis, with his brilliantly analytical mind, perhaps perceived something that others, even the gossips, had not grasped, which was that her Majesty the Queen indulged her Robin not only because he was Leicester's stepson, but because Robin's mother, Lettice, had been her hated rival, and it was to her, the Queen, that the young man gave his devotion, not to his real mother. Thwarted maternal instinct, unconscious spite. Francis Walsingham, Robin's wife, was never a problem. She stayed at home and bred. But if Essex took a mistress the Queen lashed out at him like a possessive mother, something that Lettice—who had not mourned Leicester long but had married Sir Christopher Blount, one of Robin's friends—

never did. Did the Queen, then, envy her, because in days
gone by she had not only given birth to Robin but had
been bedded by Leicester? Was envy part of her unconscious torment?

> There be none of the affections which have been noted
> to fascinate or bewitch but love and envy: they both
> have vehement wishes; they frame themselves readily
> into imaginations and suggestions, and they come
> easily into the eye, especially upon the presence of
> the objects, which are the points that conduce to
> fascination, if any such thing there be. We see like-
> wise the Scriptures calleth envy an evil eye; and the
> astrologers call the evil influences of the stars evil
> aspects; so that still there seemeth to be acknowl-
> edged, in the act of envy, an ejaculation or irradiation
> of the eye. . . .

Memoranda to be noted down by idle pens at Twickenham, and one of these days Francis decided he would
please brother Anthony, who was forever quoting Montaigne's Essays, by producing something of the kind himself.

Meanwhile he would continue to give advice to the
Earl of Essex when opportunity allowed, "for lookers on,
many times, see more than gamesters; and the vale best
discovereth the hill". Then another letter would be dashed
off to his brother, which Anthony replied "came by your
man Percy", and so the interchange of news, ideas, plans,
went back and forth between the pair of them.

Henry Percy, still the coach-companion and bed-fellow
of Francis, and so much disliked by Lady Bacon, was
trusted with all secret correspondence, much as Anthony's
letters were carried by Tom Lawson, and it is posterity's
loss that no letter from either man exists amongst the
records, save one in French from Tom Lawson to a certain
Monsieur Durant, a doctor of medicine in London. The
contents are obscure but the style is humorous, giving a
brief glimpse of Anthony's closest friend.

> "Monsieur, I am very pleased to hear you are so
> busy, and I have no doubt that these white devils
> have tried to stop you, because they are terrible

sirens who with their song draw people into their
clutches and principally those who are of your complexion. So like a good prior that loves and honours
his abbé, I am to tell you that one of these days they
will summon you to the chapter to account for your
absence. I have need of a little Benedictine laxative,
but am ignorant of the dose, so please send, as since
your departure I have taken nothing.

"I pray that the white devils will not overwhelm
their pastor.

"Your most vigilant prior, from your convent,
                    "Thomas Lawson."

The convent, presumably, is the house in Bishopsgate
Street, but the significance of the allusion to the "white
devils" is, alas, lost.

Anthony's papers for the first months of 1595 teem
with matters which, unimportant historically, nevertheless
reveal many glimpses of his London life. For instance,
the household bills. The servants—the cook, John Knight
the butler—spent a small fortune on cloth and canvas, caps
and hose, napkins, waist-bands, cuffs, suggesting that the
personal appearance of his staff was something the master
deemed important. All bought of a merchant, Mr Archer.
Horsecloth, saddles, stuffing for the saddles, here were
items from the coachman. And later in the year, with the
weather more favourable, there is a considerable sum
spent on boat-hire between London and Barn Elms,
Essex's house at Putney, and from London to the Court
at Greenwich, as well as for wine, board and lodging for
the messenger who bore the letters. Dr Morrison, the
Scottish agent, now in London, very naturally expected
Anthony Bacon to pay for items of clothing. One pair of
hose, six shillings. And he must also be taken by boat to
his various destinations, from Essex Stairs to Westminster
and back again.

Anthony's greatest extravagance, for himself and for
his friends and staff, was in the purchase, almost every
week, of beaver hats. In the spring of 1595 beaver hats
were lined with taffeta and velvet. They were bought new,
or old hats were re-trimmed. There were black beavers
and black felts, a black felt lined with taffeta was bought
"for a doctor"—Lawson's friend, perhaps, or Dr Morrison

—and for the first time the name of Anthony's new page,
"a French boye", appears, with mention of a black felt
lined with taffeta for him, and what was more he had a
cipher upon it, doubtless Anthony's family crest.

Jacques Petit, the French lad, was to figure increasingly
in future letters, and, with Tom Lawson more continuously
employed as messenger to the Earl of Essex, to Standen
and to Antonio Perez, Jacques became close to his master.
Lady Bacon had already shown her usual disapproval. She
mentions "your French cattle" in one of her letters about
this time, complaining that when on a temporary stay at
Gorhambury he had "loosened a sheet of lead near her
gate with hacking it for pellets". All was not well at Redbourne, either. Mistress Read, the housekeeper, was
"malcontent for certain implements, and the best reserved
chamber for your friends, noble or not noble, was filled
with birds, hunting or hawking, or dogs. Mr Lawson was
the nobleman lodged there, I ween; and like enough, for
he is subtle, vainglorious and makes you bleared still to
ensure all, and pay for all. One that tames the bit is become a tippler, and will be overseen with drink, but an ill
servant in your house, the fruit of idleness."

Anthony was toying with the idea of moving from
Bishopsgate to a house in Chelsea, and was in treaty with
a Lady Mary Baker for her Chelsea house. He had even
persuaded his mother to send carpets from Gorhambury
to furnish it in style. But at the last moment Lady Mary
begged to be allowed "to release myself and husband of a
promise made you for his house", so Anthony was obliged
to stay on for the time being at Bishopsgate.

Lord Mayor Spencer, now living in great style at
Crosby Hall, had a daughter ripe for marriage, whose
hand was sought by another city dignitary, Alderman
Radclyffe. Why the Alderman's letter pressing his suit
upon Sir John Spencer should be amongst Anthony's papers is a mystery, unless he offered his services as go-
between.

"There is not much odds between our years," the prospective suitor told the father, "but that mine are more by
a year or two, and if her growth be accounted by you to
be small it cannot be better helped than by a tall man.
Your Lordship's care of her is too dear to have her far
removed from you and my purpose is to live where you

shall like. I doubt not that you may have many richer offers, but one that will more love and honour your daughter I protest you shall never have."

Alderman Radclyffe was disappointed: either Sir John or his daughter Elizabeth was unwilling. Some time later she created a scandal by escaping from her father's house in a laundry-basket, let down by a rope from her balcony. Her lover was the young Lord Compton. Sir John was so furious he would not give her a dowry, not even when he heard she was pregnant, and it was the Queen herself who finally reconciled them.

The Bacon finances remained at a low ebb. Nicholas Trott, the obliging lawyer friend who had helped to negotiate the sale of Barley manor to the Lord Mayor, was still unpaid for his services. How could he be appeased? The Earl of Huntingdon, an old friend of Anthony's father the Lord Keeper, must be approached. "As the son of a father who honoured your Lordship's rare virtues so much, and loved your most honourable name and person as dearly as any other whatsoever, I venture to request . . . on behalf of a good friend of mine, Mr Nicholas Trott, whose sufficiency in law be warranted by those who make it their profession, and whose honesty, integrity, and other extraordinary good parts I dare pawn to your Lordship my poor words and credit. What favour soever it shall please your Lordship to grace Mr Trott withal I shall esteem it done to myself," etc., etc.

What came of the request is unrecorded. The Earl, who was a strict Puritan and had acted as gaoler to Mary Queen of Scots in earlier days, might not have approved of Anthony's Bishopsgate address or of his many Papist friends, amongst whom could now be counted Lord Harry Howard, younger brother of that Duke of Norfolk who had been executed for treason in 1572. Lord Harry had of late become one of the close associates of the Earl of Essex, as Lady Bacon was aware.

"Beware in any wise of the Lord H! He is a dangerous intelligencing man; no doubt a subtle Papist inwardly, and lieth in wait. Peradventure he hath some close working with Standen and the Spaniard Perez. Be not too open, he will betray you to divers, and to your aunt Russell among others. The Duke [Norfolk] had been alive but by his

practising and double undoing. . . . He is a subtle
serpent. . . ."

The gossip that Lord Harry was a homosexual perhaps
escaped her, likewise that the same smear attached itself
to Standen and to Antonio Perez. The morals of his
friends and agents did not concern the Earl of Essex. Good
company he enjoyed, and if he suddenly decided to de-
scend upon Anthony in Bishopsgate with some of his circle, then Anthony was only too happy to receive them.
But he liked warning, possibly to have his men prepared
with clean hose and cuffs and the entrance passage swept.
Standen was aware of this, hence the following hasty
word.

"As we were at supper, my Lady Rich [Essex's beautiful
sister Penelope], Signor Perez, Sir Nicholas Clifford and
myself, there came upon a sudden into the chamber my
Lord and Sir Robert Sidney, and it was resolved that tomorrow my Lord means to dine at Walsingham House and
in the way to visit Mr Anthony Bacon, and my Lady Rich
said she would go with them, and in their company, and
dismount from the coach at Mr Bacon's house. All of
which I write to you by way of advice, to the end you may
not be taken unarmed. Women's discretions being uncertain, it may be she will not dismount, and the contrary also
will fall out. . . ."

Did she dismount? It will never be known, but the image
remains, the clatter of hoofs, the coach coming to a halt
before Anthony's house, the door flung wide, young
Jacques, his beaver hat discarded, bowing and blushing
and stammering in French, and the rustle of her gown as
Penelope Rich advanced into the offending passage, her
brother and his friends in attendance; while Anthony, lean-
ing upon his stick, bade her ladyship welcome.

Chapter 13

Intelligence from France and Scotland continued to filter through Anthony's hands, and so to the Earl of Essex, through the spring and summer of 1595. In February, Henri IV had declared war on Spain, and this, combined with the sad state of his country, torn apart so long by civil strife, was a tremendous burden upon his finances and troops. He had barely escaped assassination the preceding Christmas, and the shock of this told upon his usually buoyant spirits and those of his sister Princess Catherine, who still followed him everywhere, despite the fact that he steadfastly forbade her marriage to the man of her choice, her cousin the comte de Soissons. The relationship between brother and sister became more sorely tried in the spring of this year, when the King, marching into Burgundy, found himself deserted before a battle by Soissons, on the petty excuse of having been placed second in command. Henri could not resist writing to Catherine, "Many of my young nobles showed the greatest courage, there were others who did less well, and some who did very ill indeed. Those who were not there ought to be sorry, for I was in need of all my good friends. . . ."

The King's own courage in this particular action was, according to the agent reporting from Dijon, one of the most spectacular of his life, and showed "the miraculous effects of God's favour upon him". Henri IV's bearing in this skirmish, and in those that followed, certainly roused the admiration of the Earl of Essex and whetted his own appetite for glory in the field, and for putting into effect plans of his own to succour the sorely pressed armies in France.

In Scotland the relationships between members of the royal family were also passing through a difficult phase. King James's heir, the infant prince Henry, was now nearly a year old, and his father wished to follow tradition and have the future King of Scotland brought up in Stirling Castle under the care of the Earl of Mar. This meant enforced separation from his mother Queen Anne, who was not yet twenty-one, and who was so bitterly distressed at the thought of parting from her son that she became seriously ill. Queen Anne was known to have strong Catholic sympathies, which was one factor against her having the upbringing of the heir to the throne under her own supervision; but the usual jealousy between noblemen in high authority played into her hands. The Chancellor, Sir John Maitland, was no friend to the Earl of Mar, custodian of the baby prince, and so he supported the Queen's case, as did other nobles at the Scottish Court. This rivalry, and the dispute between King James and his Queen, were officially no concern of the Earl of Essex; but since his position close to Queen Elizabeth was well known in Scotland, and both factions desired to stand well with her Majesty, it was to the advantage of them all to keep on good terms with her favourite. The cost of boat-hire between Barn Elms and Westminster or Greenwich, and stockings and beaver hats for gentlemen bearing letters from north of the border, was a small price to pay, though the money came from Anthony Bacon's pocket and nobody else's— certainly not from the Privy Purse—for information that in weeks or months to come might benefit the Earl of Essex.

The Earl, meanwhile, had become a father again. On April 14th his Countess had produced a third son, and like his two elder boys, Robert and Walter, Henry was baptised at St Olave's Church in Hart Street. Anthony almost certainly attended the christening.

Once again there is mention amongst his papers of a move to Chelsea: but when, and to whose house, remains untold. Lady Bacon, writing on June 3rd, says, "You had a mind to have the long carpet and the ancient learned philosopher's picture from hence; but, indeed, I had no mind thereto, yet I have sent them, very carefully bestowed and laid in a hamper for safety in carriage. You have now bared this house of all the best; a wife would well have regarded such things, but now they shall serve for use of gaming and tippling upon the table of every common person, your own men as well as others, and so be spoiled as at Redbourne. I should think that John, your tailor, should be fittest to look well to your furniture . . . I wish the hamper were not opened till yourself were at Chelsea, to see it done before you; for the pictures are put orderly within the carpet. You have one long carpet already. I cannot think what use this should be. It will be an occasion of mockery that you should have a great chamber, called and carpeted."

A fortnight later she continues, "The weather here very boisterous with wind, hail and rain. I fear you feeble thereof. I would, if it please God, be a few days in London the next term, but I think you will be gone to Chelsea before. Do what you can to expel the gout by diet and seasonable sleeping. Use not yourself to be twanged asleep, but naturally it will grow into a leading custom and hinder you much."

Twanged asleep . . . a delightful thought. Had young Jacques learnt to strum upon the lute, like the pages in Montauban before him, and did his master stretch himself upon his bed and fall into a pleasing slumber because of it?

In July she bids her son, "Look to your things in Chelsea. I send you oakwood strawberries gathered this morning by this bearer and others, his name is Dawes, diligent in the garden, and a zealous Christian servant, I pray you see him and speak with him yourself. He readeth the morning and evening prayers to my house heartily reverently . . . Sup not, watch not late, and sleep naturally."

There was a wedding in the family this month. The late Sir Nicholas Bacon's eldest daughter by his first wife, twice married and widowed, became the wife of Sir William Perient, Lord Chief Justice of the Common Pleas. Anthony apparently "derided" the match, and his mother was afraid this would come to the Lord Chief Justice's ears. "I pray hearken to him with all courtesy," she warned her son, "he is of marvellous good estimation for his religious mind in following his law-calling uprightly; beware, therefore, in words and deeds and speeches at table before him."

Besides, the new relative might put in a good word for her younger son, who was still unplaced as Solicitor-General.

"I am sorry your brother with inward secret grief hindereth his health," she wrote in August. "Everybody saith he looketh thin and pale. Let him look to God, and confer with Him in godly exercise of hearing and reading, and continue to be noted to take care. I had rather ye both, with God's blessed favour, had very good healths and were well out of debt, than any office. Yet, though the Earl showed great affection, he marred all with violent courses. I am heartily sorry to hear how his Lordship sweareth and gameth unreasonably." And in a postscript, "Alas, what excess of bucks at Gray's Inn; so to feast it on the Sabbath! God forgive and have mercy upon England."

Fulke Greville, who had been a friend of Sir Philip Sidney and was himself a poet, was a good ally to Francis, and like many others had urged the Queen that the post of Solicitor-General should be given to the younger Mr Bacon. "I have been like a piece of stuff bespoken in the shop," Francis told him, "and if her Majesty will not take me, it may be selling by parcels will be more gainful. For to be, as I have told you, like a child following a bird, which when he is nearest flieth away and lighteth a little before, and then the child after it again, and so on *ad infinitum*, I am weary of it; as also of wearying my friends . . ."

Thirty-four years old, and the past three years, when he could have held public office and served his Queen and country, wasted. His threat to retire to Cambridge came to nothing, as had a similar plan to travel abroad. Yet the man possessing the most brilliant intellect in the whole of England was never idle. He moved between Gray's Inn and Twickenham, his restless, enquiring mind forever in pursuit of new ideas, philosophic, literary, scientific, even horticultural—the gardens at Twickenham Park began to take shape about this time—and always the quest for motives: why did a man act thus, or a woman so, what moulded the rulers of the past, the Romans, the Kings of England? Were the stars responsible for ill, or did a man's own actions shape his destiny? Well, let it go, for the night at any rate, and for relaxation to the playhouse or to a private showing with the Earls of Essex and Southampton, to see how the Lord Chamberlain's players dealt with their scripts, enacted by Richard Burbage and his company. But before seeking relaxation at the play, one final attempt to persuade Lord Keeper Puckering to further his affairs.

"For if it please your Lordship but to call to mind from whom I am descended, and by whom, next to God, her

Majesty, and your own virtue, your Lordship is ascended; I know you will have a compunction of mind to do me any wrong. From Twickenham Park, this 19th August, 1595."

Antonio Perez, the Spanish diplomat who had attached himself to the Earl of Essex for nearly a year, hoping for some employment in which he could fully stretch his devious talents for diplomacy, was now back in Europe, on the Earl's recommendation, endeavouring to prove his same gifts to the duc de Bouillon, Marshal of France. Anthony Bacon was by no means sorry to see him go, for Perez, although good company, had been a drain on time and energy, and it was a relief to get him abroad, with a companion, Godfrey Aleyn, armed with letters of introduction asking that he might be given all possible assistance.

Perez was received with great honour by the governor of Dieppe, after which nothing was done for him, so he complained. The 525 crowns he had been promised had not been received, nor had he heard either from the Earl of Essex or from Anthony Bacon. So he went to Paris, and presuming upon his former acquaintance with the King's sister, Princess Catherine, called upon her at the Palace of St Germain, and was most "honourably entertained", so Anthony was informed, even travelling in her coach with her. But—and more protests—no money had yet come, and he was thinking of returning to England.

This would not do at all, for the Earl of Essex had just offered Anthony the suite of rooms in Essex House where Perez had previously been lodged, an invitation Anthony immediately accepted. So the house in Chelsea had definitely fallen through, it would seem; perhaps it suited the Earl to have Anthony Bacon under his own roof, or, more exactly, under one of his many roofs. Essex House near the Temple, which had been called Leicester House in his stepfather's day, and had now been refurbished and fitted up for his own use, would do very well for the purpose.

Essex House fronted the Strand, with a broad terrace to the south, extensive gardens leading down to the river, and, of course, its own landing stage, Essex Stairs. The house was of irregular shape, with a forecourt, inner paved court, great hall and galleries. The great chamber was above the south-facing hall, there were guest rooms facing east, and the Earl himself seems to have occupied a suite of rooms on the north and west sides of the paved court. His mother, who called herself Countess of Leicester still despite her marriage to Sir Christopher Blount, had her own apartments, besides her house at Wanstead, as did her sister Lady Rich and his grandfather Sir Francis Knollys. Kitchens, larders, wardrobes, armoury, banqueting house, chapel, and finally porter's lodge, the house was conceived, and kept up, in the grand scale.

Where his steward, Gilly Mericke, the numerous confidential secretaries, including the Greek scholar Henry Cuffe, and Anthony Bacon had their lodgings can only be surmised, but it seems likely that their rooms were on the third or top floor. There was a wainscotted chamber, known as the stairhead chamber, at the head of the stairs leading to the third floor. This may well have been Anthony Bacon's apartment, with a second room alongside. Any personal servant would doubtless have occupied the smaller chamber. His butler Knight, his cook, and the rest of his attendants, if they indeed remained with him, would have found quarters amongst the household servants. He presumably paid no rent, but he had to buy his own fuel for heating the apartments, which remained damp even in mid-summer, as he admitted to his mother in a letter some time later.

Lady Bacon, not surprisingly, was against the move from the start.

"I beseech God his blessing may follow you and be upon you wherever you go. The counsel to part with that London house so well agreed and most necessary was more cunning than regret for your good, being gouty as you be, but you are in such things to your great hurt credulous, and suffer yourself willingly to be abused. For the other place, though honourably offered, shall find many inconveniences not light. Envy, emulation, continual and unseasonable disquiet to increase your gout, great urging for suits, yea importune, to trouble the Earl as well as yourself. Peradventure not so well liked yourself there as in your own house . . . I fear, having as you have working about you, some increase of suspicion and disagreement, which may hurt you privately if not publicly, or both, by all likelihood these evil times. The Lord help, and I have not mentioned before your unavoidable cause of expense. The manner of your removal goes to my heart. Besides, your own stuff spoiled and lost and many incommodities.

"Mercy is gone with me, and I am but sickly and sad,

"Mater tau pia,
"AB."

Poor lonely Lady Bacon, seeing her sons so seldom, and her fretful words many a time laced with good advice. Suits and increased pressure Anthony would certainly find in Essex House, with the Earl demanding ever more of his company and assistance.

The Earl was now much preoccupied with French affairs, and in September he urged the Queen to send an army of some eight or ten thousand men to aid Henri IV against his enemies. His stout-hearted and devoted soldier-friend, the fifty-five-year-old Sir Roger Williams, had already waited upon the King, acting as go-between, and endeavouring at the same time to fob off the attentions of the agitated Perez, who kept insisting that his life was in danger from some unknown assassin.

Perez was rapidly becoming a liability, and early in October Anthony, as a gesture of goodwill, sent his young servant Jacques Petit with letters to the Spaniard from himself and from the Earl. This might serve to keep him quiet for a week or so, and Jacques Petit was instructed to tell Godfrey Aleyn, Perez's companion, to report back to England if the Spaniard became too talkative. Which indeed he did, boasting openly at table that the King of France intended to make him a Knight of the Holy Ghost and favour him with even further honours, and was likely to appoint him to his privy council; all of which Anthony, and the Earl, accepted with the proverbial pinch of salt.

How Anthony was faring himself under the roof of Essex House does not appear, but there was an awkward moment, late in October, when a letter arrived from his mother informing him that she had it on good authority that her Majesty had marvelled he had not yet been to see her in all this while. Lady Bacon ended her letter by saying, "Where you be must needs disorder your time of diet and quiet; want of which will keep you lame and uncomfortable. I hear the Lord Howard is too often with you. He is subtly deceitful. Beware! Beware! Burn this."

The Queen's remark, if indeed she had really made it, was enough to send Anthony back upon his bed, and in any event her Majesty did not deserve the bended knee from either brother, for word had finally come that the long-awaited post of Solicitor-General had been given to Serjeant Thomas Fleming.

The Earl of Essex went at once from Richmond Palace to Twickenham Park to offer his apologies and his sympathy. The following conversation then took place.

Essex   Master Bacon, the Queen hath denied me yon place for you, and hath placed another. I know you are the least part of your own matter, but you fare ill because you have chosen me for your mean and dependence; you have spent your time and thoughts in my matters. I die if I do not somewhat towards your fortune; you shall not deny to accept a piece of land I will bestow upon you. (He was referring to Edward Bacon's long lease of Twickenham Park, which now, at the latter part of 1595, would revert to the Crown.)

Francis   My Lord, for my fortune it is no great matter, but your offer makes me call to mind what I was wont to hear of the duc de Guise when I was in France, that he was the greatest usurer in the kingdom, because he had turned all his estate into obligations; meaning that he had left himself nothing, but had only bound numbers of persons to him. Now, my Lord, I would not have you imitate his course, nor turn your state thus by great gifts into obligations; for you will find many bad debtors.

Essex   Have no care of that, Master Bacon. Take the land.

Francis   My Lord, I see I must be your homager and hold land of your gift; but do you know the manner of doing homage in law? Always it is with a saving of his faith to the king and his other lords, and therefore, my Lord, I can be no more yours than I was, and it must be with the ancient savings; and if

I grow to be a rich man, you shall give me leave to give it back to some of your unrewarded followers.

When the Earl had taken his leave Francis wrote him a letter, in which he observed, "For myself, I have lost some opinion, some time, and some means; this is my account: but then for opinion, it is a blast that goeth and cometh; for time, it is true it goeth and cometh not; but yet I have learned that it may be redeemed. For means, I value that most; and the rather because I am purposed not to follow the practice of the law (if her Majesty command me in any particular, I shall be ready to do her willing service), and my reason is only, because it drinketh too much time, which I have dedicated to better purposes. A philosopher may be rich if he will. Thus your Lordship seeth how I comfort myself. . . . But without any high conceit, I esteem it like the pulling of an aching tooth, which, I remember, when I was a child and had little philosophy, I was glad when it was done. For your Lordship, I do think myself more beholding to you than to any man. And I say, I reckon myself as a common; and as much as is lawful to be enclosed of a common, so much your Lordship shall be sure to have."

The final sentence, so typical of Francis as carrying a sting upon its tail, warned Essex that the Crown would ever have first claim upon him. And so the matter was closed, and he could turn his attention to something lighter, a Device in honour of the Queen's Accession Day on November 17th, which the Earl could present to her Majesty as his own composition.

It was customary to celebrate her Majesty's accession first by a contest of arms, known as the Tilt—this had been started by the Queen's Champion Sir Henry Lee in 1580. The contest, with speeches and parades, took place in the Tiltyard at Whitehall. Stands were erected for the ladies and gentlemen of the Court, there was standing-room for citizens, and then the present champion, George Clifford, Earl of Cumberland, rode into the yard, his horse disguised as a dragon, followed by the Earl of Essex all in white.

So much for the forenoon's entertainment, but in the evening the Earl's Device was performed before her Majesty, with a Squire, supposed to represent Essex, hearing advice from a Hermit (possibly Francis himself), a Soldier, suggesting doughty Sir Roger Williams, and a Statesman, with shoulders even more hunched than those of Sir Robert Cecil. The Squire argued against all three, accepting what was good, rejecting that which seemed unworthy, and ending with vows of undying love to his Mistress, intending, of course, her Majesty.

The Device, like many another performed by amateurs, sounds somewhat laboured, and the contemporary allusions, which were right on target for November 1595, meaningless to twentieth century ears; but the Queen was apparently amused, and the Device had the effect of restoring Essex to the royal favour, which had been temporarily withdrawn during the past weeks. A book had recently been published in Antwerp relating to the succession and dedicated to the Earl, saying that no one was more worthy to succeed to the throne than Essex himself. He was as shocked as everybody else when news of the book came to England, but it took several weeks, and the help of the Device, for the Queen to be reassured that her Robin was in no way to be blamed.

International affairs, however, took priority over Devices or even scurrilous hints on the succession. The King of France had received absolution from the Pope, he was now a true Catholic in all but his secret conscience, and he sent word to the Queen of England by his own emissaries and by stout-hearted Sir Roger Williams that pressure was being put upon him to make peace with Spain, something he was in every way unwilling to do, for it would mean separating France from the alliance with England and the Low Countries. If this alliance, which was so dear to him, could be strengthened by the sending of troops from England, he need not be forced into the humility of seeking peace, or leaving the Queen of England to face the might of Spain alone.

The threat of invasion from another Armada, bringing back all the fears and excitement of seven years before, was enough to swing the Earl of Essex into immediate action. Away with passing trifles and moods of melancholy. His secretaries and his advisers, Anthony amongst them, were set to work to review the coastal defences. Ports in Scotland, Ireland, Wales, Cornwall—there had earlier in the year been a raid by the Spaniards at

Penzance—these places must be fortified, Bristol on the Severn strengthened, Plymouth well garrisoned, Sussex, Hampshire, Essex, Suffolk must all form an army and be ready to act in any direction to repel the invader and guard her Majesty's person.

Essex was in his element. This was the life, of action and leadership, for which he had been born. And if he should have her Majesty's permission to tour the country seeing to her defences, there would be none better to accompany him, and give advice, than that tough old warrior Sir Roger Williams.

It was not to be. Sir Roger, who had so often, by his own account, and indeed by those of eye-witnesses devoted to him, escaped a bloody death on the field of battle, found it, after brief illness, in his own bed at Barnard's Castle down the river from Essex House, on the night of December 12th. Cause of death, "a surfeit". Too much eating and drinking with the lads, too much seeking after fire and smoke, too much merry-making with the wenches and the roaring boys of the London and the Windsor taverns. Yet he died well, said a correspondent the following day, with the Earl of Essex at his bedside, for "none but he could make him have a feeling of his end, he died repentant". Perhaps, like the fictitious character he so much resembled, he "babbled of greene fields, his Nose as sharpe as a Pen . . . Hee's in Arthur's Bosome if ever man went to Arthur's Bosome; and went away, and it had beene a Chrystome child, between twelve and one, even at turning of the tide."

Sir Roger left his entire fortune to his beloved Earl of Essex, who spent most of his legacy in giving his old friend a martial funeral and having him laid in St Paul's. It was a sad Christmas for those who watched him go by water from Essex Stairs.

Interlude for Jacques Petit

Jacques Petit, the Gascon boy who had come from the
neighbourhood of Montauban as a page a year or more
ago, and was now promoted to even closer attendance
upon his master, was not amongst those at Essex House in
December, for Anthony had sent him upon a special assign-
ment. The true nature of his mission is obscure, but the
outward reason seems to have been to wait upon Edward
Russell, 3rd Earl of Bedford, who had succeeded to the
title in 1585 at the age of thirteen, greatly to the chagrin
of Anthony's aunt Elizabeth, whose late husband, Lord
John Russell, would have become 3rd Earl had he lived.
Edward Russell, now in his early twenties, had married
Lucy, the young daughter of Sir John Harington of Exton.
Sir John—not to be confused with his kinsman of the same
name, who was Queen Elizabeth's godson—had been a
neighbour of Anthony's in Bishopsgate. His daughter appears to have set forth with her husband on a journey to
her father's country mansion, Burley in the county of Rutland, with the purpose of arriving in time for Christmas;
and Jacques was amongst those in attendance upon the
young couple. The tour is included here as an interlude
between the events of 1595 and those of 1596, for the
picture it gives of life in a noble household at that era,
amusingly described by the naïve and somewhat bewil-
dered French boy.

The first stop was at St Albans, but certainly not at
Gorhambury, although Lady Bacon was probably aware
of the turmoil a few miles from her estate. But Jacques
Petit must speak for himself (he writes in French):

"Monseigneur,
"The principal subject of all my actions can only be
the remembrance of my duty in your service. And yet

if I do not wish to fail I cannot let any opportunity slip by without showing you whither I am bound. At 6 o'clock in the evening I arrived in this town, St Albans, where I caught up with my Lord who had left London before me. Having installed myself reasonably well I went to see him in his lodgings, quite unknown amongst many others, and my Lady for her pastime watching a tumbler do juggling tricks, and after many other clever tricks he threaded three threads in a needle of very fine quality, and unthreaded them—the ladies had provided them—turning and twisting quickly between two candles, to the sound of two violins.

"And afterwards, when the meat was served, four trumpets sounded to call my Lord as it is done at the Court for the King. These are only trifles and things of naught that I tell you, so I shall not stay long, and with my very humble and ordinary prayers to God to send you health and accomplishment of your desires, I will end, imploring you to believe that I love nothing so much as means and occasions to honour you.

"J. Petit."

The next night Jacques reports once more:

"We slept at Bedford where to welcome Monsieur le Comte (presumably he means the Earl of Bedford) the bells were rung and he was brought apples and wine by the chief men of the town. Thursday we went to the house of Sir Edward Montagu but the train was sent back a mile from there, when each was for himself at his own cost, and God for all. Friday the rendezvous for great and small was at breakfast at the knights's house, who in truth I confess treated us passably. At the parting, two or three of the household accompanied my Lord very close, waiting I think that no harm was done. Thus very late we were near to Burley, where for my part I have been welcomed and caressed by Monsieur le Doux [a French agent employed by Anthony Bacon] and others. After the deliverance of your precious merchandise and oriental present to him, I told him the news, and offered him my services. As for the state of this house, it is short of order, and of money, but I won't speak of it any more.

> "Your humble servant,
> "Jacques."

On December 14th he writes again:

"With your consent I resume once more to tell you how the world governs itself in these parts. No day passes without hunting; both Madame the Countess and the Earl with their carriages drawn by four horses. The knight Mr Harington alone pays the cost of all these pleasures, and pays dearly for the glory of the name of Countess for his daughter, and would like, from what I hear, that what is done were to be redone. He used to lease out all his lands without annual rent, being able to put in or eject whenever he pleased. Now he is forced to make a lease to this one, and a contract to that one for many years, and is bound to anyone who will provide him with ready money. Certainly he needs it, since more than 200 persons sleep and feed in the house, 30 or 40 horses, and as many couples of dogs; coming and going principally on Sundays.

"There is not an inn in London which covers so many tables as is done here. And there is much muddle and confusion this Christmas, making many useless expenditures on tragedies and games. But since the custom is for so much bad play, one keeps a good face on it. . . . Leaving the description of a thousand things that are not worth the trouble to tell you, since you will understand the worry of the rest, your humble servant kisses your hands. . . . I have a cap from Ireland, brownish-green with a wreath of white Cyprus thread, to cover my beaver hat.

> "J."

This last could, perhaps, be a message in cipher, but remembering those bills to the London hatter it is more endearing to believe that Jacques was taking pride in his personal appearance.

Then early in January:

"Monseigneur,

"After these days of holidays full of ease and pastimes I make so bold to salute very humbly your good graces by these presents which will also contain —if it please you—the excellent and magnificent rule that has been held in this house with all good men and true this Christmas. The orders were to receive and entertain 8 or 9 hundred neighbours who came every day to celebrate here. Twice a day there was a sermon in the church, morning and after dinner, and every day a new minister. Monsieur and Madame the Countess were mostly present. Monsieur the Count was served with all the honour and respect possible at dinner and supper, there was music, 30 or 40 gentlemen servants, 2 or 3 cavaliers and their ladies, in addition to many gentlemen and demoiselles who were at table, then after the meal came the dance and amusing games to make us laugh and serve as recreation. Monsieur Jean dined in hall to receive his neighbours and principal farmers, entertaining these with an excessive choice of all kinds of dishes, and all kinds of wines. His maître d'hôtel took care to see that nothing was lacking, and in addition laid out 4 or 5 long tables of meat for 80 or 100 people at a time, who having finished made way for as many others, and took their leave. After it was over, bread and wine in barrels were carried to the poor who were all satisfied, so that there were many left-overs.

"New Year's Day was demonstrated by the generosity of these people, and principally of Madame the Countess, for, from the greatest down to the smallest, she gave good evidence. I could even say a word on the subject myself.

"The comedians from London were come here to have their share. They were made to play the day of their arrival, and the next morning they were sent on their way. We had a masquerade here written by Sir Edward Wingfield, and they also played the tragedy of Titus Andronicus, but the presentation was worth more than the subject matter. Apart from all this, and which is even more to be prized, is that when one celebration was over we embarked upon another for good cheer, and pastimes are greater and amusing

because nothing spoils enjoyment more than crowds
and a too great number of rustics.

"I should be very happy if one of your people would
do me the kindness of informing me, with your good
leave, if 6 letters I have written have been handed to
you, though I know my method and style are not
worthy to be presented.

"Accept my devotion, and humble and sincere
affection, and excuse the lack of that subtle finesse and
sharpness of spirit which is used by many others. And
with this hope I kiss very humbly your poor sick
hands, to which as to your whole body I pray God to
please send you perfect health, with honour and contentment to your spirit.

"Your devoted servant,
"Jacques Petit."

So his master was crippled with the gout again, and
unable to reply. But life at Burley was not all feasting
and recreation, for Jacques sent snippets of gossip heard
at table. "It is said the Spaniard hopes to come to the
west as he did in the year 88 . . ." "That the Queen
wishes to send 20,000 men into France . . ." "That Sir
John Harington for his part must lease out his land to his
followers. The money of which I spoke in my last will go
to pay his debts, and some 200 marks were carried to
London by Wilkinson his man. . . ." "My hand is always
trembling for fear of committing some disgrace, by ignorance or otherwise, thus losing your esteem. . . ."

The new year celebrations over, Jacques was desirous
of returning to his master. But there were impediments.

"Monseigneur,

"Following my duty, which is the rudder of all my
affections, and the spring of all my actions, I must
obey you in all that you decide for me, in that Monsieur le Doux proposes that I am to stay here to teach
French to Sir John Harington's grandson. Whatever
you wish, Monseigneur, I will do it, with a joyous
heart, but it is to return to you that is my true wish.
Yet if you command me to stay in this place, then
that is my desire, so that I may give thanks to you by
my industry, and to try and win approval from these

noble lords and ladies. Advise me of your command, and I shall be content. You were my first master, and, please God, shall be my last. I shall be in despair if I am banished forever from your ocean, that is to say, from your infinite good grace, from your kindness and your love. For I have found in Anthony Bacon my Apollo and my Oracle.

"Jacques."

Surely a veritable *cri de coeur* from Rutland. But worse was to come.

"Monseigneur,

"I beg you send for me. I cannot any longer live here among fornicators and ribald domestics. I implore you to recall me, or I shall ruin M. le Doux and his 'ninain' [?], who has such villainous ideas and well in tone with those of the devil. The first confesses it to me, and then the other wishes to tell me what she can. I cannot endure any more the unseemliness of those who pay me. For the friendship that I bear you I have kept quiet, again and again, and will continue to hold my tongue, provided they clear out of this honourable house.

"Your very humble and faithful
"Jacques."

And so the letters end.

Old Gidea Hall reproduced from an engraving in the Romford public library. *Courtesy of the London Borough of Havering and the National Monuments Record.*

Miniature of Francis Bacon at eighteen, by Nicholas Hilliard. *Courtesy of the owner.*

Sir Francis Bacon as Lord Chancellor by J. Vanderbank, 1731 (*NPG*).

Sir Nicholas Bacon, artist unknown, 1579 (*NPG*).

The Lady Hobbei.

Lady Hoby by Holbein (*photo Freeman*). *Courtesy of the Trustees of the British Museum Print Room.*

Mildred Cooke, Lady Burghley, by the Master of Mildred Cooke, c. 1565. *Courtesy of the Marquess of Salisbury.*

The Cooke tomb, Romford Church, showing Mildred, Ann, Elizabeth and Katherine Cooke (*photo Christian Browning*).

The Cooke tomb, Romford Church, showing Sir Anthony and Lady Cooke (*photo Christian Browning*).

Reverendissimus in Christo Pater D.D.

IOHANNES WHITGIFT Archi Episcopus Cantuariensis.

John Whitgift, reproduced from an engraving by Vertue, 1718
(*photo the Mansell Collection*).

The interior of the Great Hall, Gray's Inn, drypoint etching by A. Williams. *Courtesy of the Greater London Council Map and Print Collections.*

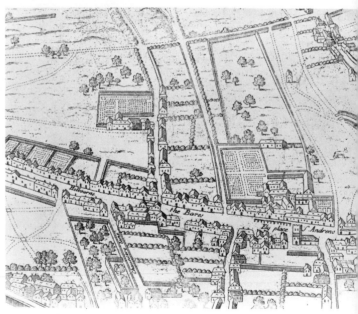

Map of Holborn showing Gray's Inn and Ely Place, from a map of North London by Ralph Aggas, 1560 (*photo Freeman*). *Courtesy of the Trustees of the British Museum Print Room.*

ABOVE Redgrave Hall, Suffolk, artist unknown, c. 1660. *Courtesy of the National Monuments Record.*

BELOW Map of Montauban, 1621 (*photo Ferlin*). *Courtesy of M. Méras, Archivist in Chief, Montauban.*

Henri IV from a portrait in the *Bibliothèque de Genève*.
Courtesy of the Caisse Nationale des Monuments Historiques.

Catherine of Navarre from a portrait in the *Bibliothèque Nationale, Paris. Courtesy of the Caisse Nationale des Monuments Historiques.*

Philippe du Plessis-Mornay (*photo Freeman*).

Court ladies in the reign of Henri III (*photo Freeman*).

Head of Montaigne from a medal by E. Gatteaux, 1817 (*photo Freeman*). *Courtesy of Librairie Larousse.*

The first Baron Burghley by M. Ghaeraedts, post 1585 (*NPG*).

Illustration by Gustave Doré from Montaigne's *Essais*, showing contemporary manners (*photo Freeman*). *Courtesy of Librairie Larousse.*

Sir Francis Walsingham after John de Critz the Elder (?), 1704
(*NPG*).

Robert Devereux, Earl of Essex, after M. Ghaeraedts (*NPG*).

Queen Elizabeth I by Isaac Oliver from the Royal Library, Windsor (*photo A. C. Cooper*). *Reproduced by gracious permission of Her Majesty Queen Elizabeth II.*

A typical seventeenth-century theatrical inn. A reconstruction of the Four Swans Inn; from Halberston's *Old Records of Old London. Courtesy of the Guildhall Library.*

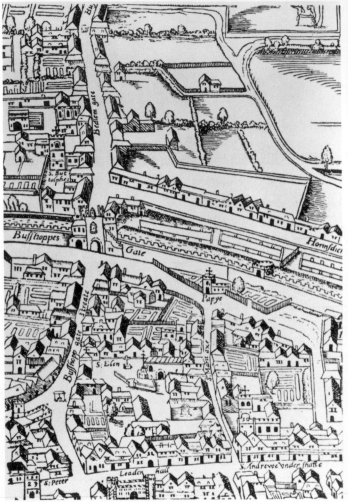

Contemporary map of the city showing Bishopsgate and Papey.
Courtesy of the Guildhall Library.

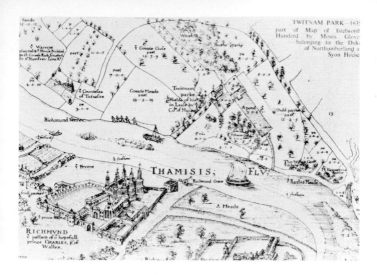

ABOVE Twitnam Park, 1635, by Moses Glover (*photo Freeman*). *Reproduced by courtesy of the Duke of Northumberland, Syon House.*

BELOW Richmond Palace in the seventeenth century from an engraving by Jan van der Guchten. *Courtesy of the Greater London Council Map and Print Collection.*

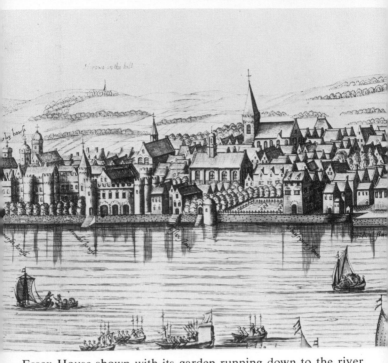

Essex House shown with its garden running down to the river (*photo Freeman*). *Courtesy of the Trustees of the British Museum Print Room.*

The Courts of the King's Bench and Chancery in the seventeenth century (the earliest known picture of the interior of Westminster Hall) from an anonymous drawing. *Courtesy of the Trustees of the British Museum Print Room.*

The Tower in 1597 by Hayward and Gascoigne. *Courtesy of the Society of Antiquaries of London.*

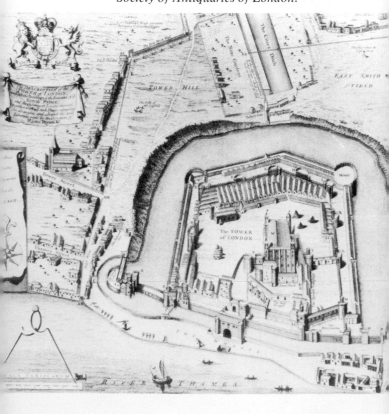

The Church of St. Olave, Hart Street. *Courtesy of the Guildhall Library*.

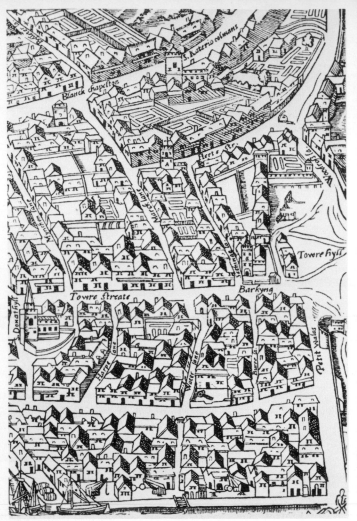

Map showing Seething Lane and its environs. *Courtesy of the Guildhall Library.*

PART THREE

Chapter 14

Whilst Jacques Petit was enduring discomfort in the household of Sir John Harington his master, Anthony Bacon, was also having some annoyance. His acquaintance Godfrey Aleyn, whom he had despatched to France as companion to the Spaniard Perez, had proved unreliable, according to reports from Perez himself. It seemed that Aleyn had been sending letters back to his father in England divulging secret matters, and one of Essex's secretaries, Henry Wotton, was despatched to France to bring him home. On arrival in England Aleyn was immediately arrested and imprisoned in the Clink. The unfortunate man protested his innocence to Anthony in the strongest terms.

"I have a suspicion," he said, "that this was purposely plotted by Signor Perez to do me some displeasure. He, seeing my unwillingness to stay with him, often told me in his anger that he would send me one day into England at my cost." He insisted also that he had written only on the most ordinary matters to his father, but admitted that he had also corresponded with Lord Zouche, the Queen's ambassador in Scotland. The sequel was that Aleyn's father was also arrested and the pair remained in the Clink, with nothing very serious proven against either, until May, when Anthony managed to have both of them released, bound over for good behaviour.

The incident was unpleasant for Anthony, making for embarrassment in the good relations hitherto existing between Wotton and himself and also amongst the staff at Essex House. Lady Bacon's judgement was proving sound. Jealousies and petty spite would and did occur, especially when every member of the household desired to hold first place in the Earl's favour.

Essex himself continued to have every confidence in

Gallicos

- La deliurance de Hierusalem in 4ᵒ · 8
- Hierusalem en rime francoise —— 3 · 6
- Cornelius Tacitus —————— · 4
- Les harangues militaires ———— 13
- Essays de Montaigne ———— 6
- Les sepmaines du Bartas ———— 6.
- Les fables d'Esope en taille doulce — 3.
- Sleidan des 4 empires ————— 2 Heny ll₄
-

2 ℔ s. ℔ 6 s

Somma Summar̃   11 ℔ 1 ℔ ·

- Il nuouo testamento latino
  e volgare ————— 3
- Le coffre de bonne esperance — 12
  Monsⁱ petit vn angelot — 10   Some 12 ℔ 6 ℔
- Onomasticon 7. linguarꝰ Junij ——— 4
- Sallustio volgare ————— 2 · 6
- Commentary Cæsaris ————— 2 6
- Sallustius latiné ——————— 2
- Terentius latiné & Italicé · in 4ᵒ —— 6
- Hercolano del varchi ———— 2 6
- Gämbular della lingua fiorentina —— 3
- Commentaires de Cæsar de Vigenere in fᵒ
- Comedie di plauto ———— 5
- Nomenclator quatrelinguis ——— 2

Some of the books in Anthony Bacon's possession in 1595

Anthony, and shared something of the latter's exasperation
with Perez, whose letters were either full of complaints
about his life in France or filled with flowery exaggeration
of the King's friendship for him.

"What are you doing in France?" asked the Earl. "You
demand of us 1,000 men with cannon, powder, other
things necessary, and this in order that you may possess
the booty. For my own part, I see the approaching fate
of both kingdoms, England threatened with a formidable
war, and France by a deceitful peace."

To which Perez replied that if peace was indeed declared between France and Spain, then "all preparations
would be turned against England, in order to reduce the
kingdom to obedience to the see of Rome", and furthermore he let it be known that Princess Catherine had said
to him, "Do you desire a bishopric or a cardinal's hat?
You shall have all you want of my brother. Or would you
like five, six or eight of my own Swiss guards to protect
you?"

The Spaniard was definitely getting too big for his boots,
and the continual payments to him and the other agents
from Anthony's own purse were a tremendous burden. Although Mr Morrison and his stockings and beaver hats
appear to have dropped out there was a new recruit to the
secret service, this time in Venice. A Mr Henry Hawkins,
nephew of the Speaker of the House of Commons, had
offered his services the previous November, and asked for
money to be sent to him regularly. Two hundred crowns
were immediately forthcoming, sent by Anthony's "good
friend Mr Jackson", a merchant, who had occasion to ply
not only between the ports of England and France, but
presumably to the Adriatic coast as well. The Spaniards,
so Hawkins reported, were more and more "fixed in Italy",
but his snippets of local gossip about the ducal families
were occasionally more colourful than useful as diplomatic
intelligence: how the Duke of Mantua, for instance, was
paying court to a fair widow whose husband had been
drowned in the canal beneath the Rialto bridge, it was
thought by the Duke's design, and the widow would not
submit to the Duke's attentions; indeed, an unknown friend
of her family had attempted to shoot the nobleman in
revenge, but had only struck his hat from his head and
scorched his ruff.

Such items of intelligence might make gossip for idle pens at Twickenham, but the Earl of Essex complained of "their trivial nature", and asked that Henry Hawkins should do better in future. The agent, disconcerted, told Anthony that he paid ten crowns a month for his chamber in Venice, besides his food, nor had he yet received the bill of exchange he had been promised. Further inroads, therefore, upon the Bacon private purse, and Anthony sent Hawkins 200 crowns.

At the end of March 1596, Italian agents were forgotten in the news that Calais was being besieged by the Archduke of Austria. It was said that the sound of the gunfire could be heard at Greenwich. The Earl of Essex went to Dover to take command of forces for the relief of the French port, but it was too late; the garrison surrendered on April 10th, and Calais was in the hands of the Spaniards. The straits of Dover were all that separated the English coast from the hostile ships of Spain.

It was evident to King Henri IV, himself at Boulogne, that had assistance from England come in time, Calais could have been saved. The Earl of Essex was well aware of this, and he and the Lord High Admiral Howard had both wished to attack the Spaniards in their own home ports, but they had been overruled in Council by the prudent Lord Treasurer and his son Sir Robert Cecil. Caution had lost Calais. Therefore *de l'audace, toujours de l'audace* must be the new order of the day, and Essex was determined that an offensive carried direct to the Spanish coast must take precedence over any plan to relieve Calais.

The King of France was not so persuaded, and sent the duc de Bouillon as emissary to confer with her Majesty and her Council. But before this the King had written a personal letter to Anthony Bacon.

"Monsieur Bacon,

"I have always held a high opinion of you through the affectionate services you have rendered me, and because of your providential handling of public affairs, which is why I now ask Monsieur de Sancy to bear this letter to you, and to inform you of my intentions, so that you may assist me in regard to my cousin the Earl of Essex, knowing full well his reliance upon you. I trust you will be able to employ yourself accord-

ingly, and when occasion presents itself, I shall most
certainly recognise this service, praying God that He
will keep you in his care.

"This XIth day of April, 1596,

"Henri."

The King, with his reference to "affectionate services",
can hardly have had in mind past events in Béarn, now
ten years old. It seems evident, from the wording of the
letter, that Anthony had sent him intelligence from England during the intervening years, possibly through Tom
Lawson, who frequently travelled to France, or by some
other trusty messenger. That he communicated with
Marshal Matignon, who had protected him in Bordeaux
as far back as 1584, is proved by an undated letter from
Anthony, written in either 1595 or 1596, offering his services, in the shape of information, at any time, and assuring
the Marshal that the Earl of Essex held him in high esteem.

It is hardly likely that Anthony Bacon acted as a "double
agent" as the term is used today, but in all matters of
diplomacy, then as now, it paid to keep your allies informed of any particular move that might concern them;
and when, as in 1596, her Majesty's Council were opposed
on foreign policy, with Essex taking a contrary view to
that of the Lord Treasurer and his son Sir Robert Cecil,
then Anthony would naturally put the Earl's interests first
and see that nothing was lacking to obtain intelligence
from any source, even if some small measure of the same
was expected in return. On this occasion he was, however,
careful to excuse himself from receiving Monsieur de Sancy
personally, pleading an infirmity which confined him to his
chair, and the actual bearer of the letter was Monsieur le
Doux, the agent who had so shocked young Jacques Petit
in Rutland. Anthony hastened to reply to Monsieur de
Sancy the following day, expressing his unbroken devotion
to his Majesty, and offering to do everything in his power
to further the King's service. The memory of Montauban,
and of what might have been but for King Henri of
Navarre, could never be erased from his memory.

On April 17th the duc de Bouillon, accompanied by
Perez and Aubéry du Maurier, who for some time had
been the Duke's private secretary, arrived at Gravesend
on the official mission to the Queen. Standen, still hovering

amongst the lesser fry at Court, wrote to Anthony that the
French emissary was expected at Greenwich the following
day, and that the Earl of Essex, not wishing to be em-
broiled, had left for Portsmouth with every intention of
going to sea. The excuse that had served Anthony in his
reluctance to meet Monsieur de Sancy must serve again
with the duc de Bouillon, whom he had also known in
Béarn, when the Duke was in attendance upon the Princess
Catherine. As for du Maurier, he had been too closely
associated with Anthony's old enemy du Plessis to find a
welcome on the third floor of Essex House. Anthony wrote
at once placing his coach at de Bouillon's disposal, but
regretting that "a severe fit of his old disorder" prevented
him from waiting upon the Duke in person. It turned out
that he need not have worried; de Bouillon was seized
with ague as soon as he set foot in England, and it was
some little while before he was well enough to attend her
Majesty.

It was one thing to plead indisposition to Monsieur de
Sancy and the duc de Bouillon, but quite another to keep
Perez at bay. He knew his way to the rooms in Essex
House that had been his own before Anthony took them
over, and had no hesitation about bursting in upon the
invalid and pouring out complaints. The Lord Treasurer
and his son "Roberto il diavolo" had slandered him; the
Queen was incensed against him, due, he felt sure, to
rumours spread about him by Monsieur de Sancy; the Earl
of Essex had left for Portsmouth without seeing him; and
the duc de Bouillon suggested that he should return forthwith to France—in short, he was totally baffled by his
poor reception in England, and felt so ill in consequence
that he must go to Bath to recover. Whether he went,
his wants supplied by the Bacon purse, is not clear, but
Anthony told the Earl, by now in Plymouth at a safe
distance from the importuning Spaniard, that he would
rather hear the cannon's roar by his side, nor would that
sound so much trouble him or hinder his rest, as the complaints, exclamations, discontentments and despair of Antonio de Perez.

"I have been advised by my physicians to retire into the
country to attend to my health and take physic there," he
added, "yet I am content to stay in town and keep Antonio
from despair."

Then another visitor arrived, Monsieur de la Fontaine, minister of the French church in London, saying that the duc de Bouillon had recovered from his ague and was shortly to see the Queen, but was disturbed that the Earl of Essex had not remained in town to see him and feared some change in his attitude. Did Mr Bacon know why this should be so? No, Mr Bacon did not know, and was sure that the duc de Bouillon had been misinformed. A hurried note was sent to the Earl in Plymouth accordingly. "I beseech your Lordship," wrote Anthony, "by one word to give me my tune and my plain song to descant hereof."

How much simpler, indeed, to hear the cannon roar, to muster men and ships, than to sit in Essex House and deal with so many complaints from those visitors to London. Tom Lawson was already with the Earl at Plymouth, and Standen too. If only Anthony's health had permitted he would have formed one of that merry company, and ridden down to Devon on one of her ladyship's greys from Gorhambury. Instead, another 200 crowns to Hawkins in Venice, and a slightly indiscreet letter accompanying the sum, acquainting the agent of the fact that her Majesty's army in Plymouth comprised 14,000 men at the least, of whom 1,500 were gentlemen volunteers; also that the duc de Bouillon and Monsieur de Sancy were likely to be ill-satisfied with their mission to the Queen.

Meanwhile brother Francis had spoken twice with her Majesty, a full hour each time, and it looked as if the long period of disfavour was over at long last.

"Thus," Anthony told his mother, "your Ladyship sees, that tho' loyalty, patience and diligence may for a time be shadowed and disgraced by malice and envy, yet it pleaseth God, the fountain of all goodness, by His extraordinary power, to make them sometimes shine to the prince's eyes, through the darkest mists of cunning and misreports."

The family hopes were raised at the same time, for a brief moment, by the sudden death from apoplexy of Lord Keeper Puckering. The place was immediately filled by the Master of the Rolls, Sir Thomas Egerton, which meant that the Mastership of the Rolls was now vacant. However, on May 15th someone else was appointed. Francis, for his part, had expected nothing; it was only that Anthony, by writing a word in due season to the Earl at Plymouth, felt that some cautious move might be made on his brother's behalf. No matter. His time would come.

On May 16th a treaty was signed between the Queen's Commissioners—the Lord Treasurer and others—and the duc de Bouillon, on the conclusion of which, although the terms were not entirely satisfactory from the French point of view, de Bouillon and his retinue prepared to take their leave, Perez amongst them. Anthony, exhausted by the continuous "importuning" of the Spaniard, accepted with intense relief his brother's invitation to Twickenham. The lodge, as they called it, was at Anthony's disposal; he could rest there in seclusion, Francis himself moving between Gray's Inn and the Court. Anthony wrote to the Earl accordingly.

"My special good Lord,

"My patience being at the last on charge, and, as I may say to your Lordship, almost turned into just anger, to see that my double torment both of stone and gout could not obtain me the privilege of rest at Signor Perez his hands; but that I must daily hear my dear Lord's honour hammered upon both by him and the French, and serve as it were, hourly, instead of a cistern, to receive his Spanish exclamations, and scalding plaints; I had no other sanctuary but to retire myself hither to my brother's pleasant lodge and fine designed garden, where, with your leave and liking, I would propose to be as private as I may, namely, till the D of Bouillon and Signor Perez, his departure, which last, I doubt not, but that my absence will haste, if the letter which I have received this morning by my man Jacques, who came in post, mar not all my former painful endeavour to get him well gone."

The fear that Antonio Perez might delay his departure, and come to seek him out in Twickenham, was ever present until the French party had definitely left Gravesend. Thus, with nerves restored, he wrote to Francis:

"Well, at the last he is gone. God send him fair wind and weather for his passage, and me but the tithe of the thanks which I have deserved; for I dare assure you, that without my watchfulness and painful patience he would have chanced upon some plot, whereby to have made an aftergame. I doubt not but that you have heard of Mr Fulke Greville's employment to carry to the two generals their royal benediction; and yet Sir Walter Raleigh's slackness and stay by the way is not thought to be upon sloth or negligence, but upon pregnant design, which will be brought forth very shortly and found to be, according to the French proverb, *fils ou fille*."

This final quip was an allusion to Raleigh's wife, who was about to make him a father, and is an amusing illustration of how Anthony changed his style to suit the recipients of his letters; intimate and light-hearted to his brother, the same though on a humbler footing to the Earl, and, in contrast to both, sober, rather distant, and with religious undertones when writing to his mother.

His style changes again, becoming imbued with deep respect, when corresponding with the Earl's two sisters, Lady Penelope, wife of Lord Rich, and Lady Dorothy, Countess of Northumberland. Her husband, the "wizard Earl" as he was termed because of his interest in science and the occult, was hardly the best choice of husband for Lady Dorothy. They were married in 1595, and in March of 1596, when she was six months pregnant, Anthony, hearing the gossip at Court to the effect that her husband was showing every sign of infidelity, took it upon himself to warn the injured Countess. His letter was unsigned, which leads to speculation as to whether he was used to anonymity and had employed the same means in other circumstances:

"Most Honoured Lady,

"If I could digest any injury offered you, I would rather conceal that which I write, than trouble you with others' folly, protesting I am as free from malice, as to keep you from being abused: so it is, that your Lord hath gotten him a chamber at Court, where one of his old acquaintance be lodged. What his meaning is, I know not, but you may perceive he bears small respect to you, that will give occasion, if any be so simple as to think he can neglect you for a ruined creature. Therefore, Madam, support cheerfully your-

self with your wonted wisdom, and let them not unworthy disquiet your mind. Proportion your affection
according to their deserts, and consider, that we are
not bound by virtue to love them, that will unloose
themselves by vice. Thus much the honour I bear you
hath enforced me to say. More I will not, for I am
one devoted to your service, and do not conceal my
name for shame or fear."

Three months later the Countess of Northumberland
gave birth to a son, but the anonymous letter, despite its
fine style, can hardly have made her pregnancy easier to
bear. Impossible to guess at Anthony's motive, unless, the
rumour of infidelity coming to his ear, he wrote at a white
heat of indignation that his own Earl's sister should be so
soon betrayed by her new bridegroom.

Lady Penelope was a different proposition. Philip Sidney's childhood sweetheart had never loved her husband
Lord Rich, and had already borne children to her lover
Charles Blount, brother to Christopher Blount and later
to be Lord Mountjoy. She had her own rooms at Essex
House, but was frequently at Barn Elms and at her
mother's house in Wanstead. Before de Bouillon departed
for France, taking Perez with him, and Anthony moved
thankfully to Twickenham for his few weeks' respite, she
wrote him the following letter:

"Worthy Mr Bacon,
　"There are many respects which lead me to an
extraordinary estimation of your virtues, and besides
your courtesies towards myself meriteth the desire I
have to requite your friendship, and so do you all
honour, praying you to believe my words, since your
merits doth challenge, more than I can acknowledge,
though I do with much affection esteem your worth.
And while I am in this solitary place, where no sound
of any news can come, I must entreat you to let me
hear something of the world from you, especially of
my brother, and then what you know of French affairs, or whether there go any troops from hence to
their aid, and so wishing you all contentment,
　"I remain, your very affectionate friend,
　　　　　　　　　　　"Penelope Rich.

"I would fain hear what became of your wandering neighbour."

The wandering neighbour was, of course, Signor Perez, but the warm tone of Lady Penelope's letter suggests that she herself might be a welcome visitor to those rooms on the third floor near the leads. Anthony could hardly wait to reply.

"Most honourable worthy Lady,
"My right honourable and dutiful thanks are the least I can render your good Ladyship for the honour of your good opinion and kind conception of me, which I humbly beseech your Ladyship to believe. I hourly expect to hear from your noble brother, and will not fail to acquaint your Ladyship of any good news I may hear from his Lordship or through others. For the French affairs, her Majesty is entered into a treaty, and is brought almost to condescend to sending three thousand men into France, the expense to be defrayed by her for five months, and certain French noblemen to remain here as hostages for payment and her Majesty's reimbursement.
"Your Ladyship may well call my neighbour wandering, if you knew as well as I do, against my will, what strange bypaths his thoughts walk in, which fester every day more and more in his mind by my Lord's silence, and the continual alarums that sound in his ear of the Queen's displeasure.
"The duc de Bouillon presseth him to be in readiness to return with him, but he refuses to go without my Lord's privity and consent.
"This is all, Madam, at this instant, and I most humbly beseech you to accept and to dispose freely of my poor service. And so I humbly take my leave.
                                    "Anthony Bacon."

On the last day of May, writing from Twickenham, he told his brother, "I purposed yesternight to have made a start to London, but it pleased God to visit me anew with a more cruel pang of the stone than ever before, which hath provoked me to vomit at the least twenty times."
Small wonder his mother wrote to him, "I fear your

drink is too strong and breedeth fancies." It is to be hoped that Jacques was on hand to "twang" him asleep, but gout and stone wre not helped by the lawyer friend Nicholas Trott, to whom both brothers owed a considerable sum of money, "storming against them with more passion than reason".

Meanwhile, down in Plymouth preparations for the great expedition against the Spaniards were almost complete. The ships were ready to sail, and now all that remained to do was to embark the army. Standen, who earlier in the year had been knighted by the Queen, to his surprise and immense gratification, told Anthony that the Lords General intended to be under sail by the end of the week—the last week in May—and that "the rich apparel, which the night before was shown in Plymouth, was beyond all the sights which he had ever seen, for at least five hundred gentlemen were covered over with silver and gold lace".

He himself was on board the *Repulse,* and had lain there in harbour for three days now. Tom Lawson had received £100 from Essex, who, according to Standen, spared neither purse, body nor spirit, and had won for himself a wonderful regard from his troops. There were four squadrons; seventeen of the vessels were her Majstey's own and seventy-six were chartered. There were over six thousand mariners and soldiers, making nearly thirteen thousand men in all, who would take part in the expedition. The Dutch formed a fifth squadron. Her Majesty composed a special prayer to be used each day in the fleet, the final words being, "We humbly beseech Thee, with bended knees, prosper the work, and with the best forewinds guide the journey, speed the victory, and make the return the advancement of Thy glory, the triumph of their fame and the surety of the realm, with the least loss of English blood. To these alone petitions, Lord, give Thou Thy blessed grant, Amen."

The fleet set sail on June 2nd, and Anthony, who despite his recurring sickness had returned to Essex House to take charge of any intelligence that might arrive, thought of what he himself had written to Henry Hawkins in Venice: "My Lord is wonderfully confident of success, and that he shall give the King of Spain so deadly a wound that he will never recover from it."

He remembered also the Earl's message to himself through his secretary Edward Reynolds: "Commend me to Mr Anthony Bacon, and tell them that are most sorry at my going, they would not wish me diverted from this army, if they saw the beauty of it", and the later personal letter, written shortly before embarking: "For yourself, I pray you believe, although your mind, which so tenderly weigheth my danger, be very dear unto me, yet for my sake you must be confident, for if I be not tied by the hand, I know God hath a great work to work by me. Farewell, worthy Mr Bacon, and know that though I entertain you here with short letters, yet I will send you from sea papers that shall remain as tables of my honest desires, and pledges of my love to you."

Brave words from the young leader, not yet thirty years old, already so popular a figure in the public eye that the memory of their older idol, Sir Francis Drake, the news of whose death had coincided with the fall of Calais, was quite eclipsed. Indeed, it seemed as if to find his equal a writer must hark back nearly two centuries to the time when a young prince, mocked by his elders for levity of spirit, sought honour in the field of battle, not aboard ship, but booted, armed and spurred.

"All furnisht, all in Armes,
 All plumed like Estridges, that with the Winde
Bayted like Eagles, having lately bath'd,
Glittering in Golden Coates, like Images,
As full of spirit as the Moneth of May,
And gorgeous as the Sunne at Mid-summer,
Wanton as youthful Goates, wilde as young Bulls.
I saw young Harry with his Bever on,
His Cushes on his thighes, gallantly arm'd,
Rise from the ground like feathered Mercury,
And vaulted with such ease into his Seat,
Af if an Angell dropt downe from the Clouds,
To turne and winde a fierie Pegasus,
And witch the World with Noble Horsemanship."

Chapter 15

When the fleet sailed on June 1st the wind was scant off
the Dodman, and the vessels were forced to return to Plymouth Sound for forty-eight hours. On the 3rd, the wind
coming fair again, the fleet set forth once more, the five
squadrons sailing well apart yet closing in when evening
came so as to hail one another. The very names of the
ships sounded on the air like clarions: *Ark Royal* (Essex's
command), *Lion, Mary Rose, Swiftsure, Dreadnought,
Nonpareil*. With the Dutch squadron, and the smaller craft
for victualling and repairs, there were some hundred and
fifty vessels overall.

It was on Sunday, June 20th, just after dawn, that the
fleet came to anchor in the bay westward of Cadiz, having
been seventeen days at sea, capturing one or two craft en
route, from which they obtained the information that the
sailing of the vessels was totally unexpected, and there was
every chance that the port of Cadiz might be taken by
surprise, notwithstanding the presence of the Spanish
ships-of-war at anchor, *St Philip, St Matthew, St Andrew,
St Thomas*, four of the largest vessels possessed by the
King of Spain.

The wind was increasing from the south-west and a
heavy sea was breaking on the shore. Lord Howard, the
Lord High Admiral, was for landing in the small boats
and seizing the town of Cadiz before attacking the Spanish
ships. Preparations had already been made to launch the
light craft in the tumbling sea—one boat was immediately
swamped and eight men lost—when Sir Walter Raleigh,
whose ship had been detained overnight in St Lucca, rejoined the fleet and persuaded the Lord Admiral that to
proceed with landing craft under such conditions of wind
and sea would mean the loss of all. The command for
landing must be withdrawn at once. This was agreed, much

to the Earl of Essex's satisfaction, for he had been for
attacking the Spanish ships before landing the troops. It
was then decided, after a council, that the following
morning the English fleet would enter Cadiz harbour.

"*Entramos . . . entramos . . .*" shouted the Earl,
throwing his hat in the sea, and at once demanded the post
of honour, that *Ark Royal* should lead the fleet into action
and his vessel be the first to open fire. This was denied
him. Her Majesty had given strict injunctions to the Lord
High Admiral that the Earl of Essex must not be exposed
to danger. Sir Walter Raleigh won the coveted post.

The fleet weighed anchor, and dropped again in the
mouth of the bay. The wind was increasing all the while,
and the seas heavier than before. No longer unaware, yet
nevertheless caught where they lay, the Spanish vessels,
both battleships and merchants, were forced to weigh anchor themselves and sail up harbour, any hope of a passage seaward blocked by the English squadrons. Then the
great ships opened fire, and the forts on land, and no
sooner did the Earl of Essex hear the sound than he drove
Ark Royal alongside Raleigh's vessel, to share whatever
should be in store, victory or defeat.

The cannons roared from seven in the morning until
past one in the afternoon, and had Anthony Bacon been
there to hear them the sound would certainly have seemed
sweeter than the plaints and moans which he had endured
from Signor Perez. The Spaniards smelt defeat as the guns
grew silent, and tried to run their ships upon the shore
and fire them. This they did with *St Philip* and *St Thomas*,
but *St Matthew* was seized where it lay by cheering Englishmen, and the vanquished Spaniards either drowned or
suffocated in the harbour mud. Now, in mid-afternoon,
with the heat from the burning vessels all about him and
the June sun blazing in the sky overhead, the Earl of Essex landed under Fort Puntales with three thousand
troops, and set about taking the town of Cadiz. The Spaniards retreated, but Essex and his men scaled the walls
and pursued them to the market-place, where for a time
the fight was fierce and bloody; and then, the Lord High
Admiral landing with more men and ammunition, the
forces of Cadiz were spent. The last of them held out
within the citadel, but next morning this final stronghold

surrendered, and the Earl of Essex's standard was raised above it.

> "Once more unto the Breach,
> Deare friends, once more;
> Or close the Wall up with our English dead."

The English losses, mercifully, were small. Some three hundred men killed in the assault, amongst them Sir John Wingfield, shot through the head in the market-place. He was the only nobleman to lose his life. The English were merciful. None of the aged touched, no woman raped, the only troops to show little forebearance were the Dutch, and because of all they had suffered for so long during the Spanish occupation of the Low Countries this could be excused and understood. The leading townsfolk of Cadiz agreed to pay a ransom of 120,000 ducats to their conquerors, but the merchant ships, laden with wealth for the Indies and forming part of the rich prize which the English had intended to carry home, had all been burnt by the Spaniards before surrender. This was a bitter blow for those whose main reason for embarking on the expedition had been to return with loot.

When a council was held by the Lord High Admiral, Essex, Raleigh and others as to the next move to be made, the general opinion was that the raid had been successful, and the wisest course now was to sail for England, visiting Spanish ports on the way and destroying what shipping they found. Essex was alone in suggesting three alternatives—to march into Andalusia and attack the Duke of Medina's forces, to hold Cadiz, or to put out to sea and waylay the West Indian fleet. He was overruled in all proposals. The Lord High Admiral was an old man, past sixty; he had fought against the Armada, and had shown much courage in the last engagement; but now he was for reporting home. Raleigh had been wounded in the leg, and others were arguing amongst themselves about the spoils of war. As a sop to disappointed hopes of wealth, the Lord High Admiral created twenty-seven knights and the Earl of Essex thirty-six.

On July 4th, having razed the town and destroyed all public buildings, respecting only churches and other places of religion, the army embarked and the squadrons put to sea. The expedition to Cadiz was over.

News filtered slowly home to England. Each day, during the latter part of June and on into July, the country waited anxiously, from her Majesty and her Council down to the humblest citizen in the land. Anthony Bacon, who was keeping his agents informed of every rumour that might come from the continent or through some merchant or fishing vessel, told Hawkins in Venice, on July 17th, that there was no news yet from the Earl, which "occasioned no small uneasiness". He had not yet received the letter which the Earl had written to him off the coast of the Algarve on July 8th:

"I pray you, let this letter serve both to satisfy you, and to commend me to your brother Francis, for I am so overwatched and have so little time, as I must crave pardon of my friends if I do not yield them full satisfaction. . . . I had thought to have rested at sea after our land travails, but our small and undefensible ships do as much strive to lose themselves, as we to save them; yet I thank God we have not lost so much as a shallop, and I hope we shall not, for if the galleys see but one good ship to defend the lesser, they will none. . . . Let this my paper deliver you my best wishes, and let all our country, and specially our particular friends, thank God for this great victory. I wish you all happiness, and rest your true friend,

"Essex.

"I once again pray you to commend me to your brother Francis. If I go not on land tomorrow I will write to him."

Then, on the last day of July, the news of victory came in a letter brought overland from Portugal by a messenger from Lord Thomas Howard, the Lord High Admiral's nephew, giving the bare details: Cadiz taken and destroyed, and with it the Spanish fleet, all well and safe aboard the English ships. It was expected that the entire fleet would be safely back in home waters by the middle of August. This letter was delivered to the Lord Treasurer so that her Majesty might be the first to learn of victory. The Lord Treasurer, as was his wont, tempered enthusiasm with caution, and some of this brushed off upon the Queen as

they pondered the cost of the expedition, the wealth of
the Indies fleet that might have been the Crown's, nothing
but smoking wreckage in Cadiz. And what was more, returning mariners and soldiers to be paid. The Treasury
would hardly stand it. . . .

No such lukewarm reception in Essex House. Messages
were coming in now from the Earl himself, and Anthony
received his long-hoped-for letter. Lady Penelope called
on him in person, and she too had a letter to show, for
her mother's husband, Sir Christopher Blount, was amongst
those sailing with her brother in *Ark Royal*. Already rumour had it that the Lord Treasurer and Sir Robert Cecil
were damping down the glowing tales of victory.

"Malicious envy," Anthony told Lady Penelope, "may
shadow for a time my Lord your brother's absence, but
the reality of his noble virtues, and the brightness of his
inestimable merits, will make that shadow serve for a more
glorious lustre, as the cunningest painters do theirs in their
principal portraits."

Not even his mother could belittle the beloved Earl's
achievement. "God willing," he wrote to her in a fever of
excitement, "I will send your Ladyship this next week a
particular true relation of the whole action, which God
be thanked hath been seconded with the taking of another
place called Faro. A Spanish merchant, much bound to
my Lord of Essex, has delivered certain dainties to the
Countess of Essex and my Lady Rich, and I am bold to
send you the best part of them. And so I humbly take my
leave."

The image is a happy one—Frances, Countess of Essex, and Penelope, Lady Rich, nibbling figs and grapes
and sweetmeats, perhaps even in the company of Anthony,
who, free of pain for the moment, or just forgetting it,
may have hobbled down the staircase from his own chamber to the spacious rooms below; while Lady Bacon,
standing in the long gallery at Gorhambury next day,
watched one of the jetting jacks ride his smutting horse
fast to deliver his package to her.

Her only comment, when she heard of the Earl's honourable, safe and happy return, "I trust it will not spend
and spoil the English soldiers whom God hath spared, nor
bring the plague into England as it did in my husband's
time. May God bless the Earl, and as He had made him

strong against his enemies, so likewise against carnal concupiscence."

If Lady Bacon felt a little sour despite the "dainties", it was partly because her nephew Robert Cecil had in July been fully established as Secretary of State, with all its authority, and her own two sons had not yet been honoured. She had warned Anthony: "I promise you, son, you have need now to be more circumspect and advised in your discoursings, doings, and dealings in your accustomed matters, either with or for yourself and others. You are said to be wise, and to my comfort I think so. But surely, son, on the other side, for want of some experience by action, and your tedious unacquaintance of your own country by continual chamber and bed-keeping, you must needs miss of considerate judgement in your verbal-only travelling."

To which her son made reply: "Pray call to mind what speech Queen Mary used, when she laid down upon the Council board the purse where the privy seal was kept, for which the old Lord Paget had been so long and earnest a suitor, having procured King Philip for his mediator—and consider what has fallen that house since. For mine own part, the reading and Christian meditation of the 36th and 37th psalms shall, with God's grace, serve to keep me from emulating any worldly prosperity or greatness, or fearing the effects of humour, power, or malice, so long as it please God to comfort and strengthen the best part of me, as hitherto He hath done with extraordinary effect. . . ."

Let his uncle and his cousin do what they will, he had other friends at hand, the new Lord Keeper Egerton amongst them, to whom, during the Earl's absence with the fleet, he had sent intelligence. And now, with Essex home, nothing else mattered. The fleet was safe in Plymouth, and on August 19th, the greatest joy of all, the Earl, posthaste from Plymouth, "surprised him at supper". They spent a whole hour together before the Earl left him for Barn Elms.

There had been much to report on matters of intelligence coming in during his lordship's absence with the fleet. The usual trouble on the border between England and Scotland, the Laird of Buccleuch attempting to seize Carlisle, for which affront her Majesty blamed King James, and King James assured her it was none of his doing; yet the troubles continued. Monsieur de la Fontaine, the Catholic minister in London, had given assurances that if Spain should attack England the King would immediately come to her Majesty's assistance. But Henri was having much trouble from his Protestant subjects since he had become Catholic: they were interfering in his financial affairs, and it was to be hoped they were not receiving encouragement from sources in England. And—of more personal interest to Anthony—the Princess Catherine, having as usual followed her brother the King into battle, had nearly been killed by a cannon-ball in the trenches, had been taken ill in a village in Picardy, and had lain on a pallet-bed open to all winds, with the moth-eaten beams threatening to fall in upon her.

In Italy, Hawkins had gone from Venice to Padua and stayed there eight days in attendance on the Earl of Rutland, who had fallen into a dangerous fever, but travelling about the country was dangerous, Spanish spies were everywhere, he feared his letters were being intercepted, and in any event he was in need of a hundred crowns. This last was being paid from the Bacon purse, and Anthony did not bother to inform Essex of it; but since much of Hawkin's information was also going to Lord Keeper Egerton, who did not understand Italian, and Anthony himself had not the time to translate the letters, he desired Hawkins in future to write in English.

Lastly there was the business of Thomas Wright the Jesuit, who, hazarding much, had come over from Spain with intelligence, lodging with the Dean of Westminster, and was now in custody. "I had rather suffer disaster in another country," he had told Anthony, "than tolerate this in my own. I lived well nigh twenty years abroad, only my allegiance brought me back. I had rather choose the Marshalsea or the Fleet, for no doubt there I should converse with Catholics, and here my whole life must be amongst Protestant ministers." Anthony had complained to the Lord Treasurer about the Jesuit's treatment, but with no result.

Essex listened to all he was told, but, like everyone home from adventure, was more eager to talk of Cadiz than keep silent and hear what had been happening in England, or elsewhere; besides, after seeing his wife and

children he must give a full account of the expedition to
the Council. This was likely to cause dissension. The Earl,
having tasted success in action, was anxious for more, not
for his own glory, but for the sake of his country. The
moment was ripe now to hit the Spaniards hard, having
blasted them already in Cadiz; he wanted more troops,
and part of the fleet to embark once again. He was well
aware, however, that this move would be opposed by the
Cecil faction, who stood for peace at almost any price.
"You are home, my Lord," Anthony had told him, "in the
nick of time. Your person has never been more necessary,
both for her Majesty and for yourself, than at this instant."
He meant by this that his uncle the Lord Treasurer and
his cousin Sir Robert had steadily decried the expedition
to Cadiz during the Earl's absence, and had influenced the
Queen accordingly.

The division of the spoils of Cadiz would be one more
bone of contention. Many who had taken part in the affray
had been dissatisfied, Sir Walter Raleigh amongst them.
The Lord High Admiral's nephew, Lord Thomas Howard,
was another. Her Majesty expected that any booty brought
back should belong to the Crown, and this claim put the
Earl of Essex at a disadvantage; he dared not oppose her
Majesty, but to fall in with her demands meant disappointment for his companions. It fell to Anthony, as usual, to
placate the disenchanted, one of whom was Katherine,
wife of Lord Thomas Howard and niece by marriage to
Lord Harry Howard, close friend to the Earl, the "papist
Lord" so much mistrusted by Lady Bacon.

"Your courtesy and kind offer of friendship to me the
last summer, good Mr Bacon," she wrote, "makes me the
bolder to trouble you, than upon a small acquaintance I
should, with a matter of some weight; because I am loath
to trouble my uncle Harry in dealing with one, whom he
honours so much, on behalf of his own nephew. My hope
was, that if anything were to be gained, my Lord should
not have been left out. It was told me certainly he would
have five thousand pounds. Yesternight, at Court, I was
told the Queen claimed all. My Lord has already spent
£20,000 in the Queen's service. It were hard, that in this
action, wherein none are forgotten but those that lack
friends, he should be thus forgotten."

So the lady's ruffled feelings must be appeased and a

word in season whispered to the Earl, who told him, in an aside, "I assure you, I am as much distasted with the glorious greatness of a favourite, as I was before with the supposed vanity of a courtier, and call to mind the words of the wisest man that ever lived, 'Vanity of vanities, and all but vanity'."

Then Anthony had to deal with the lesser fry. Tom Lawson, although he had been made a captain by Essex, had gained nothing at Cadiz, so Standen, through love for Mr Bacon, had made him a sharer in thirty bales of paper and a great chest of Venetian mirrors. Tom Lawson was appeased. Not to one of the Earl's secretaries, Edward Reynolds, who had been chief messenger overland throughout the whole expedition. Poor Reynolds returned home to find that one of his underlings had usurped his place, and furthermore that a fifth secretary had been engaged to do the work that should be rights be his.

"You will find my papers in good order," Reynolds told Anthony, deeply offended. "I desire never more to be seen of his Lordship." Anthony placated him too. Peers of the realm, their ladies, friends, staff, all must be soothed, and Anthony the only one at Essex House suited to perform the task.

Meanwhile brother Francis at Twickenham was hard at work on a collection of essays which, so he told Anthony, would rival those of the Frenchman Michel de Montaigne, and he was also considering writing a letter of advice to the Earl on his future conduct of affairs. Anthony hoped his lordship would take note of it. And finally his mother sent him a present of "peascodde". "Let it be tenderly soaked, and if you taste it take it at dinner and not at night or soaked in good beer." No matter, swallow it down, and no harm done provided that Jacques Petit was on hand to twang him asleep afterwards.

Chapter 16

The Earl's success at Cadiz had been widely acclaimed both in the Low Countries and in France, and in the last week of August the duc de Bouillon arrived in London for the solemn signing of the defensive league, which had been agreed in May, between the King of France and the Queen of England. He was received graciously by her Majesty and fêted at Court, while the Earl in turn gave a splendid banquet for the French guests at Essex House, costing 1,000 marks. Anthony does not seem to have been present, but as a lodger under the Earl's roof he could hardly refuse this time to receive the duc de Bouillon in his chamber, and a meeting took place on Sunday, September 5th, before de Bouillon and his train left again for France. "But for my indisposition," Anthony assured the French emissary, "I would be the last to stand on the shore till the wind carried you from my sight", words which were doubtless repeated to King Henri IV, along with some further remarks by Mr Bacon to the effect that there were others, whom he would not name, who would not express the same devotion to the duc, to the King, and to the fair country of France. He alluded, naturally, to the Cecil family.

And now, in this first week of September, Anthony found himself in some trouble with the Lord Treasurer. The whole business was brought about by his aunt Elizabeth, Lady Russell, who, like her sister Lady Bacon, liked to meddle in other people's affairs. Not content with bullying her sons Edward and Thomas Posthumous Hoby— both had sailed in the expedition to Cadiz—she next took it upon herself to call upon her nephew at Essex House and give him what can only be termed a piece of her mind. She was now sixty-seven, a year younger than Lady Bacon, and had never really recovered from the fact that her hus-

band, Lord John Russell, had died before succeeding to the
title of Earl of Bedford. She liked to sign herself Elizabeth
Russell, Dowager; and although Lord John was buried in
Westminster Abbey she had erected a superb tomb to her
first husband, Sir Thomas Hoby, and to his brother in the
church at Bisham, where she lived, with the figure of herself in widow's weeds kneeling beside it in prayer and, as
a final gesture, wearing a coronet upon her head.

What Lady Russell thought of Anthony's quarters at
Essex House does not appear, but the conversation between them was fully documented. She arrived one September afternoon with a gentlewoman in attendance, and
whether she found Anthony abed is not stated, but she
must have taken him by surprise.

Lady Russell Good nephew, are you not bound to
your aunt, that will make such a posting journey to
see you with only one gentlewoman? First in a coach
to Paris Garden, and then in a wherry over here to
see you, to visit you and perform a very kind office?
Anthony Madam, your query and my obligation is
very great, but not greater than the thankfulness of
my heart.
Lady Russell Marry, nephew, it is that same heart
that must ease my heart, which is almost choked with
grief to see what you do.

Here she paused, to see what effect her words should
cause, but instead of being dismayed Anthony's spirits rose
to the occasion.

Anthony Nay, good madam, go on and spare me not
any misreport you may have heard of me, or any
wrongful imputation. I shall hope to ease your heart
thoroughly and justify myself.
Lady Russell Well, nephew, seeing you so well
armed I won't flatter you a whit, but will tell you that
all your bodily pains grieve me not so much as the
alteration in your mind, which is said to be cor-
rupted in religion, factious and busy, undutiful and
unnatural; and all this I tell you from the Lord Treasurer, who protests upon his salvation he has always

loved you as a fond father, and hath never as much wronged you even in thought.

So, it was as he had expected; the Lord Treasurer was behind it all, and his aunt had come post-haste from him and the Court at Nonsuch Palace.

Anthony Madam, here are very heavy propositions, and a protestation of great price. For the first, I hope their proofs will be as light.
Lady Russell Well, nephew, answer my proofs. What of your familiarity with Standen, a fugitive, and Wright, a seminary priest?
Anthony Give me leave to help you, madam. And my Lord Harry Howard, whom you should have done the honour to name first.
Lady Russell Aye, and him too.

Here they were interrupted by Anthony's man entering the room to say that Lord Harry Howard was below in person, but on being informed that Lady Russell was with Mr Bacon had made great haste to go away. Her ladyship was not surprised.

Lady Russell The daily resort of these unto you, nephew, makes you odious. Secondly, you are too well known and beloved in Scotland to be a true Englishman, and busy yourself with matters above your reach, as foreign intelligence and entertainment of spies. You have not only abandoned the kind old nobleman your uncle, but you do him ill offices, not only with the Earl here in Essex House, but in France and Scotland by means of your acquaintance. In one word, you oppose yourself more directly than any nobleman in England durst do, how great soever.

This was too much, and Anthony interrupted her.

Anthony Madam, I do not see why an honest poor gentleman may not apprehend my Lord Treasurer's greatness as a rich nobleman, whose estate may make courage more pliable. *Je vais me servir de toutes mes pièces jusqu'au fond de mon sac;* in other words, I

can prove myself as clearly as daylight, that I am not
guilty, neither in part nor in whole.

Her ladyship settled herself to hear her nephew defend
himself as he would in a criminal court of justice. Anthony
could have done with his brother Francis to act as counsel
for the defence; nevertheless, he embarked upon the long
recital of his life since he had first left England in 1579.

Anthony   The Lord Treasurer should call to mind
the confidence he had in the firmness of my religious
beliefs when he sent me over to France seventeen
years ago, and persuaded me to meet with the traitor
Parry. He assured both her Majesty and the Earl of
Leicester, that Parry would never shake either my religion nor my honesty. Let him recall how I lodged
with Théodore Beza, who dedicated his Meditations
to my mother. Let him recall how I visited the King
of Navarre and his sister the Princess Catherine in
Béarn, and later in Bordeaux roused the hostility of
certain Jesuits there, and found protection from the
kindness of the Marshal Matignon. Then at Montauban . . .

It was the turn of Lady Russell to interrupt.

Lady Russell   The Lord Treasurer confessed he was
offended with you for falling out with du Plessis.
Monsieur du Plessis complained of it at home. You
also conversed with a bishop and other bad fellows,
and had about you one man in particular, Lawson or
Lawton, as bad and lewd a fellow as could be.
Anthony   Madam, Monsieur du Plessis's prejudice
against me rose because of his wife. I censured her
hair apparel and would not marry her daughter. My
circumstances were so impoverished at that time I was
obliged to borrow from the Bishop of Cahors. As for
Mr Lawson, the Lord Treasurer kept him in durance
for ten months, all through false surmises and suggestions of du Plessis and his wife. . . . And if you
wish for further good confirmation of my character
I will read you a letter written some thirteen years
ago by the late Secretary of State, Sir Francis Wal-

singham, to me in her Majesty's name, expressing her gracious acceptance of my poor endeavours, and the assurances of her princely favour and good opinion.

Anthony handed his aunt the letter to read, and when she had finished it she turned to him again.

Lady Russell God's body, nephew, thou art mightily wronged; for here is not only warrant but encouragement.

Anthony Yes, madam, and if I had come home to find Sir Francis alive, he would have made that good, and more too. Is it not a hard case, that an honest and loyal subject, son of so faithful a servant and true patriot, should reap no other fruits than jealousies, suspicions, and misinterpretations? I deny not, that in France I encountered many Scots gentlemen both well and ill-affected, but never sought them out until I received the warrant you have seen; since when I confess to have tilled, as industriously as I could, so barren a soil, only for her Majesty's service, which I hope the Lord Treasurer will grace with fitter names than faction and *outrecuidance,* seeing such poor fruits as grew in my own ground have hitherto come free both to her Majesty and to his Lordship.

And let her carry that and more to the Lord Treasurer and see what relay she had from him.

Lady Russell By my faith, nephew, if thy tale be true, then Topnam has turned French [a contemporary catch-phrase].

Anthony Ask my uncle what makes him so loath to advance his nephews, madam. And this my brother and myself have found too true, howsoever it pleases him to protest to the contrary. And his son, Mr Secretary Cecil, has sworn that he holds me for a mortal enemy, and will make me feel it when he can.

Lady Russell Vile urchin! Is it possible?

Anthony Whether it be true or not, I refer you to my mother, who marvelled that I laughed when she

told me of it. Do you know the Gascon proverb *Brame d'âne ne monte pas au ciel?*
Lady Russell By God, nephew, your cousin Robert is no ass.
Anthony Let him go for a mule, then, madam, the most mischievous beast there is.

Thereupon his aunt rose to her feet, laughing, her temper recovered, and desired him to write everything down so that she could report back to his uncle the Lord Treasurer.

Anthony God forbid if, by such an arrogancy, I should derogate from your merit. If I had not full assurance in yourself, and your kindness toward me, I would have excused myself from ever beginning.

She insisted, however, and rather than exasperate her on parting he agreed to do so, and they embraced better friends than he had dared to hope on first sight of her. Lady Russell departed to catch her wherry back to the south bank, or, if the day was drawing in, she might well have gone for the night to her own house at Blackfriars, about which neighbourhood she was almost as concerned as she had been about her nephew's conduct, for to her horror it had come to her ears that a Mr Burbage had bought property there, and this with the deliberate intention of turning it into a common playhouse. There must be a petition to stop it. She was appalled to think of the noise of drums and trumpets so near to the church, disturbing the minister and people at divine service, quite apart from the type of low person who would come to the district.

Anthony, exhausted from the visit, notwithstanding did his best to commit to paper all that had transpired between them, but the letter satisfied neither his aunt nor the Lord Treasurer, as Lady Russell informed him a few days later. His uncle complained that when he had gone early to Windsor, hoping to present his nephew to her Majesty, Anthony had pleaded his sickness and returned to Twickenham. And if his nephew reproached him for not paying Mr Standen, now Sir Anthony Standen, for monies said to be due to him, this was not his business, the monies should have been paid by Sir Francis Walsingham. But the Lord Treasurer was sorry for his nephew's sickness, and he had no recollection of having ever said— this had been repeated by Lady Russell—that Anthony's ill health was partly his own fault for being too good a trencherman.

Well, there it was, apologies and excuses on both sides, neither relenting, and Anthony sent a detailed account of everything that had passed, in blunter, more racy, language, to the Earl of Essex, who commented, "I took so great pleasure in reading it, at my going to bed, I found it ran in my head all night."

The only information missing, both in the conversation between Anthony and his aunt and in that between Lady Russell and the Lord Treasurer, and also in the long letter written to the Earl of Essex, was any allusion, even the barest hint, of those serious and very embarrassing charges which had been brought against Anthony Bacon at Montauban in the year 1586. So . . . nobody knew. Henri of Navarre, King Henri IV of France, had kept his word. Not a murmur from de Bouillon, nothing from du Plessis. The records lay in the files at Montauban and would remain there, unread, through centuries. The King, moreover, continued in his friendship. The message of loyalty which Anthony had sent him through de Bouillon at the end of August won a reply on October 21st.

"Monsieur de Bacon,

"I was very pleased to have news of you through the letters you wrote me, confirming your affection, of which my cousin the duc de Bouillon gave me such good proof, hence I wished to thank you by this letter.

"Pray rest assured of my good wishes on every occasion, this you well know. I ask God to keep you in His Holy care.

"Written at Rouen, the 21st October, 1596,

"Henri."

Neither the Lord Treasurer nor Sir Robert Cecil would have been gratified to learn on what good terms their relative was with the King of France, having the edge, as it were, on their own diplomacy; nor would they have been any the better pleased with the letters he received

from Scotland, or the calls to his rooms in Essex House
of David Foulis, who had formerly been one of Anthony's
Scottish correspondents, and was now James VI's ambassador to the Court of Queen Elizabeth. Particularly as Mr
Foulis let it be known that his reception by certain of her
Majesty's Council had been less than warm, meaning very
naturally the Cecils, father and son.

Lady Russell had spoken no more than the truth when
she told Anthony that her brother-in-law found his
nephew too friendly with the Scots. Anthony's correspondence and interviews with Scottish agents and emissaries
was part of a deliberate policy to ensure that King James
VI should be kept well informed of all pertaining to the
Earl of Essex, so that King and nobleman should be on the
best possible terms. If the Cecils neglected to do the same,
then their diplomacy was at fault. "It makes me blush,"
Anthony told Essex, "to see my sovereign so ill-served,
and a King so absolutely scorned with dangerous and
damnable insolency."

So on once more with correspondence to and from
Italy, Scotland and France. Jacques Petit, having attended
upon Lord Rich in France, was presently to go to Holland
with Anthony's nephew William Woodhouse, and find life
rather more active and to his liking than he had done in
Rutland; but Lady Bacon was once again in troublesome
mood, having heard that the Earl of Essex had some clandestine relationship with a lady about the Court. What
was more, she had the nerve to write and tell him so. She
wrote to the Earl on December 1st, having herself visited
Court and heard the common gossip. "Some late back-
sliding doth appear," was the hint contained in her letter,
"and the infaming of a nobleman's wife, so near about her
Majesty. Yet she is utterly condemned as bad, unchaste,
and impudent. . . . It is a great pity she is not delivered
to her husband, and the Court cleansed by sending away
such an unchaste gaze and common by-word. But you, my
good Lord, have heard the holy words, 'This is the Will of
God, that ye should be holy, and abstain from fornica-
tion'." And so on and on . . . She sent the letter to her
son to deliver to the Earl, which Anthony did, though
appalled at his mother's lack of tact. The Earl took it in
excellent spirit, and returned his thanks.

"Madam,

"That it pleased you to deal thus freely with me, in letting me know the worst you hear of me, I take it as an argument of God's favour in sending so good an angel to admonish me. But I protest, that this charge, which is newly laid upon me, is false and unjust; and that since my departure from England towards Spain, I have been free from taxation of incontinency with any woman that lives. I never saw or spoke with the lady you mean but in public places. But I live in a place where I am hourly conspired against and practised upon. . . . Worthy lady, think me a weak man, full of imperfections; but be assured I do endeavour to be good, and had rather mend my faults than cover them. . . . Burn, I pray you.

"At your Ladyship's commandment,

"Essex."

This pacified her somewhat, and she wrote once more, asking God to "send his holy angels and pitch about your army, and with fulness of good days and years in this life, preserve you to his heavenly kingdom forever". Nevertheless, she took the opportunity of murmuring to her son about the cost of lodging at Essex House, to which he made reply, "The expense of coals I confess for four summer months are great, but consider first my sickness, then the extraordinary moistness of the season, and the situation of my lodgings, and the honourable helpers I have had to spend since my Lord's return."

Perhaps it was the damp so near the leads that made him request the Earl, on December 22nd, "that your Lordship would vouchsafe to procure me Mr Broune's lodging". Who Mr Broune was, and in what part of Essex House he lodged, is not revealed. It is to be hoped it was near the pump court, handy to the buttery door, so that the partridges, which his mother frequently sent him by carrier, could be drawn and hung and later roasted without giving offence to those who might be walking in the galleries above.

So for the second time Anthony spent Christmas at Essex House. Writing to Hawkins in Venice he said, "Altho' it is Christmas Day, I take more contentment to speak with you, being absent, than to confer with many whom

I see almost daily, and therefore instead of cards and dice, I betake myself to pen and paper."

To the Earl, a few days previously, he had advised that, "I will be seeing Mr Hudson from Scotland, and his Lordship must not censure the silence of the agent Bruce nor the Scots ambassador David Foulis, for they both appreciated Mr Secretary's ambuscades and interceptions, and will defer to write till they meet with some confident messenger, whom I expect daily. Your Lordship knows the French proverb *Un chien en chaud craint fort l'eau froid;* and if a public minister's letters to a king, his master, and the king's to him, have been laid to wait for, and opened, how much more letters betwixt private friends."

On New Year's Eve he was happy to acquaint his mother with the good news that "Brother Francis has received gracious usage and speech from her Majesty at Court, and that I hope will, at the last, exemplify her good words by some princely real effects", and that, wonder upon wonders, his cousin Robert Cecil had declared himself ready to do "Anthony Bacon any kind office, if Anthony would but make proof of him".

Time would show what 1597 would bring—whether favours and friendship from the Cecil faction or a continuance of the old reserve, more skirmishes against the might of Spain or an ill-timed, patched-up peace. Above all, would the Earl of Essex heed what brother Francis had advised him in October? "To stay close to the Queen, as the late Earl of Leicester and Lord Chancellor Hatton had done, to divert her Majesty's mind from the impression the Earl gave of martial greatness, for she loved peace, and loved not the charge of war; to take care in his personal habits, what he wore, his gestures and the like; to speak against popularity and popular courses, this should be handled tenderly; to be careful of his estate; and lastly, to be plain, to have the altering of some of his officers about him, though this could not be done but with time." Wise counsel, and how closely brother Francis had observed his subject; and yet . . . he would never be as close to the moody, volatile commander as was Anthony himself, who loved and questioned not.

Chapter 17

In February of the new year, 1597, Francis published his first volume of essays, ten in number, and dedicated them to his dear brother, Anthony Bacon.

Loving and beloved brother [the dedication ran], I do now like some, that have an orchard ill-neighboured, that gather fruit before it is ripe, to prevent stealing. These fragments of my conceit were going to print. To labour the stay of them had been troublesome, and subject to interpretation: to let them pass, had been to adventure the wrong they might receive by untrue copies, or by some garnishment, which it might please any that should set them forth, to bestow upon them. Therefore I held it best discretion to publish them myself as they passed long ago from my pen, without any further disgrace than the weakness of the author. . . . Only I disliked now to put them out, because they will be like the new half-pence, which tho' the silver were good, yet the pieces were small. But since they would not stay with their master, but would needs travel abroad, I have preferred them to you, that are next myself, dedicating them, such as they are, to our love; in the depth whereof, I assure you, I sometimes wish your infirmities translated upon myself, that her Majesty might have the service of so active and able a mind, and I might be with excuse confined to these contemplations and studies, for which I am fittest. So commend I you to the preservation of the Divine majesty.

From my chamber at Gray's Inn, this 30th of January 1597,

Your entire loving brother,

Fran. Bacon.

187

In later years, in 1613 and again in 1625, these essays would be enlarged and bear different dedications, but in 1597 brother Anthony was the "begetter", and indeed, with his known admiration for Montaigne, the source of the inspiration. The very choice of subject matter was suited to his temperament—"Of Study", "Of Followers and Friends", "Of Suitors", "Of Expenses", "Of Regimen of Health"—and in each appears some phrase or sentence which had undoubtedly sprung from discussion between the brothers, whether in early days at Cambridge, or when they shared chambers at Gray's Inn, or more recently by the river banks at Twickenham—Francis, with his biting wit that stung if it did not wound, and Anthony with an equally swift rejoinder, culled from the French, yet sometimes disenchanted.

Thus, in "Studies", the reader can have a picture of Francis pacing up and down, his eye upon a recumbent Anthony, saying, "If a man write little, he had need have a great memory; if he confer little, he had need have a present wit; and if he read little, he had need have much cunning, to seem to know that he doth not." And swiftly, before Anthony could interrupt, "Nay, there is no stand or impediment in the wit, but may be wrought out by fit studies: like as diseases of the body may have appropriate exercise; bowling is good for the stone and reins; shooting for the lungs and breast; gentle walking for the stomach; riding for the head and the like." Then reaching down and lugging his brother to his feet, who answered, "Aye, so if a man's wit be wandering, let him study the mathematics; for in demonstrations, if his wit be called away never so little, he must begin again."

The essay on "Followers and Friends" applied very closely to both brothers, with their band of personal attendants, some of whom pass from the records, others, like Tom Lawson, Jacques Petit and Francis's Henry Percy, remaining steadfast throughout, possibly with too great power behind the scenes. "There is a kind of followers likewise," said Francis, "which are dangerous, being indeed espials; which enquire the secrets of the house, and bear tales of them to others; yet such men, many times are in great favour; for they are officious, and commonly exchange tales." And again, "It is good discretion not to make too much of any man at the first; because one cannot hold out that proportion. To be governed (as we call it) by one, is not safe; for it shows softness, and gives a freedom to scandal and disreputation. . . . Yet to be distracted with many, is worse; for it makes men to be of the last impression, and full of change. To take advice of some few friends is ever honourable; for lookers on many times see more than gamesters; and the vale best discovereth the hill."

Both brothers might well have taken heed, which they did not, of the truths Francis expounded in the essay upon "Expense": "He that is plentiful in expenses of all kinds, will hardly be preserved from decay. In clearing of a man's estate, he may as well hurt himself in being too sudden, as in letting it run on too long; for hasty selling is commonly as disadvantageable as interest. Besides, he that clears at once, will relapse; for finding himself out of straights, he will revert to his customs; but he that cleareth by degrees induceth a habit of frugality, and gaineth as well upon his mind as upon his estate."

The most pointed essay of reference to his brother Anthony was certainly that on "Regimen of Health", every word of which told upon the original begetter. "Beware of sudden change in any great point of diet, and, if necessity inforce it, fit the rest to it, for it is a secret, both in nature and state, that it is safer to change many things than one. . . . To be free-minded and cheerfully disposed at hours of meat, and of sleep, and of exercise, is one of the best precepts of long lasting. As for the passions and studies of the mind, avoid envy, anxious fears, anger fretting inwards, subtle and knotty inquisitions, joys, and exhilarations in excess, sadness not communicated. Entertain hopes, mirth rather than joy, variety of delights, rather than surfeit of them . . . I commend rather some diet, for certain seasons, than frequent use of physic, except it be grown into a custom, for those diets alter the body more, and trouble it less."

And lastly, Francis had no great opinion of physicians, some of whom were always on call at Essex House. "Physicians," he wrote, "are some of them so pleasing and conformable to the humour of the patient, as they press not the true cure of the disease; and some other are so regular in proceeding according to art for the disease, as they respect not sufficiently the condition of the patient.

Take one of a middle temper; or, if it may not be found
in one man, combine one of either sort: and forget not
to call as well the best acquainted with your body, as the
best reputed of for his faculty."

Anthony's first response, on receiving his own copy of
the essays, was to forward another to the Earl of Essex on
February 8th: "To your Lordship, to whose disposition
and commandment I have entirely and inviolably vowed
my poor self, and whatsoever appertaineth unto me, either
in possession or right", adding on behalf of his brother,
"Your Lordship's singular kindness towards us both will
vouchsafe first to give me leave to transfer my interest
unto your Lordship, and then humbly to crave your honourable acceptance and most worthy protection."

Francis, doubtless, approved of the gift, knowing that
a great deal of what the essays contained by way of advice would apply to the noble lord almost as much as it
did to Anthony, especially where the choosing of followers
and friends was concerned. Essex had been indisposed for
some weeks, keeping to his bed at Barn Elms and supposedly out of favour with her Majesty, the reason being
the increasing influence of the Secretary of State, Sir
Robert Cecil. It still annoyed her Majesty that the expedition to Cadiz had brought so little in the way of financial return, and Essex was convinced that this irritation
was deliberately fostered by Robert Cecil, an opinion which
Anthony also held. "The just cause of your Lordship's
undeserved discontent of mind is far more irksome to me
than my own bodily pains," he told Essex. There was talk
of the Earl going to his estates in Wales and staying
there until the Queen should soften towards him; while
the Queen, for her part, was resolved to break him of his
pride, and was heard to say that this same pride he inherited from his mother Lettice.

Gossip was rife at Court, of discontent, of reconciliation, of discontent once more, and there was further argument concerning the Earl's sister Dorothy, the Countess
of Northumberland, and lands she held to be hers through
her former husband. The Attorney General, Edward Coke,
thought fit to intervene for the Crown, which Anthony
deemed "intolerable insolency".

Essex was once again overruled when Lord Cobham,
Lord Chamberlain and Warden of the Cinque Ports, died

early in March. The Earl had asked the Queen that the position of Warden might be given to his friend Sir Robert Sidney, but she made the new Lord Cobham Warden instead. That Lord Cobham, whom Essex detested, should be preferred to Sidney added further fuel to his smouldering fires of discontent. Moreover, since Robert Cecil was married to the late Lord Cobham's daughter, this meant that the new Warden was Cecil's brother-in-law—so yet another member of the Cecil family had been shown favour by the Queen. It appeared to Essex and to his friends and supporters that the Cecil faction was growing in strength daily.

Anthony was powerless to intervene. He could only continue his unceasing correspondence in the Earl's name with agents in Italy, France and Scotland, sending and gathering what intelligence there might be, and every few days writing messages of support to his loved employer, as this, on March 3rd, when the Earl was still toying with the idea of going into Wales: "Alarm is taken by the proposed journey into Wales, which, if your Lordship hath resolved to perform, I can but pray to God by the most cordial defensive of His divine grace to reserve her Majesty's royal heart, if not her ears, from the venomous injections of those two pestilent vipers, sovereign jealousy and subaltern unquenchable envy." (Allusions to the advice that might be given to the Queen by Lord Cobham and Sir Robert Cecil during the Earl's absence from Court.)

The King of France continued to press for further assistance from the English sovereign. He was desirous that Essex should command an army and relieve Calais, still in the hands of Spain; but the Queen, prompted by her own instinct and supported by the prudent Sir Robert Cecil, returned an answer through her ambassador at the French Court that if her army should recover Calais, then she desired that it should rest in her own hands until she was reimbursed for all expenses. "This," Anthony Bacon told the Earl, "so infuriated the King he was ready to strike the ambassador, but checking himself in time, asked him to leave the chamber. Whether this be fiction or truth, I doubt not but your Lordship knoweth. If the first, it is not without design. From whencesoever it springeth, if the circumstances be true, some effects, no doubt, will follow, if they be not in time prevented."

The King of France then sent a personal envoy, one
Monsieur de Fouquerolles, to have a private audience of
her Majesty, but he was coldly received, and the entertainment provided for him at Court was poor. His royal
master asked for the continuation of English troops in
France, and for a further supply of as many more, upon
the Queen's pay. The answer came, "Her Majesty could
not tell what she would do in this request."

Anthony, whose letters to Henry Hawkins in Venice
were frequently indiscreet, wrote him a full account of the
whole affair, and how Monsieur de Fouquerolles was so
enraged at his reception that an Italian neighbour in the
adjoining room heard him stamp about the floor in anger.

"Come, dine with me and forget your business," said the
Italian.

"What—dine?" repeated de Fouquerolles. "I had such
a bellyful this morning I am full of it still and ready to
vomit."

"How is that, monsieur? Some drollery with your old
acquaintances?"

"Old in truth," replied the Frenchman, "and I mean by
old that senile Lord Treasurer of England, to whom I
paid court today on behalf of my royal master. Tossing
his Majesty's letter amongst the papers on his table he
asked me if my French King had so little conscience that
he could ruin all the English, waste their resources, lose
good cities in France, and all for love of a whore—
referring to Madame Gabrielle d'Estrées, my master's most
respected mistress. Well, the King of France deceives himself, says my Lord Treasurer. We intend to keep our hands
out of his poor game, for we can see very well the folly of
hoping for anything good out of Henri de Bourbon."

Monsieur de Fouquerolles continued to stamp up and
down the room before his Italian neighbour.

"God's blood," he went on, "I was never more astounded
in my life to hear that old lunatic rave thus, and could
hardly contain myself from letting him have it with my fist
rather than with my tongue. But the privilege of old age,
and the honour with which I hold my master, kept me
back. I merely told him I would reply if he would send
his servants from the room, as I would the gentlemen who
accompanied me, from respect for my master the King.
'Oh, indeed,' rejoined the Lord Treasurer disdainfully, 'I

have no time to amuse myself with your reply. We have had enough of all these fanfares. The last envoy, the vicomte de Turenne who calls himself duc de Bouillon, hasn't yet paid up the 20,000 écus he owes for all his grandeur.' So that was it, and for my part," added Monsieur de Fouquerolles, "I'll be off tomorrow, and cannot get away soon enough."

The whole conversation was repeated verbatim to the Earl of Essex, and, "Thus your Lordship sees," said Anthony, "the untimely morosity of an old Englishman, and the indiscreet manner of a Frenchman to a stranger, namely an Italian, between whose stayed judicious nature and the French giddy impotent impatiency is such an extreme antipathy."

What brother Francis thought of the Lord Treasurer's "untimely morosity" towards the French emissary does not appear. Doubtless when he heard of it he kept silent, for it would not have suited his plans at this moment to join in argument against the Cecil family. The Lord Treasurer's granddaughter, the enchanting Elizabeth, with whom he had flirted since she had been a girl in her teens, but who had married Sir William Hatton, had suddenly become a widow, her husband having died in March. She was barely twenty, herself childless, though stepmother to her husband's young daughter by his first marriage, and she had inherited the whole of the Isle of Purbeck, with Corfe Castle as its centre, and the imposing Hatton House in Holborn, which had once belonged to the see of Ely.

Hatton House was within strolling distance of Gray's Inn, and the gardens were famous for their beauty and design, with fountains, fishponds, arbours, lawns and alleys, terraces and trees. Francis, who had planned much of the lay-out of the garden at Twickenham and later was to do the same for Gorhambury, was no stranger to Hatton House or to its lady, even after her marriage. She was not only beautiful, witty, possessed of great spirit and temperament; she was also rich. The fact that she had been devoted to her late husband, who as a young man had fought beside Sir Philip Sidney and the Earl of Leicester, was no barrier to the urging of his suit. Others were after the same game, amongst them his friend Fulke Greville. There was little time to lose, for young widows of property and fortune were expected to remarry almost

as soon as they had put on their widow's weeds. But
Francis was virtually penniless, and without position. A
barrister just turned thirty-six, without prospects—unless
his brother Anthony should die and leave him Gorhambury—and with only his brains and his ever-ready pen to
support him, would stand small chance with the best catch
of the season, however much she chose to laugh and argue
with him, unless he had friends at hand to urge his suit.

The Earl of Essex, very naturally, was the first of these
to come to mind. The timing of a suitable letter was all-
important, and to importune too soon might mar success.
Here was the rub. The Earl, in May, was appointed chief
commander of the fleet that was shortly to set sail against
Spain, her Majesty having finally agreed to another expedition; and with so much preparation for war on hand, and
Essex going backwards and forwards to Chatham to see to
the fitting-out of the ships, it was hardly the moment to
press his lordship towards the urging of a marriage suit.
Nevertheless, a letter was penned and sent to Sandwich,
where the Earl was staying, and while the greater part
concerned other matters, and the hopes for divine providence in the forthcoming voyage, one sentence refers, most
assuredly, to his courtship of Lady Elizabeth Hatton. "My
suit to your Lordship is for your several letters to be left
with me dormant, to the gentlewoman, and either of her
parents: wherein I do not doubt, but as the beams of your
favour have often dissolved the coldness of my fortune;
so in this argument your Lordship will do the like with
your pen."

The Earl, despite all his preparations for the voyage,
obliged instantly, writing first to Sir Thomas Cecil and
then to his lady.

"Sir,
"I write this letter from the seaside, ready to go
aboard, and leave it with my secretary to be by him
delivered to you, whensoever he shall know, that my
dear friend Mr Francis Bacon is a suitor to my Lady
Hatton your daughter. What his virtues and excellent
parts are, you are not ignorant. What advantages you
may give yourself and to your house by having a son-
in-law so qualified, and so likely to rise in his profession, you may easily judge. Therefore to warrant my

moving of you to incline favourably to his suit, I will only add this, that if she were my sister or daughter, I protest I would as confidently resolve myself to further it, as now I persuade you. And tho' my love to him be exceedingly great, yet is my judgement nothing partial; for he that knows him so well as I do, cannot but be so affected. In this farewell of mine I pray you receive the kindest wishes of your most affectionate and assured friend,

> "Essex."

The second letter was to Sir Thomas's lady.

"Madam,

"The end in my writing to your Ladyship now is to do that office to my worthy and dear friend, which, if I had stayed in England, I would have done by speech; and that is to solicit your Ladyship to favour his suit to my Lady Hatton, your daughter; which I do on behalf of Mr Francis Bacon, whose virtues I know so much, as I must hold him worthy of very good fortune. If my judgement be anything, I do assure your Ladyship I think you shall very happily bestow your daughter. And if my truth be anything, I protest, if I had one as near me, as she is to you, I had rather match her with him than with men of far greater titles. And if my words do carry credit with your Ladyship, you shall make me very much bound to you, and shall tie me to be, at your Ladyship's commandment,

> "Essex.

"Sandwich, the 24th of June, 1597."

The trouble was that her ladyship's daughter had a strong will of her own and many wealthy and noble suitors at her feet. She was in no hurry to remarry. She could pick and choose amongst the best of them. Meanwhile, let each and every one call upon her at Hatton House and take a stroll in the famous gardens, Francis Bacon not the least; she could match her wit with his, as she had done in the past, and play him off against his rivals.

An undated letter from Francis to his uncle makes no mention of the marriage-suit, but is obviously intended to show respect and even offer service, should opportunity arise, as the following extracts make decidedly plain.

> "The time is yet to come that your Lordship did ever use or command or employ me in my profession, in any services or occasions of your Lordship's own, or such as are near to your Lordship; which hath made me fear sometimes that your Lordship doth more honourably affect me, than thoroughly discern of my most humble and dutiful affection to your Lordship again. Which if it were not in me, I knew not whether I were unnatural, unthankful, or unwise. . . . And in like humble manner I pray your Lordship to pardon mine errors, and not to impute unto me the errors of any other (which I know also themselves have by this time left and forethought); but to conceive of me to be a man that daily profiteth in duty. . . . And so again, craving your Honour's pardon for so long a letter, carrying so empty an offer of so unpuissant a service . . . I cease, commending your Lordship to the preservation of the Divine Majesty."

The words "the errors of any other" signify, without a doubt, his brother Anthony, whose antipathy to their uncle could hardly have been ignored by the Lord Treasurer. Francis had no desire to become involved in any such dispute, more especially at the present time, with schemes of marriage to Lady Hatton in the forefront of his mind. It was politic, therefore, to keep on civil, even obsequious, terms with uncle Burghley, and no hasty or indiscreet word would drop from his lips in company, or from his pen on paper; something quite otherwise with brother Anthony, and his talk of "the untimely morosity of an old Englishman, *vieillard lunatique*".

Plans and schemes, however, must rest in abeyance for the time being, with all men's thoughts on the progress of the fleet down-channel, from Sandwich to Weymouth, from Weymouth to Plymouth, the Earl in tremendous heart and spirits, once again in high favour with the Queen and on good terms with his comrades—even the Cecils, father and son, for once showing cordiality to the Earl, as supreme commander of the expedition. There were 120 ships in all, English and Dutch, divided into three squad-

rons. Lord Thomas Howard was Vice-Admiral and Sir
Walter Raleigh Rear-Admiral. Lord Mountjoy was
Lieutenant-General of the troops on board the squadrons,
and his brother Sir Christopher Blount, Essex's father-
in-law, was Colonel-General of the Foot. Many other earls,
knights and gentlemen, who with their followers numbered
five hundred, came as volunteers. Once again, as in the
expedition to Cadiz, the flower of England had embarked
for battle.

By July 8th the whole fleet was in Plymouth Sound.
Back in London Anthony Bacon, stricken as usual with
gout and in some pain, left Essex House to join his brother
Francis at his lodge in Twickenham. It could be that the
quiet by the river, and the air, would relieve his trouble,
but it was also true that brother Francis, plunged into
debt, was hardly pressed by his lawyer friend Nicholas
Trott, who had lent him so much cash already that he himself was in the hands of creditors. There was nothing for it,
Anthony was persuaded, but to sell land in Hertfordshire,
possibly the tithes and manor of Redbourne, in order to
repay Trott and help free his brother Francis from debt;
but these negotiations must wait until the autumn; concern
for the Earl's safety took precedence over family matters.

The expedition was ill-starred from the first. The fleet
set sail from Plymouth on July 10th, but two days later,
off Ushant, contrary winds blew in the Channel, freshen-
ing to a full gale from the southwest, and some of the
ships parted company with the main portion of the fleet,
Sir Walter Raleigh's vessel amongst them. "On Saturday
night," Raleigh wrote later to the Secretary of State, "we
made account to have yielded our souls up to God—our
ship so open everywhere, all her bulkheads rent, her very
cook-room of bricks shaken down into powder." Essex,
in *Mere Honour,* had his decks and upper works give way,
his seams open, his main-mast and fore-mast cracked, and
he bore up his helm and limped back into Falmouth under
jury rig with all hands to the pumps. The rest of the fleet
fared little better. All were back in port, either in Falmouth or in Plymouth, by July 20th. It was not a happy
augury. The venture must now be postponed for nearly
a month, half the fleet refitted, the numbers reduced, troops
discharged—and, indeed, many of the volunteers left
forthwith, unwilling to serve again.

Storm and gale could not be blamed upon the leader, and for once the Earl of Essex and the Cecils, father and son, found themselves exchanging regrets without recriminations. The Lord Treasurer, who was now seventy-seven and suffering from a flux in the left eye, piously referred to God's will and recommended the Earl to read the 107th psalm, while his son so far forgot his customary caution as to tell Essex, "The Queen is now so disposed to have us all love you, as she and I do talk every night like angels of you". It was something of a *volte face* on the part of the Cecils, but it suited Essex well since he wanted the fleet refitted.

As for Anthony, at Twickenham, he too found himself caught up in the current flow of courtesy, and not only introduced one of his agents to Robert Cecil—his name unknown, but possibly a friend of Henry Hawkins in Venice—but expressed a desire to visit his cousin in person. This was a strange request from Anthony, who professed himself so great an invalid that he called upon no one and had never yet attended Court, and whose personal attendants were careful to screen him from unwelcome visitors. Why did he suddenly ask for a personal interview with "Roberto il diavolo", the cousin he so disliked? He received, what is more, a somewhat curt answer. "It may discommode you, in regard of your indisposition," Robert Cecil told him, "and whereas I can catch an opportunity hereafter to see you, where you are, I assure you if I would appoint you the time with certainty to find me, I would break it a thousand to one, such are the distractions, which my service in that kind affords me."

The reason for the request remains a mystery. Some have thought that Anthony was planning a transference of allegiance from the Earl of Essex to his Cecil relatives. This is so unlikely, and so out of character, that it can be discounted. Anthony had earlier been in correspondence with Robert Cecil, with Essex's full knowledge, about the placing of one of the Earl's secretaries, Edward Reynolds —he who had been so put out the year before when Essex had recruited additional staff—and Anthony might well have thought he could bring up the matter in personal interview. But the main purport of conversation more assuredly would have been financial, with Anthony suggesting to his cousin that the Treasury might share some of the intelligence he received from abroad, and recompense the agents, thus sparing his own purse and the Earl's as well. He, Anthony, did all his work for love, having only his lodging free at Essex House. He believed himself fully paid by the Earl's friendship and complete confidence. But agents demanded cash, and too often had to be satisfied, or partially satisfied, by the Bacon purse alone; and with brother Francis forever out of funds, and a possible marriage in the offing, that purse had its limits.

In any event, the outcome of the temporary *rapport* between cousins remains unknown. And on August 17th, when the Earl of Essex sailed from Plymouth for the second time, he left with a letter from Anthony in his pocket, penned not by Anthony himself, who had gout in both hands, but by their mutual friend and go-between, Lord Harry Howard.

"Mr Bacon," said Lord Harry, "desired me to recommend his affectionate and humble service to your Lordship, which has no date but his life's ending. The world is quick, and pens are nimble in reporting wrongs; in respect whereof rather doubting, lest some of your pretended friends, in respect of Mr Bacon's alliance with a certain person, might out of humour, without any ground, lend him a charity, than you to continue in retaining a firm impression of his devoted faith." (This is an obvious allusion to the correspondence between Anthony and Robert Cecil, open to misconception.) "He hath required me, as a constant witness of his love to you, by way of caution to put in a bar to any wrongful plot, that might be preferred to his prejudice. He knows your gentle disposition, and hath often had experiment of your facility in acquitting persons guilty, as he cannot fear your hard conceit against him, that ever will be innocent, believing your most noble favour to be grounded upon principles of ancient experience, too strong to be shaken with any blast of emulation. His brother, as the world doth know, is dear to him; and yet I dare be sworn, that he would rather wish him underground, than he should live to your prejudice." This last a significant pointer that Anthony was not unaware of the letter which brother Francis had written to the Lord Treasurer offering service in return for furthering of the marriage suit.

As to the expedition . . . more gales, further misfortunes, the fleet once again split up, the intention to seize the Spanish harbour of El Ferrol discarded because of head winds and so countermanded, and the command ignored by Sir Walter Raleigh, who seized the harbour and landed on his own initiative, thus making bad blood between the leaders. The chief object of the expedition, which was to pursue and seize the rich prize of the West Indian fleet, ended in failure; the ships eluded capture. The Azores islands of Graciosa and Flores surrendered to the Earl of Essex, but there was small glory in this, and little return. The weather was breaking once more, provisions were scarce, men were sick.

"All protested," said Essex, "that if we stayed to attend change of winds, and did not instantly seek a watering-place, both men and ships were absolutely lost."

The fleet re-watered at Villa Franca on St Michael's, but could not penetrate further. The mountains were impassable for troops, the surf impeded and threatened the landing of small craft. On October 15th it was recognised that the only course left was to reassemble and sail north, but even now, before England and safety were reached, further gales were encountered on the passage home.

The Earl of Essex, in his dispatch, concluded with these words, "We hope her Majesty will think our painful days, careful nights, evil diet and many hazards deserve not now to be measured by the event. The like honourable construction we promise ourselves at the hands of all my Lords of the Council. As for others that have sat warm at home, and do now descant upon us, we know they lack strength to perform more, and believe they lack courage to adventure so much."

Chapter 18

A battle won, no matter what the cost in material and men, is counted victory. Honours are heaped upon the commander, glory surrounds him. Even if the battle is merely a temporary achievement, a tactical success, ground won and held and later, through weight of opposing numbers, lost, the commander does not forfeit prestige. His early victory is remembered. Not so when he fails altogether in his objective. This is not forgotten, nor is he forgiven. There is a black mark against him through the rest of his career.

It was so with Robert Devereux, Earl of Essex. Loved by the men who served under him, supported by his friends, acclaimed by the populace of London, he found a very different reception when he returned to Court at the end of October. The Queen laid the full blame of ill-success upon his shoulders. The whole expedition had been mismanaged from first to last. He had neglected to destroy the Spanish fleet, and he had missed the rich prize of the West Indian merchantmen into the bargain. She should have listened to wiser counsel from older heads before she ever promoted him to his command. As it was she had seized the opportunity, during his absence, to make Robert Cecil Chancellor of the Duchy of Lancaster, a highly lucrative post, while Lord Admiral Howard had been made Earl of Nottingham and Lord Steward of the Household, taking precedence over his peers.

Essex had spoken truly indeed when he had written, "As for others that have sat warm at home, and do now descant upon us, we know they lack strength to perform more, and believe they lack courage to adventure so much." Another earlier leader, and a king, who won not failure but victory on St Crispin's Day, had somewhat similar, though prouder, words put into his mouth by a playwright.

> "And Gentlemen in England, now a bed,
> Shall thinke themselves accurst they were not here;
> And hold their Manhoods cheape, while any speakes
> That fought with us upon Saint Crispines day."

Harry the King did not fail in his objective: Robert Devereux did, and failure is not forgiven a commander on the field of battle or upon the seas.

Essex retired to Wanstead, the estate of his late step-father, the Earl of Leicester—not to sulk and nurse his pride, as his detractors amongst the Cecil faction hinted, but to brood upon the "slings and arrows of outrageous fortune", which the same playwright put into the mouth of another character. He had expected no reward for the last voyage; nevertheless it seemed to him that some honour, some expression of approval should have been bestowed upon him in recognition of last year's capture of Cadiz—and it was for this that the Lord Admiral had been created Lord Steward and Earl of Nottingham. The old man, who had been all for pushing home instead of keeping to the seas, had been preferred to Essex, who had breached the city walls and destroyed the shipping. So much for martial prowess and for courage. . . . Musing at Wanstead he may have remembered the advice which Francis Bacon wrote to him in October a year ago: "Divert her Majesty from this impression of a martial great-ness . . . abolish it in shows to the Queen . . . for her Majesty loveth peace. . . . Pretend to be as bookish and contemplative as ever you were . . You say wars are your occupation, whereas, if I might have advised your Lordship, you should have left that person in Plym-outh. . . ."

Left him in Plymouth both last year and this? Re-mained a courtier, a pseudo-statesman, like a rudderless vessel changing course with every wind that blew? This was not the way of a man of action. Francis Bacon was a lawyer and a scholar, Essex a soldier, a leader of men. It was easier to listen to the counsels of those closer to hand, his stepfather and contemporary, Sir Christopher Blount, for instance, his steward, Sir Gilly Mericke, his personal secretary and close assistant, Henry Cuffe. They could move with him from Wanstead to Barn Elms, ever ready with suggestions and advice, whereas Anthony Bacon, gout in both hands, unsteady upon his legs, was hardly mobile enough to travel between Twickenham and Essex House.

Meetings were few, therefore, between Anthony and his beloved Earl during the autumn of 1597, but in the latter part of November it was rumoured that the Earl might soon return to Court, where her Majesty was prepared to receive him. On November 26th Anthony wrote to Henry Hawkins in Venice, "I was resolved to have continued my silence so long as my Lord continued his absence from Court: and had so done, if I were not more than in hope, that this day shall be the last of the eclipse; and that the beams of his Lordship's virtue, fame, and merit can be no longer shadowed by malice and envy, which, you know, reigns in Courts; not doubting but that ere twenty-four hours pass, he shall be Lord Marshal of England, and have a royal reward of his peerless prowess and deserts."

It was nearer twenty-four days than twenty-four hours before the Earl of Essex received what was, to him, the satisfaction of taking precedence over the Earl of Nottingham. He was created Earl Marshal—the precise position which Francis had warned him against filling—and Nottingham, piqued, resigned the staff of Lord Steward.

Anthony was doubtless thankful that Essex had received his just deserts, but he was at this time in such financial stress on his own and his brother's behalf that the threatened lease of lands was obliged to take place. A certain Robert Prentis of Breyston, in Norfolk, appears for the first time amongst his papers; he seems to have been a personal attendant. Anthony's old friend of former days, Edward Selwyn, reappears, along with a Thomas Crewe of Gray's Inn. An indenture was drawn up between all four persons regarding lands in Hertfordshire—Redbourne amongst them—under the terms of which Selwyn and Crewe should hold them for a year in the event of Anthony's death, with the purpose of raising £2,000.

It is not clear whether any loan was forthcoming at the time of signature, but in August of the following year, 1598, the Redbourne lands, house and tithes were sold—not to any of the above three gentlemen, but to one Edmund Bressey.

Francis, meanwhile, had been returned as Member of
Parliament for Ipswich and his brother for Oxford, though
Anthony obviously never took his seat. Francis, however,
not only attended in the House but rose to his feet and
spoke, the first time against enclosures and the second in
favour of a bill of subsidy, thus speaking for the Crown
and for the Bill instead of against them, as he had done,
with ill consequences to himself, four years previously.

"For enclosure of grounds brings depopulation," he said
in the first speech, "which brings forth first idleness, secondly decay of tillage, thirdly subversion of houses, and
decrease of charity and charge to the poor's maintenance,
fourthly the impoverishing the state of the realm." In his
second speech he spoke with great eloquence of the dangers from invasion, mentioning *en passant,* "that ulcer of
Ireland, which hath run on and raged more, and cannot but
be a great attractive to the ambition of the counsel of
Spain." He praised the expedition to Cadiz in 1596 and the
more abortive voyage in the present year of 1597: "The
second journey was with notable resolution borne up
against weather and all difficulties. . . . Sure I am it was
like a Tartar's or Parthian's bow, which shooteth back-
ward, and had a most strong and violent effect and opera-
tion both in France and Flanders, so that our neighbours
and confederates have reaped the harvest of it, and while
the life-blood of Spain went inward to the heart, the outward limbs and members trembled and could not resist."

The bill for subsidy was passed on all three readings,
met with no obstruction, and was presented to the Queen
at the closing of the session. How much was due to the
eloquence of the honourable member for Ipswich remains
conjecture, but her Majesty this time was satisfied, and the
voyage itself, besides its leader the Earl of Essex, spared
further calumny.

Francis Bacon, close on thirty-eight, a member of the
House of Commons without office or position, was feeling
his way towards a command of the English language that
would seldom, if ever, be surpassed. Certain of his phrases
read like verse—"Our neighbours and confederates have
reaped the harvest of it" and "While the lifeblood of Spain
went inward to the heart".

Brother Anthony, touching forty years and feeling older,
had not even the satisfaction of a well-phrased speech in

Parliament to content him. He was busy writing about his physical condition to a Dr Barker of Shrewsbury, a relative of his one-time tutor in Gray's Inn.

"Good Mr Barker,

"Having understood first by my servant Mainwaring, then by mine ancient special good friend your kinsman Mr Richard Barker, that God of his goodness had moved and disposed your heart, though otherwise a stranger unto me, to employ your best skill and experience to reintegrate my health, or at the least to ease my much pain, I can but render you most hearty thanks for your free goodwill and friendly offer, the performance whereof with your good leave I will be bold earnestly to request by your repair hither. I know you too well by report to enter into protestations what confidence and thankfulness you shall find in me, and therefore referring myself to your judgement and proofs, I will shortly set down certain particulars by way of advertisement to prepare your consultation and advice thereupon.

"My late father was much troubled both to the gout and the stone, and consequently myself by birth subject hereunto. My complexion sanguine, my constitution of body even from my youth sickly and rheumatic, having been at 14 years of age in danger of losing both mine eyes. Then began to be made a piste [?] of physic. At 27 I travelled into France where having remained 7 years I wrenched my right foot, which outward mischance finding my body otherwise indisposed began to draw down the rheum that way, which, little by little, did so encroach upon me as at the last it grew to a running gout, which held me in my shoulder, mine arm and my hand, otherwise in my knee and my foot, in which state I have continued these seven years, sometimes more, sometimes less pained, and yet not lost, God be thanked, the use of any limb nor have gotten any formed knottiness, but rather a stiffness and weakness in my joints.

"The rage of my gout, considering my years being towards 40, is nothing fiery nor red hot, but bringeth with it a swelling and dissolution of my sinews. It takes me by fits as well in the summer as winter, specially if I take never so little cold it removeth often from one place to another very suddenly. My diet is not offensive. My stomach weak and subject to wind. My head free from all headache but exceeding moist and fruitful in defluctions at this part. My body hath been evacuated both by light purifyings or late vomits.

"Thus, sir, have I been bold to confess myself unto you, even from my cradle to this time, for the state of my body, and will only add this one thing, without ostentation, God knoweth, but in truth for your right information, that I have never been troubled with any kind of *leues veneria*, nor committed any act to occasion it, for the which modesty I have by some physicians been rather censured than commended, noting my *abundantia seminis*. And so, good Master Barker, committing the consideration thereof to your good meaning, knowledge and experience, I commend myself most heartily unto you, and you to God's safe protection.

"Your entire loving friend,

"A.B."

Many crippling diseases other than gout and rheumatism come to mind: arthritis, neuritis or disseminated sclerosis —Anthony Bacon may have suffered from any of these, with a contributing psychological element. The fact remains that his condition did not improve, though whether or not Doctor Barker from Shrewsbury came to London to treat him never appears. It is significant that the negotiations with regard to his lands, and the naming of his trustees, Edward Selwyn and Robert Prentis, were made at this time, although no copy of his will has yet been traced.

The frankness of the letter is somehow touching. Near forty and virgin still? The fondling of those pages in past years producing *abundantia seminis* and nothing more? He would hardly have lied to Dr Barker or any other physician.

And his mother Lady Bacon? What had been her counsel through the past months? Unfortunately, her many letters for this period are undated and increasingly confused, and only here and there, scattered from one letter to another, is it possible to pick out some contemporary allusion. "God bless you with needful health inward and outward. . . . You purge still. Me thinketh it should make nature neither to work digestion nor strength, being so long still pulled. What custom of physic hath done in you God knows . . . I would gladly know when and how you sell Redbourne. Do wisely and be out of debt as soon as you can. Look to your health and may God bless you with a good marriage for your comfort."

Little hope in this advice, and she must have known it, yet in a further letter she returns to the theme. "Bruit goes here you would sell Napsbury. I hope you mean it not. The chiefest manor hereabouts. Yesterday being the Lord's day, at church one asked me the question, and said that Mr Fuller desired a friend in these parts to hark out some manor for him to buy. Have you no hope of posterity? Only my children counted in the world unworthy their father's care for and providing for them. Barley and Pinner, if you had kept them, would have been above 95 marks a year to you. Do not, I pray you, make yourself a by-word both here and to such as are but your half-friends, by so selling to your great lack and encumbrance to this house. Young sons in latter time are blessed posterity, and it would be well used for them. I should have been happy to have seen children's childer, but France spoiled me and mine."

Poor lonely old woman, her desire for grandchildren forever unfulfilled, and the last dig, "France spoiled me and mine", showing how bitterly she still resented Anthony's long years abroad.

Another letter had more practical advice. "I pray God hourly to give you strength to bear and his healing help to overcome safely the whole cause of your present pain. No doubt, by all likelihood of your present thick troubled urine and other tokens, the past calamity is yet behind. You must in any wise be special careful you take no violent things to break it, for it will so cut you and raw the place, that the smart thereof will be intolerable and very dangerous. I know you should anoint you beneath, and also camomile oil might help it. I remember your father once with ravens' quills or crows' helped to turn it in the passage if need were. I would Dr Smith were with you."

Her remedy sounds more painful than the bearing of

the pain, yet how earnestly she writes, adding the post-script, "I pray let me hear, and the Lord take care of you and safely ease you. Whensoever it comes, I will come quickly. Deo . . ."

First instinct of a mother, to leave all at a moment's notice and go to the bedside of her son. She was somewhat stricter where Francis was concerned. "Your brother promiseth too much. He knoweth too well upon what late cause I have cause to give not only motherly but godly advice. His profession is not, and ought not to be, of vain device or unprofitable. Let him read the Epistle to the Ephesians touching unclean speech and thought. Trust in the Lord with all thy heart sayeth the Wisdom of God, and not in their own. Let him be a fool in this world that he may be wise. Read not my letters either scoffingly or carelessly."

Whether she knew about Francis and his expectations of the lady in Hatton House is possible: Lady Elizabeth's reputation as a flirtatious widow would hardly be endearing to one of Lady Bacon's moral standards. She might be the granddaughter of the Lord Treasurer, but she was hardly fitted to become the daughter-in-law of Lady Bacon and of her late husband the Lord Keeper, nor suited to be mistress of Gorhambury in days to come. In any event, no more was heard of Francis's suit, either in the family or in public. Gossip at Court was concerned with the Earl of Essex, said to be trifling with Mrs Brydges, an old love, and also with a Mistress Southwell, and rumour was rife too that his close friend, the Earl of Southampton, had got one of the Queen's maids of honour with child.

The Earl of Essex was certainly at Court in the spring, and diligent in his attendance upon the Queen, hoping, during the absence of Sir Robert Cecil on a mission to King Henri IV in France, that he might regain some of the ground he had lost the preceding year. Sir Robert himself was in no happy mood at this time; his wife, to whom he had been devoted, had lately died, and his father the Lord Treasurer was becoming more frail every day. The full burden of State appeared to rest upon his shoulders, his "crooked" shoulders, as his cousin Anthony would have termed them. He had embarked for France on February 17th, with a small group of noblemen in attendance, including, curiously enough, the Earl of Southampton and

Lord Harry Howard, both so close to the Earl of Essex, but he had for support his brother-in-law Lord Cobham.

The Earl of Essex gave a lavish entertainment at Essex House once they had left for Dover, with his guests amusing themselves until one in the morning while a group of actors performed two plays before them. What the plays were can only be conjectured. *Romeo and Juliet* had been published in quarto in 1597—and this would have staged well in the great hall or gallery of Essex House—while *Love's Labour's Lost,* though not yet printed, had been presented before her Majesty at Christmas, and with the mission departing to the Court of France might have been deemed highly contemporary, with its King of Navarre, its Princess of France, its fantastic Spaniard Dom Adriano de Armado—so like Signor Perez, who, incidentally, fussed around the Secretary of State almost as soon as Cecil set foot in France.

Speculation is idle. The guests at Essex House were entertained, and hardly was the party over than there came a sudden rumour that Spanish ships had been observed in the Channel. It was a case of panic stations. The Earl of Essex was ready to go to Kent and Sussex, Lord Mountjoy to Portsmouth, Sir Walter Raleigh to Cornwall, the Lord Chamberlain to the Isle of Wight (though what he could have achieved there is a mystery); and then the scare subsided, the enemy passed up the coast to Calais, still in Spanish hands, and everyone relaxed.

The Secretary of State remained at the French Court for two and a half months and returned at the very end of April, having achieved little. Henri IV had made a separate peace with Spain and seemed unconcerned with the danger to his English allies. He had, however, treated Sir Robert with great cordiality, invited him to shoot wolves, and introduced him to Madame his sister and to his mistress Gabrielle d'Estrées. It seems that Cecil described Princess Catherine as "well-painted, ill-dressed, and strangely jewelled", which would have offended the loyal Anthony Bacon had he heard it. (The unfortunate princess, still passionately attached to the comte de Soissons, was to be harried into marriage with Henri of Lorraine, whom she did not love, the following year.) The worst news this spring, however, was that the Irish leader, Hugh O'Neill, Earl of Tyrone, had made an agreement with the

King of Spain, who had agreed to furnish him with troops and money so that he could achieve a free and united Ireland. The question was, should England join with France in making peace with Spain, or continue to fight without allies? And who was to put down the rebel Irish? Inevitably the Council was divided, the Cecil faction for peace, Essex and his supporters for war. It was now, in late May, that the Earl drafted a long treatise on the subject, calling it *An Apologia,* and dedicating it to Anthony Bacon.

Chapter 19

Part of the Earl's *Apologia* had been written after his return from Cadiz in August 1596, when, despite the capture of the Spanish port and the success of the expedition, he had nevertheless found some criticism at home. Henry Cuffe, his private secretary, had given the text to Anthony, who had copies made, translations too, which were sent to Scotland, the Low Countries and France. The *Apologia* of May 1598 was an expansion of the earlier material with a discussion of the current problem of whether to continue the war against Spain, or take the easier way out and agree to a problematical peace.

The *Apologia* is of interest because it shows that the Earl still felt so close in sympathy and friendship to Anthony Bacon that he dedicated the work to him, and also because it gives much insight into how Essex looked upon the problems of his day. A few extracts from the latter part of it illustrate this, omitting the details of the Earl's earlier life, his bookishness as a boy, his venture to the Low Countries at nineteen, his comradeship-in-arms with stout-hearted Sir Roger Williams, and the two expeditions to Spain, all of which he recounts in some detail. He writes proudly, which was his nature: "I am not one to lean on other men or sit at home like merchants," runs an early line, and, "Since the Queen early used my service, she must count me amongst the men of war" is another. "Our dependence as a nation is upon our ships" has, to a modern ear, a fine Churchillian ring, and, "I know that great scandal lies upon arms, but that is the fault of the possessors and not of the profession" would find an echo in many a military or naval heart in later centuries.

"I see no sign that Spain wants peace with us," the Earl continues. "What chance have the Low Countries of maintaining war if we abandon them? . . . Our navy was

211

never stronger, our nation never so martial. France has
left us. Ireland is our sole burden. Her Majesty's Treasury
has drawn deep, and poor husbandmen by late hard years
have scant means, but England cannot be considered poor
from sumptuous buildings, surfeiting diet, prodigality in
garments, infinite plate and costly furniture. With our ex-
penseful vanities cannot we arm ourselves? Is England so
bare an estate? . . . When our country was far poorer
we made great conquests in France, even to the Holy
Land. . . . Ours is a degenerate age, but we have some
seed left of our ancient virtue. Thanks be to God we have
a Queen who will sell her plate and jewels to defend her
people. Turn silken coats to iron ones. . . . Peace will
encourage the enemy. He will bring us asleep in the name
of Peace till he rouse us with a thundering war. . . .

"These, these, worthy Mr Bacon, are my apprehensions
and doubts. I will embrace an honourable and durable
peace with both my arms. . . . But till then, a just war is
our necessity."

A century and a half later Essex's *Apologia* was in-
corporated in an edition of the works of Francis Bacon.
This was declared ,to be an error. The sentiments were
certainly the Earl's and not those of Francis, who, like his
cousin Robert Cecil, was more inclined to peace and prudence at this time. Yet it is possible that he, or brother
Anthony, or all three, could have had a hand in the composition. Whether this is so or not, the language is Elizabethan English at its most stirring, awaking perhaps even
greater understanding and sympathy in loyal and patriotic
hearts today, after two world wars, than it did in 1598,
and finding as little response amongst those who, then as
now, sought only ease, comfort and good living.

The Earl of Essex was accused of favouring his
companions-in-arms and all fighting men, and perhaps his
strongest words were employed in their defence.

"I do entirely love them. . . . Now that I know their
virtues, I would choose them for friends if I had them not,
but before I had tried them, God in his providence chose
them for me . . . I love them for their virtue's sake, for
their greatness of mind, for their understanding, for their
affections—for soft-living men love ease, pleasure and
profit, but those that love pains, dangers and fame, show
that they love the public more than themselves. I love them

for my country's sake, for they are England's best ancient armour of defence, and weapons of offence; if we have peace, they have purchased it; if we have war, they must manage it; yea, while we are doubtful and entreat, we must salve ourselves with what may be done by our men of action."

Essex may have declared that her Majesty would be prepared to sell her plate and jewels, but in the Council chamber this assertion seemed more remote. Debates were long and devisive; the Cecil faction called Essex a warmonger, and the old Lord Treasurer one day went so far as to take out a prayer-book and read from the Psalms, "The bloodthirsty and deceitful men shall not live out half their days". Nevertheless, measures were taken by the Council to provide assistance to the Low Countries, who were still hard-pressed by Spanish forces.

Then the question came up regarding the appointment of a new governor for Ireland, and here once more Essex found himself in disagreement with the Cecils and with her Majesty herself. The Queen wished to send the Earl's uncle, Sir William Knollys, while Essex urged the merits of Sir George Carew, one of the Cecil faction, who would thereby be removed to a safe distance. The famous quarrel ensued in which the Earl of Essex turned his back upon the Queen, and she boxed his ears for his bad manners, whereupon he laid his hand on his sword and declared he would not have suffered such an indignity from Henry VIII himself. The Earl of Nottingham, he who had been Lord Admiral Howard, intervened; but the damage had been done. The Queen bade Essex go hang himself, and he left Court immediately and retired to Wanstead. Whispers of a serious breach between monarch and favourite spread from Whitehall and throughout London and beyond. It was an unhappy setback for Essex and his supporters.

The immediate reaction at Essex House is not known, but Anthony Bacon was still in active correspondence with the Earl's friends. Reports from Scotland and the border continued to reach him for forwarding to his lordship at Wanstead, and foreign intelligence from overseas, from Venice and from France, was also dealt with during those summer months of 1598.

On August 4th William Cecil, Earl Burghley, Lord

Treasurer, died, aged seventy-seven, and if his nephews Anthony and Francis Bacon were not greatly affected it was a crushing blow to her Majesty and a sad loss for England. He was a great man and a great statesman—possibly none wiser or more devoted has ever served an English monarch; and what over-caution he was apt to show, what narrowness of mind in some particulars, must be forgiven him. Certainly some family rivalry, a desire to favour his astute son at the expense of his equally talented nephews, remains a shadow on his reputation; but this is a basic fault, natural to most men through the ages. Perhaps, had things been otherwise, Cecil dying in early middle-age and the Lord Keeper Sir Nicholas Bacon surviving him, the same accusation might have been levelled at the latter's door, Anthony and Francis exalted to high favour and Robert Cecil ignored, left without position.

The Lord Treasurer's funeral was a solemn and stately occasion attended by five hundred mourners and all his family, children, grandchildren and great-grandchildren. The Earl of Essex was present, "carrying the heaviest countenance of the company", it was reported at the time, and that same evening retired once more to Wanstead, still out of favour with her Majesty. Another reason for this was that the maid of honour who had been courted by the Earl of Southampton, Essex's close friend, was six months pregnant and was staying at Essex House. Southampton, in fact, married her in secret about this time, which so infuriated the Queen when she came to hear of it that both he and his bride were imprisoned in the Fleet.

It had been an anxious, unhappy year for her Majesty. Now sixty-five, affairs abroad and at home weighed heavily upon her. She had lost her most trusted and faithful servant, Lord Burghley; she was estranged from her loved Robin Devereux, who had dared to oppose her in open Council; her maids of honour flaunted her, thereby causing young courtiers to laugh behind her back; and every day the "ulcer of Ireland", as Francis Bacon had termed it, swelled and erupted. The commander of the English troops was killed in battle with 1,500 men, fighting the rebel leader Tyrone; she must appoint a new commander, a new governor, a new Lord Treasurer, the whole weight of the final decision resting upon herself.

The weeks following Burghley's death had been fraught with anxiety for Francis Bacon also, though from a very different cause. On August 28th brother Anthony had sold the manor and tithes of Redbourne to Edmund Bressey of London and Gray's Inn for £1,800, but much of this money was already forfeit to Anthony's own debts—monies due to agents abroad—and little could be spared for Francis. Friends had been touched too often to be approached again. Relatives were useless. Those half-brothers Nicholas and Nathaniel in Suffolk and Norfolk would do nothing for him, despite their joint fortunes and large estates. To whom, then, could Francis turn, like most of his contemporaries, but Jews and money-lenders?

A goldsmith, one Sympson of Lombard Street, had held a bond of his for £300 since the early summer, but had agreed to wait for its forfeiture until Michaelmas Term began in October. Meantime, Francis was engaged in the examination of a certain John Stanley, accused of a conspiracy against the Queen; and although his part in the examination was a minor one, it necessitated going every day to the Tower of London and taking depositions. The matter of the bond may not have been uppermost in his mind as he walked to and from the Tower, for he was preoccupied with another matter which dismayed him greatly. The man whom he most detested in the legal world, the Attorney-General Sir Edward Coke, had become a widower in June, and with his wife scarcely two months dead he had had the nerve to approach Sir Thomas Cecil, now the 2nd Earl Burghley, for the hand of his daughter Lady Elizabeth Hatton. Coke was now a man of property, with an estate in Norfolk and £30,000 from his late wife; the fact that he was forty-six years old and had ten children would not count against him in the eyes of the new Lord Burghley, who would undoubtedly find it extremely useful to have the Attorney-General in the family. The young lady herself would hardly favour him, though he was not ill-looking, and his powerful mind and caustic tongue would match her own; but the £30,000, added to the persuasion of her parents, might sway her opinion, and it was no use blinking the fact that Edward Coke was a formidable rival to a penniless barrister deep in debt, despite the friendship that had grown ever since, wandering from Gray's Inn to those famous gardens at Hatton

House, he had given her advice on plants and shrubs. If, indeed, friendship was all that took place between them.

On September 23rd, walking homeward from the Tower, Francis was arrested and seized at the instigation of Mr Sympson the goldsmith, although it wanted a full fortnight still to Michaelmas Term, when the bond for £300 would fall due. In a matter of hours he would have been confined in the Fleet, and indeed he was detained for a short while by the officials sent to arrest him; but he managed to send a message to Sheriff More, a personal friend, with whom he had fortunately dined two days previously, and was at once transferred to a house in Coleman Street where he could spend the night in comfort, and from there send urgent messages to his brother and his friends. Unfortunately, no trace remains of a letter sent to Anthony or of Anthony's response, which would have been immediate. The only reference to the whole affair consists of two letters written by Francis on September 24th from Coleman Street, one to Sir Robert Cecil, the other to Sir Thomas Egerton, Keeper of the Great Seal. The letters were discovered in a collection at Hatfield House a century and a half later, around 1760. There is no mention of Francis's arrest in the common gossip of the day, so presumably the debt was promptly paid, Francis released, and the unfortunate affair hushed up. The two letters have, of course, been published since in biographies, and it is of some interest to include them here.

"To Sir Robert Cecil, Secretary of State.
    "It may please your Honour,
    "I humbly pray you to understand how badly I have been used by the enclosed, being a copy of a letter of complaint thereof, which I have written to the Lord Keeper. How sensitive you are of wrongs offered to your blood in my particular, I have had not long since experience. But herein I think your honour will be doubly sensitive, in tenderness also of the indignity to her Majesty's service. For as for me, Mr Sympson might have had me every day in London; and therefore to belay me, while he knew I came from the Tower about her Majesty's special service, was to my understanding very bold. And two days before he brags he forebore me, because I dined with Sheriff

More. So as with Mr Sympson, examinations are not
so great a privilege, *eundo et redeundo,* as Sheriff
More's dinner. But this complaint I make in duty,
and to that end have also informed my Lord of Essex
thereof; for otherwise his punishment will do me no
good. So with significance of my humble duty, I commend your Honour to the divine protection. From
Coleman Street, this 24th of September, 1598.

"At your honourable command particularly,
                                "Fr. Bacon."

The letter he enclosed to Lord Keeper Egerton gives
fuller detail.

"It may please your Lordship,

"I am to make humble complaint to your Lordship
of some hard dealing offered me by one Sympson, a
goldsmith, a man noted much, as I have heard, for
extremities and stoutness upon his purse; but yet I
could hardly have imagined, he would have dealt
either so dishonestly towards myself, or so contemp-
tuously towards her Majesty's service. For this Lombard (being admonished by the street he lives in I
give him this name) having me in bond £300
principal, and having the last term confessed the action, and by his full and direct consent respited the
satisfaction till the beginning of the term to come,
without ever giving me warning either by letter or
message, served an execution upon me having trained
me at such time as I came from the Tower, where
Mr Waad can witness, we attended a service of no
mean importance. Neither would he as much as
vouchsafe to come and speak with me to take any
order in it, though I sent for him divers times, and
his house was just by; handling it as upon a despite
being a man I never provoked with a cross word, no,
nor with any delays. He would have urged it to have
had me in prison; which he had done, had not Sheriff
More, to whom I sent, gently recommended me to
an handsome house in Coleman Street, where I am.
Now because he will not treat with me, I am enforced
humbly to desire your Lordship to send for him, according to your place, to bring him to some reason;

and this forthwith, because I continue here to my
further discredit and inconvenience, and the trouble
of the gentleman with whom I am. I have an hundred
pounds lying by me, which he may have, and the rest
upon some reasonable time and security; or if need
be, the whole; but with more trouble. . . ."

The letter then repeats something of the same matter
contained in the covering note to his cousin Sir Robert
Cecil, and ends with his humble duties.

In all probability the Earl of Essex came to the rescue
first, but there is no proof of this, nor of what action was
taken by Sir Robert Cecil or the Lord Keeper. Francis
may have remained in Coleman Street a day or a week.
Certainly the debt must have been paid, the bond cancelled, and Mr Sympson the goldsmith of Lombard Street
in some way satisfied, if grudgingly.

> "Ile have my bond, I will not heare thee speake,
> Ile have my bond; and therefore speake no more,
> Ile not be made a soft and dull ey'd fool,
> To shake the head, relent, and sigh, and yeeld
> To Christian intercessors: follow not,
> Ile have no speaking; I will have my bond."

Shylock, Merchant of Venice, drove a harder bargain with
his demand for a pound of flesh than Sympson the goldsmith did with Francis; nevertheless, the similarity of the
cases would have caused those few in the know to nod and
smile when the play first appeared in quarto two years
later.

Whether news of the arrest ever came to the ears of
Lady Elizabeth Hatton is open to speculation. Six weeks
after his arrest she married Sir Edward Coke, secretly by
night at Hatton House, the only witnesses her father and
the minister who performed the service. The date in St
Andrew's parish register, Holborn, is November 2nd 1598.
She was twenty years of age. The secret marriage, without
banns or licence, was at her own insistence, and she declared that although now wife to Edward Coke she would
continue to be known as Lady Hatton.

Naturally the marriage remained a secret for a few days
only. Men in the position of Lord Burghley and Edward

Coke could not deceive the world. The Queen must be informed, and the Queen ordered that the marriage should be made public, and that the Archbishop of Canterbury should take up the matter in the Ecclesiastical Court and somehow legalise the marriage by giving a dispensation to the offending couple, who otherwise might have been imprisoned and excommunicated. The Attorney-General, incidentally, pleaded ignorance of ecclesiastical law, which saved his face and reputation, but why Lady Elizabeth had insisted on secrecy in the first place remains a mystery. Many a battle followed between them, in later years, regarding the property of her first husband, Sir William Hatton, and in other matters too; but she stuck to her guns, and was always known, at Court and elsewhere, even at Stoke Manor, the Attorney-General's house, as Lady Hatton.

The marriage was the talk of the town. "The seventh of this month," wrote the gossip John Chamberlain to his friend Mr Dudley Carleton, "the Queen's Attorney married the Lady Hatton to the great admiration of all men, that after so many large and likely offers she should decline to a man of his quality, and the world will not believe that it was without a mystery."

The mystery remains. And the rumour that she was pregnant by another man could not be proved or disproved when nine months later, in mid-August 1599, she was "brought to bed of a daughter". But this is to anticipate.

Francis, presumably either at Twickenham Lodge or at the Inn of Glaucus, endeavoured to bury mortification in a manner common to most writers, by employing his own and other idle pens in forgetting the whole sorry business. What was past was past. The future beckoned. And Anthony, his anxiety for his lordship's cause temporarily relieved, since Essex had been received back at Court by the Queen with partial favour, could turn to a letter addressed to him by the new French ambassador, lately arrived in London, saying that the King his master, "Could not have conferred his favours upon a more worthy person than Mr Bacon, or upon a gentleman of more merit, or more mindful of the courtesies he had received in France; that he deserved a thousand more courtesies than he had received, and Mr Bacon might, when opportunity offered, certainly expect this from the King, who,

as a prince, had a greater affection and regard for her
Majesty than could be expressed, and consequently for
the brave gentleman of England, whom the ambassador
was ready to serve."

The brave gentleman of England had so far received
nothing more concrete from his Majesty King Henri IV,
with the exception of kind protection in 1586, than he had
from her Majesty Queen Elizabeth, or indeed from his
beloved Essex, beyond board and lodging—perhaps not
even board and certainly not fuel; but there was always
consolation in the knowledge that his lordship trusted him,
and that, despite the jealousy of others in the entourage,
his had been the name upon the *Apologia* written in May.
When plagued by gout and rheumatism and the stone, he
could forget his unpaid labours and turn up a poetic conceit penned by an anonymous European who at least
thought him worthy of much praise.

ANTHOINE BACON

A. *Anglais phenix de celeste origine,*
N. *Né pour orner et la terre et les cieux,*
T. *Ton renom bruit jusques aux envieux:*
H. *Honneur te sert, et vertu te domine:*
O. *Ornement seul de sagesse et doctrine,*
 I. *Jour, et clairté de tout coeur genereux:*
N. *Nous ne sçaurions regarder de nos yeux*
E. *Eternité qui devant tol chemine.*
                    Bacone.
B. *Bacon fior di virtu, raro e perfetto*
A. *Animo pronto, angelico intelletto,*
C. *Chiaro lume d'honor e caritade,*
O. *Ornamento e beltà di nostra etade,*
N. *Natural real di fideltà pieno*
E. *Essempio d'ogni ben sempre sereno.*

Chapter 20

January 1599 opened with the decision not yet made as to who was to be Lord Lieutenant of Ireland, although most of the Council were inclined towards Lord Mountjoy, and her Majesty was said to be wavering between him and the Earl of Essex. In any event, the Earl was restored to favour and was now pressing his own claim to the position; and it was observed that upon Twelfth Night, when the Queen was entertaining the Danish ambassador at Whitehall, she "danced with the Earl of Essex very richly and freshly attired". Whether this description refers to her Majesty's own apparel—she was invariably gorgeously dressed and be-jewelled—or to Robin Devereux's own costume is not clear. He was apt to be negligent in this respect, and had been warned of his error in the letter which Francis Bacon had written to him twelve months previously. Nor is it really clear either from the gossip of the day or from historical records how passionately determined the Earl of Essex was to become her deputy in Ireland; like her Majesty, he too blew now hot, now cold on the appointment. One thing is evident: if he was finally offered the position he wanted to accept it on his own terms, with a strong enough army to support him and fellow-officers he could trust, and no niggardly pay arrangement from the Treasury.

Throughout February and March the matter remained unsettled, and then, on March 24th, the Queen signed the document appointing the Earl of Essex Lord Lieutenant of Ireland, a decision that was immensely popular amongst the ordinary people, but was accepted with some reserve by the Council and even by certain of his closest friends. The position required a man of great experience, judgement and political understanding, and with some knowledge of the Irish people. The Earl was untested in these

qualities, and his predecessors in Ireland, who had possessed them in some measure, had not been conspicuous
for their success. Lady Bacon's cousin, Sir William Fitzwilliam, had been one of them. From 1588 until 1594 he
had striven hard to bring some sense of justice and equanimity to the troubled, and troublesome, island; sometimes
acting with too firm a hand, laying waste part of the
countryside so that "not a house was left standing or a
grain of corn unburnt", sometimes attempting pacification. When at the age of sixty-eight he gave way to his
successor, Sir William Russell, Fitzwilliam, like his second
cousin Anthony Bacon, was "old in body, sick in stomach,
racked with the stone, bed-ridden with the gout". How
much these disabilities could be laid at Ireland's door and
how much to a constitution inherited from Fitzwilliams
before him—this last might well have been Anthony's inheritance too—remains conjecture.

Sir William Russell, brother-in-law to Anthony's aunt
Elizabeth, had trodden an equally dusty road in Ireland.
He told Anthony in 1596 that, "Since we have entered
into treaties of pacification and cessation from arms, her
Majesty hath received more loss by the cunning and treachery of the rebels, than in any likelihood could have befallen her by a course of war in twice so much time, insomuch, if it be not speedily looked into, and horse and foot
presently sent over, the whole kingdom is likely to be
endangered."

The Earl of Essex, at thirty-two, having scaled the walls
of Cadiz and shown great gallantry in the field, certainly
believed he could succeed where older men had been defeated. When he took horse on March 27th from Walsingham House and rode through Cheapside, with all the
people acclaiming him and crying out "God bless your
Lordship!", the Earl himself "very plainly attired", it was
noticed by some that the sky was calm and clear, which
was a good omen for the days ahead of him; yet before
he had passed Islington a black cloud came out of the
northeast, followed by thunder and lightning, hail and rain,
and this was not a happy augury.

There was foul weather awaiting him in Wales, fog and
much rain, and the passage to Ireland rougher and more
dangerous than had been known in years. His close friend,
the Earl of Southampton, was with him, appointed Gen-

eral of the Horse, but his nearest adviser at this time, his stepfather Sir Christopher Blount, had been forbidden by the Queen to accompany him to Ireland, which rankled with the Earl as further proof of the Queen's lingering hostility to his mother, and indeed to most members of his family. Edward Reynolds, his personal secretary, who had been offended two years earlier by what he considered some neglect on the Earl's part, was now appeased by being appointed liaison officer in London between the new Lord Lieutenant and the Council, while Anthony remained as usual at Essex House to deal with foreign intelligence. What he thought of the Earl's appointment in Ireland does not appear in any correspondence, but brother Francis had more presumption and some definite ideas on the subject, and wrote a letter of advice to his lordship before he left London. The letter has been often quoted since, and extracts from it give his line of reasoning.

"Your Lordship is designed to a service of great merit and great peril; and as the greatness of the peril must needs include a like proportion of merit so the greatness of the merit may include no small consequence of peril, if it be not temperately governed. For all immoderate success extinguisheth merit, and stirreth up distaste and envy . . .

"The goodness and justice whereof [he refers to the cause on which the Earl was employed in Ireland] is such as can hardly be matched by any example; it being no ambitious war against foreigners, but a recovery of subjects, and that after lenity of conditions often tried; and a recovery of them not only to obedience, but to humanity and policy, from more than Indian barbarism . . .

"And if any man be of opinion, that the nature of the enemy doth extenuate the honour of the service, being but a rebel and a savage, I differ from him. For I see the justest triumphs that the Romans in their greatness did obtain, were of such an enemy as this; that is people barbarous and not reduced to civility, magnifying a kind of lawless liberty, fortified in woods and bogs, and placing both justice and felicity in the sharpness of their swords. Such were the Germans and and the ancient Britons, and divers others. Upon which kind of people, whether the victory were a conquest, or a reconquest upon a rebellion or a revolt, it made no difference that ever I could find in honour. . . .

"Advice . . . is that which is left to me, being no man of war, and ignorant in the particulars of State. For a man may by the eye set up the white right in the midst of the butt, though he be no archer. Therefore I will only add this wish, that your Lordship in this whole action, looking forward, would set down this position, that merit is worthier than fame . . . that obedience is better than sacrifice. For designing to fame and glory may make your Lordship in the adventure of your person to be valiant as a private soldier, rather than a general."

If the advice was not heeded—and Francis was well aware that there was little likelihood of persuading the Earl of any course of action that he did not sincerely believe had been instigated by himself—it was because confrontation, then, now, and always, is not only between the commander in the field and the enemy he seeks to subdue, but also between the men of action on the ground and the politicians back at home. The opposing views are seldom if ever reconcilable. Francis Bacon feared for the Commander-in-Chief in Ireland, knowing that, wisely or unwisely, he would be willing to listen to brother officers close to him, but would never bend to the will of civilian gentlemen in England, members of the Council and advisers to her Majesty the Queen. Today the commander who has been overruled is posted to a lesser command or retires to write his memoirs. The politician who suffers reverse retreats to the back benches, hoping for office at a later date. In 1599 both commanders and politicians, when subject to reverses of fortune, were more often put to death. The Tower and the axe awaited them.

One of the most striking things about that fateful campaign in Ireland was the fact that then, as in the 1970's, nearly four hundred years later, the Irish employed guerrilla tactics, and regular troops could make little or no impression upon them. Equally, opinion at home failed to realise the nature of the terrain, and the Earl of Essex, trained in battles of assault in France, found Francis Bacon's warning of "woods, and bogs, and lawless liberty" fully justified. He wrote to the Council from Kilkenny, on May 20th:

"This people against whom we fight hath able bodies, good use of the arms they carry, boldness enough to attempt and quickness in apprehending any advantage they see offered them; whereas our new and common sort of men have neither bodies, spirits, nor practice of arms like the others. The advantage we have is in our horse, which will command all campaigns; in our order which these savages have not; and in the extraordinary courage and spirit of our men of quality. But to meet these with our helps, the rebels fight in woods and bogs, where horses are utterly unserviceable; they use the advantage of lightness and swiftness in going off when they find our order too strong for them to encounter; and I protest to your Lordships how unequal a wager it is to adventure the lives of noblemen and gentlemen against rogues and naked beggers, which makes me take more care to contain our best men, than to use their courage against the rebels."

By the end of May Essex had come to know the terrain better, and the type of warfare and defensive measures likely to be undertaken by the enemy; nevertheless, he had not the advantage of trained and disciplined troops, his army being largely raised from levies at home without experience in any sort of battle, let alone ambush from wood and thicket. He admitted, in a dispatch to the Council, that he had difficulty in getting his men "to stand firm, to keep order, to forbear noises and speeches of fear and amazement".

This want of experience amongst the English came as a bonus to the rebel Irish and their leaders, who could lie in wait, then engage in sudden skirmish at will. It was superior numbers, more money, and more victuals that the Earl of Essex needed, and he wrote to the Council from Waterford demanding them. His letter to the Queen showed a farsighted appreciation of the situation as he saw it.

"In their rebellion," he told her, "these people have no

other end but to shake off the yoke of obedience to your
Majesty, and to root out all remembrance of the English
nation in this kingdom. I say this of the people in general;
for I find not only the greater part thus affected, but that
it is a general quarrel of the Irish; and they that do not
profess it are either so few or so false, that there is no
account to be made of them. The Irish nobility and lords
of countries do not only in their hearts affect this plausible
quarrel, and are divided from us in religion, but have an
especial quarrel to the English government, because it
limiteth and tieth them, who ever have been, and ever
would be, as absolute tyrants as any are under the sun."

The same sentiments have been held by many during
the twentieth century, and by substituting Irish Unionists
for the nobility his words make sense in the 1970's.

"No war can be made without munition, and munition
this rebel cannot have but from Spain, Scotland, or your
towns here. If your Majesty will still continue your ships
and pinnaces upon the coast, and be pleased to send a
printed proclamation that upon pain of death anyone doth
traffic with the rebel, I doubt not that in a short time I
shall make them bankrupt of their old store, and I hope
our seamen will keep them from receiving any more." He
warned her Majesty that the course of action he proposed
would in the end be successful though costly, and many
would be sacrificed in the quarrel.

This was not what the Queen wanted to hear, nor the
Council. They did not realise that the native Irish were a
people who would continue fighting, in their own guerrilla
fashion, no matter how tremendous the odds against them,
until the hated English were driven from the territory that
was Irish soil. The Earl was blamed for wasting his men
and resources by useless marches through the countryside;
yet it was only by doing this that he had learnt what to
expect from the Irish people and how long-term the
struggle was that lay before him.

But the Earl of Essex was not only Lord Lieutenant of
Ireland; he also held a very special place in the Queen's
affections, and it was imperative that he should continue
to keep this position. Long absence from her Majesty's
side, as he knew only too well, meant that others at home
would have the royal ear, and take measures to discredit
him. It had happened before, after Cadiz, and after the

expedition to the Azores. It could happen again, and judging by warnings from friends at home was indeed likely, more especially since the Queen had expressed dissatisfaction with his conduct of affairs in Ireland up to date. She had relented in that Sir Christopher Blount was now there, but she had demanded that the Earl of Southampton should be replaced and the Earl of Rutland recalled, another vexing factor to the Earl of Essex, who very naturally resented interference in his chain of command; she also desired that he should now march north with his army to the Ulster border and engage the Earl of Tyrone, leader of the Irish rebels, in decisive battle. What was more, she did not wish him to return to England until the enemy was entirely routed and victory had been achieved. This was a royal command.

Despite reinforcements, the troops were in poor shape, some unwilling to continue, a number pretending sickness, others deserting or actually going over to the rebels. It was not a force of which a commander could be proud, nor one, saving a miracle, which he could have the remotest hope of leading to victory.

"My Lords" (he wrote from Dublin on August 28th) "I am even now putting my foot into the stirrup to go to the rendez-vous at Navan; and from thence I will draw the army as far, and do as much, as duty will warrant me, and God enable me. And so, commanding your Lordships to God's best protection, I rest at your Lordships' commandment,

"Essex."

And two days later, to the Queen:

"From a man that hates himself and all things that keep him alive, what service can your Majesty reap? Since my services past deserve no more than banishment and proscription into the most cursed of all countries, with what expectation or to what end shall I live longer? No, no, the rebel's pride and successes must give me means to ransom myself, my soul I mean, out of the hateful prison of my body. And if it happen so, your Majesty may believe that you shall not have cause to mislike the fashion of my death,

though the course of my life could not please you.
      "Ardbracken, the 30th of August.

                                                    "Essex."

   The sequel is known to history. The drawing-up of the
opposing sides and the Earl's proposal to attack Tyrone
overruled in a council of war, Tyrone's troops being more
numerous and better placed. Then the request by Tyrone
to have a private parley with Essex. The request granted,
the upshot, after a second conference and a third the following morning, being a truce for six weeks, and to continue from six weeks to a further six weeks, and this truce
not to be broken by either side without fourteen days'
notice. Tyrone then withdrew into his own province, and
the Earl, having dispersed his army, retired to Drogheda,
it was said to take physic.
   An inglorious finale to an inglorious campaign. Had the
Earl of Essex been killed in battle, even if that battle had
been lost, he would still have been acclaimed a hero. A
truce, in those circumstances and in that century, amounted
to a defeat, as Essex well knew. It was, of course, a
basic flaw in his character that he should so suddenly go
to pieces, but it must be remembered that in those days
of plot and counter-plot a highly strung personality would
tend to paranoia even more swiftly than his counterpart
in modern times. He was convinced that enemies at Court,
Robert Cecil and Lord Cobham and others, had been the
instigators of the many angry letters from the Queen that
he had received in Ireland, that they were determined to
displace him for good and so break him entirely.
   During his private meeting with the Irish leader, Tyrone
had drawn a promise from him that he would communicate
the result of their discussion personally to her Majesty,
and not in any written document. It seemed to him that
his only course was to break the Queen's express command to remain in Ireland, return home and throw himself
upon her mercy, ask forgiveness for any errors that he
might have committed in the campaign, and explain the
reasons for the truce with Tyrone. Having won her over,
he would then be in a strong position to confront his
enemies in the Council. He was, apparently, supported in
this proposal by both the Earl of Southampton and Sir
Christopher Blount.

Immediately after the conference with Tyrone, Essex, at his fateful moment in his life, sent Tom, now Captain, Lawson to England with a dispatch to the Queen, though he did not explicitly state in it that the truce had been signed. Lawson arrived at Court on September 16th and delivered his dispatch. The Court was at Nonsuch Palace at the time. The Queen had her answer ready the following day. It is hardly conceivable that Lawson did not take the opportunity, during the twenty-four hours or so that he was near London, to cross the river and call on Anthony at Essex House, and receive some personal message to take to the Earl. No document exists to prove it. The only surviving letter is that written by her Majesty herself, signed and sealed and dated September 17th. She complained that the "management of our forces hath not only proved dishonourable and wasteful, but that which followeth [i.e. truce with Tyrone] is like to prove perilous and contemptible. . . . To trust this traitor upon oath is to trust a devil upon his religion."

Tom Lawson started immediately for Ireland, and it must be presumed that he arrived in Dublin on September 21st or 22nd. On receipt of the letter the Earl summoned his friends and the decision was made. He appointed the Earl of Ormonde to command the army in Ireland, and he himself sailed for England on the 24th, arriving in London on the 28th, accompanied by the Earl of Southampton, the rest of his household that had been with him in Ireland, and a number of captains and gentlemen.

The sequel, like the campaign, belongs to history; how the Earl rode to Westminster, crossed the river to Lambeth, seized horses belonging to others, and riding furiously arrived at Nonsuch at ten in the morning. "He stayed not till he came to the Queen's bedchamber, where he found the Queen newly up, the hair about her face; and he kneeled unto her, kissed her hands, and had some private speech with her, which seemed to give him great contentment: for, coming from Her Majesty to go shift himself in his chamber, he was very pleasant, and thanked God, though he had suffered much trouble and storms abroad, he found a sweet calm at home."

The calm lasted a few hours only. During a second interview at midday all still seemed well, and her Majesty gracious towards him, but after dinner things were different; she had had time to reflect. That evening, between ten and eleven, Essex was commanded by the Queen to keep to his room.

The news of his arrival spread through London the following day. Some of his household would have stayed at Essex House on the morning of arrival, Tom Lawson undoubtedly, the Earl of Southampton and others; Anthony Bacon would have been amongst the first to learn what had happened, and a message sent to his brother.

Francis went at once to Nonsuch Palace and managed to have a letter delivered to the Earl, still confined in his room. The letter, scattered with Latin phrases, complimented his lordship as "coming up in the person of a good servant to see your sovereign mistress", and ended with hopes that he might attend him. He was granted an interview of a quarter-of-an-hour, and the Earl asked him his opinion of the Queen's decree that he should be confined to his room.

"My Lord, it is but a mist," Francis replied. "If it go upwards, it may haps cause a shower, if downwards, it will clear up. Carry it so, as you take away by all means all umbrages and distastes from the Queen. . . . And observe three points. First, make not this peace which is concluded with Tyrone as a service wherein you glory, but as a shuffling up of a prosecution which was not very fortunate. Next, represent not to the Queen any necessity of estate whereby she should think herself enforced to send you back to Ireland, but leave it to her. Thirdly, seek access, seriously, sportingly, every way."

Essex was willing to hear him but spoke very little, and shook his head sometimes, as if thinking Francis was in the wrong. And there the interview ended. Francis returned to his lodging, whether he was then at Twickenham or Gray's Inn, and would certainly have reported to his brother at Essex House.

The Earl remained confined to his room at Nonsuch. On September 30th his wife gave birth to a daughter, who was christened Frances like her mother. The Earl was denied permission to visit wife and child, and the next afternoon he was taken under escort in the Earl of Worcester's coach to York House, to be detained there in the custody of Lord Keeper Egerton.

It is easy to picture the state of mind of his family and

friends, gathered at Essex House. His mother-in-law, anxious for her daughter's health, humbly asked permission that the Earl might at least be allowed to write to his wife: her request was refused. The Earl's sister, Lady Rich, and the young Countess of Southampton were both at Essex House, and the usual number of attendants, servants, friends and acquaintances coming and going. Rumour of company being there apparently gave offence, and Lady Rich and the Countess of Southampton removed themselves to the country. The Earl himself was allowed no visitors at York House, except for his guardian, Lord Keeper Egerton, the new Lord Treasurer Buckhurst, who had succeeded Lord Burghley, and the Secretary of State Sir Robert Cecil. He had two personal attendants only.

Then rumour had it that he had fallen ill and was "troubled with a flux". He asked that the Queen's own physician might come to him, but this was refused until early in November, when the Queen relented, and sent Dr Brown to York House. The physician did him little good, apparently, for by the end of the month the Earl was suffering from "the stone, strangullion, and grinding of the kidneys, which takes from his stomach and rest". His wife, dressed all in black, went to Court hoping to move the Queen for her husband, but she was refused the royal presence, and told not to appear at Court again. His sisters the Ladies Northumberland and Rich fared little better, and the French ambassador, Monsieur de Boissise, who had been instructed by His Majesty King Henri IV to intercede for the Earl's liberty, found her Majesty "very short and bitter on that point".

It was a very different story amongst the common people. The Earl was still widely popular, and that the hero of Cadiz should be confined to York House in custody, not allowed to see his wife and child, aroused great hostility. Pamphlets were scattered in the streets and pinned upon walls, the Queen was blamed for excessive harshness, preachers denounced his secret enemies from the pulpit. When the Earl of Southampton went to the playhouse—which he did that autumn almost every night—he was acclaimed because his friendship with the hero was well known.

And Anthony Bacon? Not one letter to or from him survives this anxious period. His correspondence with

friends, with agents, ceases. No letter to his mother. No
letter to his brother. The only significant record, indeed,
dates back to the preceding autumn, while Essex was living
in retirement at Wanstead, having temporarily fallen from
the Queen's favour. The letter, written on September 24th,
was from Sir William Cornwallis to Sir Robert Cecil, and
said, "Mr Anthony Bacon, who lies at Essex House, has
sent a gentleman to me to entreat he might be my tenant
at Bishopsgate, saying that since he can never hope to live
but like a bird in a cage, he would very fain have a fair
cage. I could be content he had it so I might get some
other place in the other end of the town for the dead time
of winter; which makes me presume to make the question
if I might be your tenant, if you mean to leave your lodging next my Lord your brother's, as I have heard."

Bird in a cage Anthony certainly was, whether at Essex
House or elsewhere, and becoming, it would seem, increasingly crippled. Nor is it surprising that he should have
written to Sir William Cornwallis for asylum. This gentleman wrote essays after the style of Michel de Montaigne,
and lived a life of "studious retirement". They would have
suited one another well.

Nothing came of the request, and the reason for it remains a mystery. Anthony stayed in his lodging at Essex
House, and continued there throughout the following year,
during which Essex became Lord Lieutenant of Ireland
and returned home to face disgrace. It was not Anthony,
possibly bedridden by now, who could offer himself as
mediator between her Majesty and his beloved Earl, but
brother Francis.

Chapter 21

It had been towards the end of August or very early in September, while the Earl was still in Ireland before proceeding north to meet Tyrone, that Francis had occasion to attend the Queen at Nonsuch Palace upon some legal business. He had done so before from time to time, but it is significant that this appears to be the first occasion when she drew him aside for personal conversation. Her Majesty, one of the most astute persons in her own kingdom, knew very well that Anthony Bacon had been employed by the Earl since he had returned from France in 1592, and that he now lodged at Essex House—indeed, the fact that Anthony had never come to Court and paid her his humble duties had been an omission she could hardly have passed over. She knew the brothers were close to each other, that Anthony handled all the Earl of Essex's foreign intelligence and private correspondence besides, and by drawing the one she might probe the other, so informing herself of matters pertaining to Essex.

How alert Francis was to this manœuvre on the part of his sovereign it is difficult to tell. He wrote of it later, after the death of the Queen, and there is no other account of these encounters between sovereign and subjct.

"The Queen one day at Nonsuch," wrote Francis, "a little, as I remember, before Cuffe's coming over [Francis alludes to the Earl's private secretary, who brought letters to the Queen from Ireland in early September], I attending her, showed a passionate distaste of my Lord's proceedings in Ireland, as if they were unfortunate, without judgement, contemptuous, and not without some private end of his own, and all that might be, and was pleased—as she spoke of it to many that she trusted least—so to fall into the like speech with me. Whereupon I, who was still awake and truc to my grounds which I thought surest for my Lord's good, said to this effect: 'Madam, I know not the particulars of estate, and I know this, that princes' actions must have no abrupt periods or conclusions, but otherwise I would think if you had my Lord of Essex here with a white staff in his hand, as my Lord of Leicester had, and continued with him still about you for society to yourself, and for an honour and ornament to your attendance and Court in the eyes of your people, and in the eyes of foreign ambassadors, then were he in his right element; for to discontent him as you do, and yet to put arms and powder into his hands, may be a kind of temptation to make him prove cumbersome and unruly. And therefore if you would send for him and satisfy him with honour here near you, if your affairs which, as I have said, I am not acquainted with, will permit it, I think were the best way.' "

Francis says nothing of her Majesty's reply to this advice, which, if she had followed it and sent straightway for the Earl, would have prevented his rash decision to return of his own accord. The Earl did return and was confined to his room, and Francis saw him for a brief interview. Afterwards Essex was taken in custody to York House. Francis takes up his account once more.

"During the while since my Lord was committed to my Lord Keeper's, I came divers times to the Queen, as I had used to do, about cause of her revenue and law business, as is well known; by reason of which accesses, according to the ordinary charities of Court, it was given out that I was one of them that incensed the Queen against my Lord Essex. These speeches, I cannot tell, nor I will not think, that they grew any way from her Majesty's own speeches, whose memory I will ever honour; if they did, she is with God."

It was inevitable, of course, that those at Court should gossip in such fashion, the Queen never having singled out the young barrister Francis Bacon before, indeed, having disapproved of him strongly in earlier years and prevented him from gaining promotion in his profession. She now acted even more strangely, though it must have encouraged Francis at the time that his own particular star was likely to be in the ascendant at long last.

"Being about the middle of Michaelmas term [i.e., late October or early November] her Majesty had a purpose to dine at my lodge at Twickenham Park, at which time I had (though I profess not to be a poet) prepared a sonnet directly tending and alluding to draw on her Majesty's reconcilement to my Lord, which I remember also I showed to a great person, and one of my Lord's nearest friends, who commended it: this, though it be, as I said, but a toy, yet it showed plainly in what spirit I proceeded, and that I was ready not only to do my Lord good offices, but to publish and declare myself for him: and never was so ambitious of anything in my lifetime, as I was to have carried some token or favour from her Majesty to my Lord."

The Queen's sudden curiosity to see Twickenham Lodge, having lived opposite it for years without interest whenever the Court moved to Richmond Palace, shows an intense desire on her part, surely, to learn more of Anthony Bacon's relationship with the Earl of Essex, which, by dining privately with his brother Francis, might be revealed. Was Anthony staying at Twickenham that night? Was he at last presented to the Queen? If so, why the secrecy? Even more intriguing is the mention of the sonnet which Francis had prepared for the Queen, "tending to draw on her Majesty's reconcilement to my Lord."

"The quality of mercy is not strain'd,
It droppeth as the gentle raine from heaven
Upon the place beneath. It is twice blest,
It blesseth him that gives, and him that takes,
'Tis mightiest in the mightiest, it becomes
The throned Monarch better then his Crowne."

No sonnet, true, but pertinent to the subject discussed; and remembering Francis Bacon's experience with Mr Sympson the goldsmith the year before, and what idle pens at Twickenham might have made of it, the link with Shylock's bond and Portia's speech is interesting. The first quarto of *The Merchant of Venice* was printed in 1600. The Queen dined at Twickenham Lodge in October 1599. As to the "great person" to whom Francis's sonnet was shown, the Earl of Southampton, Will Shakespeare's patron, comes readily to mind, though Francis does not name him. Nor does he record what the Queen thought of his verse, but that her interest had been aroused in certain other literary matters is shown by a further discussion that apparently took place between sovereign and subject.

> *Francis* About the same time I remember an answer of mine in a matter which had some affinity with my Lord's cause, which though it grew from me, went after about in others' names. For her Majesty being mightily incensed with that book which was dedicated to my Lord of Essex, being a story of the first year of King Henry IV, thinking it a seditious prelude to put into the people's heads boldness and faction, said she had good opinion that there was treason in it, and asked me if I could not find any places in it that might be drawn within case of treason.

Now, here is another example of probing on the part of the Queen. John Hayward's book on Henry IV had been published just after Christmas 1598, and had greatly incensed her Majesty, being an account of the deposition of Richard II by Bolingbroke, afterwards King Henry IV. The dedication to the Earl of Essex offended her in particular. John Hayward was tried in the Star Chamber and sent to the Fleet. Why, then, did the Queen wait some nine months before asking Francis Bacon what he thought of it? And did she connect it with a play on the same theme, entitled *The Life and Death of King Richard II*, which had appeared in quarto in the same year as Hayward's publication, and had been acted by the Lord Chamberlain's players? The Queen evidently thought there was some collusion somewhere, and suspected that Francis and his brother Anthony knew the answer.

"Her Majesty asked me," continues Francis, "if I could not find places for treason [in Hayward's book], wherein I answered, "Treason, surely none, Madam. But for felony, very many.'"

> *The Queen* Wherein?
> *Francis* The author has committed very apparent theft, for he has taken most of the sentences of Cornelius Tacitus, translated them into English, and put them into his text.

The Queen was apparently not content with this reply, and brought up the subject again.

The Queen It hath some mischievous author, other than he whose name is upon it. I will have him racked to produce the real author.
Francis Nay, Madam, he is a doctor, never rack his person, but rack his style; let him have pen, ink, and paper, and help of books, and be enjoined to continue the story where it breaketh off, and I will undertake by collecting the styles to judge whether he were the author or no.

Francis then seems to have led the Queen back to the main subject of the Earl and away from discussion of the offending history, beseeching her not to bring his lordship's case into public discussion, but to "wrap it up privately, and to restore him to his former attendance, with some addition of honour to take away discontent". And when she informed him that she was minded to have the case brought before the Star Chamber, Francis told her he was utterly opposed to this.

"The people, Madam, will say that my Lord is wounded upon his back, and that Justice hath her balance taken from her, which ever consists of an accusation and a defence."

This plain speaking seems to have offended her Majesty, for writing of the months that followed, November, Christmas, and into the new year of 1600, Francis admits that "her face and manner were not so clear and open to me as it was at the first". Furthermore, she disregarded his advice about not taking the case to the Star Chamber. A Court was held on November 29th before a large assembly. The Lord Keeper, the Lord Treasurer, the Secretary of State and the Lord Admiral were all present, as well as Lord Cobham, Sir Walter Raleigh and Fulke Greville— friend to both Essex and Francis—but Francis Bacon himself, though expected to be present, did not attend. This may have been a factor contributing to her Majesty's cooler attitude towards him.

A statement was issued afterwards, listing the Earl's offences in Ireland which had caused him to be confined in custody, and warning the public that it was no concern of theirs. The statement reassured no one. The hero of Cadiz continued to gain sympathy among the masses, the Queen and Council to lose what popularity they held. Essex himself grew worse in health, according to common report. Eight doctors attended his bedside on December 15th, sent, so it was said, by her Majesty; they told the Queen that "they found his liver stopped and perished, his entrails and guts exulcerated, they could not tell what now to minister but gentle glisters to keep him clean within." Hearing this, the Queen sent another of her own physicians, Doctor James, to see him and take him broth; she also permitted his wife to visit him at long last.

On December 19th the Earl was not expected to live more than a few days, and the city bells began to toll for him. The Countess was allowed to sit beside her husband every day, but neither his sisters—who were now staying at Essex House—nor his mother were granted access.

Still no record of how Anthony Bacon received this grave news, and whether, like his loved employer, he also was confined to his bed. No record either of whether his brother came to Essex House to condole with him. It seems possible that the rumours circulating at Court and elsewhere of Francis having prejudiced the Queen against the Earl may have actually arisen under the roof of Essex House itself. If this were so, Francis would certainly not have been *persona grata* at his lordship's house, or made welcome by his staff.

That he was unpopular amongst the Earl's supporters is evident from two letters he wrote about this time, one to the Queen and one to Sir Robert Cecil. In the first, to her Majesty, he apologises for not having attended the deliberations in the Star Chamber, saying, "I most humbly entreat your Majesty, not to impute my absence to my weakness of mind or unworthiness. . . . Never poor gentleman had a deeper and truer desire and care of your glory, your safety, your repose of mind, your service: wherein if I have exceeded my outward vocation, I most humbly crave your Majesty's pardon for my presumption. . . . My life hath been threatened, and my name libelled, which I count an honour. But these are the practices of those whose despairs are dangerous, and yet not so dangerous as their hopes."

To his cousin, Secretary of State Sir Robert Cecil, he

writes, "It is blown about the town, that I should give opinion touching my Earl of Essex's cause, first that it was a *praemunire;* and now, last, that it reached to high treason. . . . The utter untruth of this report God and the Queen can witness; and the improbability of it every man that hath wit more or less can conceive. . . . The root of this I discern to be, not so much a light and humorous envy at my accesses to her Majesty, which of her Majesty's grace being begun in my first years, I would be sorry she should estrange in my last years; for so I account them, reckoning by health not by age, as a deep malice to your honourable self, upon whom, by me, through nearness, they think to make some aspersion. But as I know no remedy against libels and lies; so I hope it shall make no manner of disseverance of your honourable good conceits and affection towards me; which is the thing I confess to fear. For as for any violence to be offered me, wherewith my friends tell me to no small terror that I am threatened, I thank God I have the privy coat of a good conscience; and have a good while since put off any fearful care of life or the accidents of life."

These letters show that Francis wished it known, both by the Queen and by her Secretary of State, that he was first and foremost loyal to the Crown and desired to place this on record. A third letter, dated December 3rd 1599, was to Lord Harry Howard, that devious nobleman who liked to have a foot in either camp, and who had always been a far closer friend to Anthony Bacon and to Essex than he had to Francis. In this letter Francis reiterates much of what he had said to his cousin Robert Cecil, and continues, "And therefore, my Lord, I pray you answer for me to any person that you think worthy your own reply and my defence. For my Lord of Essex, I am not servile to him, having regard to my superior duty. I have been much bound to him. And on the other side, I have spent more time and more thoughts about his well doing, than ever I did about mine own. I pray God you and his friends amongst you be in the right. For my part, I have deserved better than to have my name objected to envy, or my life to a ruffian's violence. But I have the privy coat of a good conscience. I am sure these courses and bruits hurt my Lord more than all."

It was evident that Francis hoped this letter would be

shown to one of the Earl's family, possibly the Countess
of Essex, and its contents conveyed to the sick man himself. Had he been granted access to Essex House, or been
in communication with his brother, this would not have
been necessary. Speculation indeed arises as to whether
the brothers had become estranged since Essex had been
confined to York House, and Anthony's silence was deliberate. Where was Anthony's confidante, Tom Lawson,
at this moment? Where was Francis's trusted attendant,
Henry Percy? Did rumour and counter-rumour pass between them? When Francis wrote, "I have deserved better
than to have my name objected to envy, or my life to a
ruffian's violence", to what ruffian did he allude? Some
hanger-on amongst the Earl's staff? The questions are
manifold, and no answer is forthcoming.

Christmas was undoubtedly not a joyous one for the
Queen, or for the Earl of Essex and his family. His New
Year's gift to her Majesty was not accepted. The fact that
his health was mending, despite the tolling of those December bells and the solemn prayers in church, inclined the
sovereign to believe that his illness had been exaggerated,
a mere pretence to win her sympathy.

Amongst the gifts offered to the Queen that new year
of 1600 was the following: "By Mr Francis Bacon, one
pettycote of white satten, embrothered all over like feathers
and billets, with three brode borders, faire embrothered
with snakes and frutage." It was the custom to send the
sovereign gifts at the new year; nevertheless there is something touching about Francis's effort to appease, to atone,
in the new year of 1600, the beginning of a new century
which would be fateful to Elizabeth and to all her loyal
subjects. "A pettycote of white satten" to the monarch of
sixty-eight. The letter that accompanied the gift was not
published until after the donor's death.

"Most excellent Sovereign Mistress,
    "The only new year's gift which I can give your
Majesty is that which God hath given to me; which is
a mind in all humbleness to wait upon your command-
ments and business: wherein I would to God that I
were hooded; that I saw less, or that I could perform
more: for now I am like a hawk, that baits, when I
see occasion of service, but cannot fly because I am

tied to another's wrist. But meanwhile I continue my
presumption of making to your Majesty my poor obla-
tion of a garment, as unworthy the wearing as his service that sends it: but that approach to your excellent
person may give worth to both; which is all the happiness I aspire unto."

Tied to another's wrist . . . the metaphor is a curious
one. Tied to whose wrist? If the law was so personified,
the law also served her Majesty. And Francis Bacon, unlike his brother, was bound to no man, so his meaning
remains obscure. Perhaps her Majesty, standing in front of
a long mirror in the satin petticoat while her ladies
robed her for the day, understood the reference.

The Earl of Essex was so far recovered by January 5th
that he was able to sit up and eat at table. His wife,
however, was still only permitted to visit him at stated
times, and his mother and sisters not at all; while his
eldest boy Robert, now nine years old, went back to
school at Eton without having seen his father either at
Christmas or in the new year.

If the Earl's bodily health improved his mind seems to
have become more unbalanced as the months passed. He
was cut off from all serious counsel or good advice, and
whatever medical attention he received certainly did nothing, could do nothing, to counteract his increasing paranoia. Robert Cecil and Lord Cobham were the chief ob-
jects of his unreasoning hostility. He believed that neither
man would rest until he, Essex, was destroyed. Plotters
were everywhere, in England, on the continent. Now that
he no longer received foreign intelligence from Anthony
the rumours that came to him at York House were garbled
and distorted.

It was said that peace was to be made with Spain at last.
King Philip II had died in September 1598, and some pro-
Spanish factions in England were known to have murmured amongst themselves that his daughter, the Infanta,
had a better right to the succession on the death of Queen
Elizabeth than had King James VI of Scotland. Essex
began persuading himself that Robert Cecil, Cobham and
others had the Infanta in mind when considering plans for
peace between the two countries. Yes, there was evidently
a scheme of this nature to be carried into effect once he,

Essex, was put out of the way for good. He must get
messages to Scotland. King James, his especial friend,
must be warned. Some trusted messenger must be sent.
And so his mind raged to and fro, himself the victim of his
own fevered imagination.

The Queen, hearing that he was once more ill, relented,
and the order she gave was to prove fatal in its ultimate
consequences.

> 10th March. By her Majesty's express command,
> Lady Leicester, Lord and Lady Southampton, Mr
> Greville, Mr Bacon, are all removed from Essex
> House; and this day my Lord of Essex is looked for
> there, to remain with two keepers, Sir Drue Drury
> and Sir Richard Barkely, and none to come to speak
> with him but by her Majesty's leave. Whether my
> Lady shall remain with him, or come in daytime to
> him as she now doth, is not yet known.

On Maundy Thursday, March 19th, at about 8 o'clock
at night, the Earl was removed to Essex House, Sir
Richard Barkely having all the keys and his servant being
porter. Nobody to be admitted without leave, and Lady
Essex only in the day. At the end of March his mother,
Lady Leicester, also obtained leave to see him.

Meanwhile Lady Leicester presumably went to her
house at Wanstead, and the Countess his wife either to
Barn Elms or her mother's house in London. And Anthony
Bacon? If he was on good terms with brother Francis,
then surely to Gray's Inn or to Twickenham Lodge. The
silence continues. The man who, in his own words, could
"never hope to live but like a bird in a cage" was removed
to an unnamed lodging.

Chapter 22

The assumption by historians that on quitting Essex House in March 1600 Anthony Bacon destroyed all correspondence after 1598 which might in any way be compromising is a reasonable one, though why personal letters from his mother, his brother, and his friends should also have disappeared is puzzling. The massive pile of documents before this date was presented to the Lambeth Palace library by Archbishop Tenison some time after 1695, and has reposed there to the present day. How he acquired them in the first place is not known. It is possible that they came in some way through William Rawley, a personal friend, and son of the Dr Rawley who became Francis Bacon's chaplain and amanuensis when the latter was appointed Lord Chancellor in 1618. It is hardly likely that Anthony neither received nor wrote any letters after March 10th 1600. If he was crippled he was at least capable of attending to his personal business, as the Hertfordshire Manorial County Records show; for on April 30th, along with Edward Selwyn of West Dean, his old friend, and Thomas Crewe of Gray's Inn, he witnessed a release of land comprising a house, orchard and some fifty acres of land to Thomas Fynche and Richard Laseby.

He had already sold the manor of Redbourne; now he was selling still more land. And that he was hard pressed financially is corroborated by Francis himself, who, in a letter to the Queen on March 12th, writes frankly as a suppliant. His suit is for a gift of certain manorial lands belonging to the Crown. This letter, like others from his pen, remained in obscurity until 1729, 130 years later. The request was modest, the value of the Crown land being £80 or so, and he gives three reasons for his supplication.

"First my love to my mother, whose health being

worn, I do infinitely desire she might carry this comfort to the grave, not to leave my estate troubled and engaged. Secondly, these perpetuities being now overthrown, I have just fear my brother will endeavour to put away Gorhambury, which if your Majesty enable me by this gift I know I shall be able to get into mine own hands, where I do figure to myself that one day I may have the honour and comfort to bid your Majesty welcome, and to trim and dress the grounds for your solace. Thirdly, your Majesty may by this redemption—for so I may truly call it—free me from the contempt of the contemptible, that measure a man by his state, which I daily find a weakening of me both in courage and means to do your Majesty service."

The result of his suit is unknown, but the information the letter contains is valuable. His mother's health was worn, but, more important still, Anthony had it in mind to sell Gorhambury, which his brother naturally expected to inherit. As to Lady Bacon, the last letter in Volume VIII of the Lambeth correspondence—undated, but presumed to have been written some time in 1598 or 1599—certainly gives proof of this. It is written in a style even more rambling than usual, the meaning sometimes quite obscure; and for almost the first time she speaks of her own failing health.

"Though my increased pain in *superficie cutis* be extraordinary to me, and may partly support some venom to be drunk with those black worms I took in drink and twice, about half a pint of them, yet you know the learned do call senet *gipsum morby*. Since my quartan fever I find by diverse accidents to be true and very painful and I humbly acknowledge God's mercy that moveth my mind to take age, sickliness and infirmities being natural as well as you. And yet I use such good means by counsel and diet as may make my uneasy warranted pain more tolerable, and I find much ease by the diet wholesome and earlier suppers before six, and clean usual drink never in the night and seldom in morning or betwixt meals. Your continual uncomfortable state of body doubleth what

griefs God sendeth me, therefore patience in your disease, and the Lord have pity on his children . . . I
lament your continual bodily impotence the more because you are so thereby as it were cast off and un-
abled. . . . Labour therefore by hearty prayers. . . .
God keep the good Earl safe."

This last line suggests that the letter may have been
written in the summer of 1599 while the Earl was in Ireland. In any event, it is the last we have from her, although she had some ten more years to live.

As for Gorhambury, while Anthony was living in Essex
House his creditors could probably not have gained access
to him. Once he had left there—and it is significant that
his brother's suit to the Queen was written on March 12th,
two days after the household had been commanded by her
Majesty to leave—he was prey to anyone with a sheaf of
unpaid bills in his pouch. That there were many such
solicitors is obvious. Merchants who had brought back
messages from agents on foreign service; the agents themselves, unpaid by the Earl of Essex; tradesmen, clothiers,
hangers-on: all knew the Earl had fallen into disgrace and
could no longer employ Mr Anthony Bacon. Those who
had fawned upon him once because of his position as
friend and personal confidante were now ready to turn and
rend him. No man is more scorned by underlings than one
who has lost position, who has no means of defence.

It is possible that he did, during the month of March,
become Sir William Cornwallis's tenant in Bishopsgate,
and return to the quarter that he had known so well in
1594. He need never have stirred abroad—indeed, it is
doubtful if he could—and the secret of his whereabouts
would have been close guarded. Anthony could never
have broken off all contact with Essex, to whom he was so
devoted; and once the Earl had returned to Essex House,
despite the security measures commanded by her Majesty,
there must have been some means of communication between them, and Anthony's whereabouts known to his former employer. Anthony knew too many secrets, and even
if the papers relating to these secrets had been destroyed,
much of their contents would be stored in his memory.
It was Anthony who had gathered and sent information to
Scotland, even to King James himself. In March of 1596,

for instance, Mr. Hudson, the King's Scottish agent, delivered letters from Anthony personally to his Majesty, all other persons being forbidden the chamber and a guard kept upon the door. King James, so Hudson reported back, "read some of them with great respect, and some with much mirth, thankfully and kindly accepting of them, and commanding Mr Hudson to return Mr Bacon his very hearty and loving thanks for them, and for many acceptable courtesies and good offices done by him". These papers, said Mr Hudson, had won a promise from the King that he would continue a full and sound correspondence with Mr Bacon, and the papers were then burnt in his Majesty's presence.

The question arises, therefore, to what extent it came to the knowledge of others that letters had passed between Anhony Bacon, acting on behalf of the Earl, and his Majesty of Scotland. Spies were everywhere, and those who during the summer of 1600 believed that the Earl of Essex, despite all precautions, was in secret correspondence with King James VI may have wondered if a sick man in his bed, crippled with gout, his hiding-place unknown, could have been the brain behind the pen.

In November of the preceding year, when the case of the Earl of Essex had come up before the Star Chamber, Francis Bacon had not been present. On June 5th 1600 the Queen decided to bring the case before eighteen Commissioners at York House. This time Francis was instructed to speak for the Crown after the Attorney-General and the Solicitor-General had concluded their accusations against the Earl of Essex, and that he consented to do so was not forgiven him either by his contemporaries then or by historians later. However, in 1600 a lawyer of small renown did not disobey the command of her Majesty herself, and that she did so order him is evident from Francis's own testimony three years later.

Once again he was in attendance upon her over some business, and she told him she was thinking of bringing up the Earl's case before an assembly of Councillors. This would be towards the end of the Easter Term.

"Madam," Francis replied, "it is now far too late, the matter is cold, and hath taken too much wind."

Her Majesty was offended, but later on, in May, mentioned the matter once more.

"Why, Madam," he said on this occasion, "if you will needs have a proceeding, you were best have it in some such sort as Ovid spake of his mistress, *est aliquid luce patente minus*, to make a counsel-table matter of it, and there an end."

The Queen was not so pleased to have the proceedings informal, and the assembly was commanded for June 5th. Francis wrote privately to the Queen asking that he might be spared from appearing for the Crown, but this request was not granted. Indeed, his instructions were explicit: to bring before the Commissioners the affair of John Hayward's book, with its theme of Bolingbroke's deposition of Richard II. This book, dedicated as it was to the Earl, had already been discussed by Francis and the Queen when she had visited him at Twickenham Lodge the previous year. Her Majesty's curiosity about the book is significant. If the subject of Richard II's deposition so riled her why did she not also allude to the play of *Richard II*, which had been published in quarto and had been acted by the Lord Chamberlain's players? Or did she? Were these frequent encounters between the Queen and Francis a further attempt to probe the authorship of John Hayward's book? She believed that some other "mischievous author" was involved, and suspected some sinister motive in the writing of it, a motive that might bring into question the right of succession to her own Crown. The Earls of Essex and Southampton had always been keen play-goers; they were on familiar terms with writers and actors, who had been invited to perform in the past at Essex House. The Queen knew this, and she knew also that Anthony Bacon, before living at Essex House, had lodged in Bishopsgate amongst the acting fraternity. Clearly, then, Mr Anthony Bacon must know more about matters of plays and books and dedications to his master than most men; and if Mr Anthony Bacon was so sick that he could not hold a pen or leave his bed, then his brother Francis must answer for him. Indeed, Mr Anthony Bacon's name need not be mentioned in the proceedings at all at any time, if his brother Francis would guarantee to speak for the Crown. This would seem to be the reason for Francis's appearance on June 5th.

For Francis to take the stand after his hated rival Edward Coke, the Attorney-General, had made a harsh and embittered speech for the Crown, listing the Earl's alleged misdemeanours and disloyalty to ther Majesty, combined with his disregard for the state of the army, his shameful treaty with a rebel, etc, etc, was certainly the most difficult moment of the thirty-nine-year-old barrister's career. It did not matter to the Attorney-General if he was disliked, even hated, by the Earl's supporters and the public as a whole; it did matter to a lawyer without means or position that he should be shunned as one who, having received much favour and kindness from the Earl, must now accuse him. Nor could the sight of Essex himself, who stood to hear the proceedings, carrying himself with great calm and dignity, have made the situation any the easier.

Francis's speech was brief, coming as it did after the tirade from the Attorney-General and a more temperate address by Solicitor-General Fleming. He began by praising her Majesty for allowing the Earl to appear before his peers and the assembly rather than before the Star Chamber, and continued by quoting passages from a letter which Essex had written to the Lord Keeper in 1598 in which he had said, "Her Majesty's heart was obdurate". If, declared Francis, "his Lordship intended comparing her Majesty to Pharaoh, such a comparison was odious . . . By the common law of England, a prince can do no wrong."

He concluded his address, as he had been told to do, by alluding to the book by John Hayward. This, he affirmed, was an old matter, and was not relevant to the rest of the charge; but his lordship had been in error in not suppressing the book immediately, instead of waiting for a week after publication, and then only drawing the Archbishop's attention to it in a formal letter. Forbidden things, said Francis, are the most sought after.

The speech was mild and inoffensive, and could have carried little weight as far as the Assembly was concerned; while the Earl himself, kneeling, and speaking in his own defence, was so humble in confessing his many errors, and so sincere in his expressions of loyalty and devotion to her Majesty, that his speech drew tears from many eyes. He showed passion only in refuting with great firmness some of the more bitter accusations of the Attorney-General. In conclusion, he gave himself to her Majesty's mercy and favour, and was ready to suffer whatever punishment she should inflict upon him.

The Lord Keeper, the Lord Treasurer and Secretary Cecil all spoke, and finally censure was passed, emphasis being laid that it was censure only and not a sentence, as it would have been in the Star Chamber. Essex would be barred from the Council and dismissed from his position as Earl Marshall, and he must return to his own house, there to remain a prisoner until it should please her Majesty to release him. The proceedings then finished, having lasted from eight in the morning until nearly nine at night.

The next day, Francis sought an audience of the Queen.

"You have now, Madam," he told her, "obtained victory over two things, which the greatest princes in the world cannot at their wills subdue; the one is over fame; the other is over a great mind. For surely the world is now, I hope, reasonably well satisfied: and for my Lord, he did show that humiliation towards your Majesty, as I am persuaded he was never in his lifetime more fit for your Majesty's favour than he is now. Therefore, if your Majesty will not mar it by lingering, but give over at the best, and now you have made so good a full point receive him again with tenderness, I shall then think, that all that is past, is for the best."

The Queen told Francis to write down a full account of the proceedings at York House the previous day, and, when completed, to read it to her. This seems a curious request from the sovereign to a junior barrister. It was true that clerks had been barred from the Assembly and no record of the proceedings taken, yet the Lord Keeper or the Secretary of State would have given her all the information necessary. Possibly she wished to compare their statements with that written down by Francis Bacon. In any event, he complied with her command, and she was apparently much moved by what he told her, especially when he read to her the Earl's answer to his accusers.

Queen You speak his part well. I perceive that old love does not easily die.

Francis I hope by that, Madam, you mean your own.

She then agreed that his written account of the proceedings should not be made public.

The Earl had himself, since mid-April—and it was now early June—been given rather more freedom at Essex House. He had been allowed to walk on the leads and in the garden, and even play tennis. His wife the Countess came more often to him, and they read aloud together (plays, poems, history? . . . curiosity is aroused), but one thing in particular angered him, and this was that his *Apologia*, dedicated to Anthony Bacon in 1598, had suddenly been reprinted without his sanction at the beginning of May. Here is another puzzle. Who authorized the reprint of a pamphlet which had annoyed the Queen when it first appeared? And was this one of the factors which had decided her Majesty to bring the Earl's case up before the Assembly in June? Francis does not mention it. Nor did anyone at the Assembly. The only person to draw attention to it was the Earl himself, in one of his many letters to the Queen written in May. "The tavern-haunter speaks of me what he lists. Already they print me, and make me speak to the world; and shortly they will play me in what forms they list upon the stage. The least of these is a thousand times worse than death."

Strange and indeed prophetic words from a man now torn by doubt and indecision. Paranoia gripped him, there was no one he could trust. He wrote to the Stationers' Company asking them to suppress the *Apologia*, saying there were two persons already in prison because of it. Who were these two persons? The mystery deepens.

During the remainder of June and July, after the censure of the Assembly, he continued to write letters to the Queen, pleading for access to her, or at least for permission to retire into the country, if not to his own house at Barn Elms then to the Oxfordshire house of his uncle, Sir William Knollys. And all this while Francis Bacon was granted the access that the Earl demanded in vain. What information could it be that her Majesty sought so assiduously to draw from him? Was she still harping on John Hayward's book and its treasonable implications? The Queen herself was surely becoming paranoiac. Then, one day, she enquired after his brother, possibly not for the first time. She was speaking of someone who had under-

taken to cure or ease Anthony of his gout, and asked
how it went forward.

Francis Madam, at first he received some good by it,
but after in the course of the cure he found himself
at a stay, or rather worse.
The Queen I tell you, Bacon, the error of it: the
manner of these physicians, and especially these em-
pirics, is to continue one kind of medicine, which at
the first is proper, being to draw out the ill humour,
but after they have not the discretion to change their
medicine, but apply still drawing medicines, when they
should rather intend to draw and corroborate the part.
Francis Good Lord, Madam! How wisely and aptly
can you speak and discern of medicine administered
to the body, and consider not that there is the like
occasion of physic administered to the mind: as now
in the case of my Lord of Essex, your princely word
ever was that you intended ever to reform his mind,
and not ruin his fortune: I know well you cannot
but think you have drawn the humour sufficiently
. . . and therefore it were more than time . . . that
you did apply and minister strength and comfort unto
him.

Thus the dialogues continued, round and about the Earl's
case, Francis speaking on his behalf, her Majesty listening
and noting what he said, yet nothing admitted, nothing
decisive confirmed, and always the spectre of Anthony's
presence hovering in the background. So much so, indeed,
that Francis, shortly after this—and according to him
with Essex's, but not his brother's agreement—composed
two letters to be shown in private to the Queen, the first
purporting to be from Anthony to Essex, the second the
Earl's reply, affirming the Earl's loyalty and devotion to her
Majesty. Francis admitted in after years that Anthony was
not the author of the letter which purported to come from
him; and it seems clear, indeed, that he had no knowledge
of either letter. It was a devious experiment, and suggests
that the brothers were not at this time in agreement as
to policy. In any case the stratagem failed. The Queen was
apparently not "cozened", and during the latter part of the

summer her manner towards Francis changed once more: in his own words, "She would not as much as look on me, but turned away from me with express and purpose-like discountenance wheresoever she saw me: and at such time as I desired to speak with her about law business, ever sent me forth very slight refusals."

Earlier, before composing the bogus letters, Francis had apologised to the Earl for the part he had been forced to take before the Assembly, saying, "I confess I love some things much better than I love your Lordship, as the Queen's service, her quiet and contentment, her honour, her favour, the good of my country and the like, yet I love few persons better than yourself, both for gratitude's sake and for your own virtues, which cannot hurt but by accident or abuse. Of which my good affection I was ever and am ready to yield testimony by any good officers but with such reservations as yourself cannot but allow: for as I was ever sorry that your Lordship should fly with waxen wings, doubting Icarus' fortune, so for the growing up of your own feathers, especially ostriches, or any other save of a bird of prey, no man shall be more glad. And this is the axle tree whereupon I have turned, and shall turn."

The Earl returned a brief though courteous reply.

"I can neither expound nor censure your late actions; being ignorant of all of them save one; and having directed my sight inward only, to examine myself . . . Your profession of affection, and offer of good offices, are welcome to me. For answer to them I will say but this; that you have believed I have been kind to you, and you may believe that I cannot be other, either upon humour or mine own election. I am a stranger to all poetical conceits, or else I should say somewhat of your poetical example. But this I must say, that I never flew with other wings than desire to merit, and confidence in my Sovereign's favour; and when one of these wings failed me, I would light nowhere but at my Sovereign's feet, though she suffered me to be bruised with my fall. And till her Majesty, that knows I was never bird of prey, finds it agree with her will and service that my wings should be imped again, I have committed myself to the new.

No power but my God's, and my Sovereign's, can
alter this resolution of
     "Your retired friend,

                                        "Essex."

These two letters were written in the third week of
July, Francis's from Gray's Inn, the Earl's from Essex
House.

In late August the Queen allowed the Earl his liberty
and he was permitted to retire into seclusion at Barn
Elms. He continued to write to her Majesty pleading for
access to her, but was still refused. In October he returned
to Essex House. He was rumoured to live very "privately" there, "his gate shut day and night", yet this was
not in accordance with other reports, which said that his
steward Sir Gilly Mericke, whose influence with him had
increased greatly during the last two years, kept open
house for all: recusant Catholics, tenants from the Welsh
estates, dissatisfied soldiers returned from Ireland, and
every sort of malcontent.

The Earl, like Anthony Bacon, had now reached bed-
rock financially. His main source of income had been one
which his stepfather the Earl of Leicester had enjoyed
before him, the monopoly of the duty on sweet wines. The
lease had expired at Michaelmas, and her Majesty had
not renewed it. He was close to despair. Something must
be done to restore his fortunes, support must come from
somewhere, from the King of Scotland, perhaps, from
the warm-hearted populace of London which had always
cheered him in the streets and had prayed for his recovery
last November and for his release in the spring. If he could
appeal to honest citizens throughout the kingdom they
would, they must, uphold him; once he had gained access
to the Queen she would restore him to favour as she had
done in the past.

The disordered mind plotted, schemed, turned truth to
fantasy, and the year crept onward to its close; while
somewhere, near at hand, the caged bird Anthony awaited
his own release.

Chapter 23

If Anthony in his hidden lair could no longer write, no longer move about at will, even his eyesight failing, as it had done once before when he was fourteen, one of his faithful attendants would have taken letters, books, plays, and read them aloud—Jacques, perhaps, Tom Lawson, Robert Prentis or even Ned Selwyn, riding up from his Sussex estate to keep Anthony company. The first quarto of *King Henry V* had been printed that year, so much of it reviving memories of what the hero of Cadiz had been himself in happier days, when all his thoughts and aims had been set on victory and a foreign enemy's defeat. When King Harry stood with his lords before the French, it could have been Robert Devereux himself waiting to breach the Spanish citadel.

". . . Take a trumpet Herauld,
Ride unto the Horsemen on yond hill:
If they will fight with us bid them come downe,
Or voyde the field: they do offend our sight.
If they'll do neither, we will come to them,
And make them sker away, as swift as stones
Enforced from the old Assyrian slings.
Besides, weele cut the throats of those we have;
And not one alive shall taste our mercy."

King Harry had been proud, and the Earl too; but the first had been dead nearly 180 years, and the second had lost his fire and perhaps his reason. A good thing his doughty comrade-in-arms, Sir Roger Williams the old Welshman, had not lived to see his hero now. Anthony, dreaming of the past, thought of the drinking and the laughter in the taverns, the old warrior boasting of his exploits, and the times the Earl had called on him in

Bishopsgate to ask what news there was from France, from Venice and the Netherlands.

When the Earl, first fallen from favour after the Azores expedition, was living in retirement down at Wanstead, the first quarto of *King Richard II* had been printed. Ned Selwyn or Robert Prentis could read a speech aloud.

> "I have bin studying, how to compare
> This Prison where I live, unto the World:
> And for because the World is populous,
> And heere is not a Creature, but my selfe,
> I cannot do it . . ."

As Anthony thought back, even the moans and plaints and fastidious conceits of Antonio de Perez seemed harmonious. "My Lord hath provided him here of the same office those eunuchs have in Turkey, which is to have the custody of the fairest dames," thus Standen had written, mocking the Spaniard, with his protestations of a close acquaintance with the Princess Catherine of France, poor lady now married to a man she did not love, and of how he had once travelled in a coach with her from St. Germain into Paris. How tedious the King of France had found him too!

> "Our Court, you know, is hanted
> With a refined travailler of Spaine,
> A man in all the worlds new fashion planted,
> That hath a mint of phrases in his braine:
> One who the musicke of his owne vaine tongue
> Doth ravish, like inchanting harmonie:
> A man of complements whom right and wrong
> Have chose as umpire of their mutinie."

So the King of Navarre describes Don Adriano de Armado in *Love's Labour's Lost.* As well that Antonio de Perez had been out of England in 1598, or he might have seen the play performed at Essex House.

King Henri of Navarre had been Anthony's first hero; now, as Henri IV of France, he had married a new queen, Marie de Medici, this October. The world had changed, was changing, all about the sick man in his caged retreat, and his second hero, Robert Devereux, had altered almost out of recognition, one moment indecisive, wavering, weary of life, the next listening to advice from meaner men who were only seeking their own ends. There was no quarto published yet of the tragedy of another man suffering from the same sense of oppression as Robert Devereux —it would be nearly three years before Hamlet's utterances found their way on to the printed page; but in the late autumn of 1600 the play may well have been in the process of composition.

A play with a very different theme was to go into rehearsal very shortly, so that it could be shown before the Queen and her Court on Twelfth Night, when she would be entertaining the Duke of Bracciano, cousin to the new Queen of France. There would be celebrations around the clock thrugh Christmas-tide, her Majesty footing it with the best of them, partly to show how little she thought of her sixty-eight years, and partly to prove she was not thinking of the Earl of Essex, whose absence would be noted by everyone present and, from discretion, not remarked upon anywhere near the royal presence. The play would be a merry one, befitting the occasion. Sir William Knollys would be made a butt and a figure of fun, with his known passion for Moll Fitton, one of her Majesty's maids of honour. The title of the play? *Malvoglio*.

Brother Francis would certainly be of the company, and Lady Hatton was listed amongst those attending the Queen. No doubt Francis and his idle pens devised some new conceit to entertain the distinguished visitor at the Inn of Glaucus. But Anthony, the caged bird, never had, and never would, look upon Whitehall in all its brilliance, never see Nonsuch, or Richmond except from the grounds of Twickenham Lodge, or Windsor Castle save from the windows of his coach. It had been his own choice, and there let it rest. The Court of Navarre had been good enough for him, and Princess Catherine de Bourbon less formidable a royal personage than her Majesty of England.

Meanwhile, at Essex House in mid-December, the Countess of Essex had been safely delivered of a daughter, and this over the Earl could summon all his friends for consultation, but for better security have them meet at the Earl of Southampton's London seat, Drury House. Southampton himself was present, naturally, and his friend

Sir Charles Davers, who had corresponded with Anthony Bacon in the past when he was a student in Paris and Anthony was living in Bordeaux, as well as Sir Ferdinando Gorges, governor of Plymouth, Sir John Davis, Surveyor of the Ordinance, and others, including, of course, Sir Christopher Blount. There were said to be at least one hundred and twenty noblemen and gentlemen sworn to the service of the Earl of Essex.

The possibility that Anthony Bacon knew of these consultations at Drury House, or that he formed any part of the growing conspiracy, has never been suggested. He was known to be bedridden, sick, and therefore out of action, of no account. Nevertheless, it is strange that his name nowhere appears. Either he was so ill by this time as to be paralysed, or he was virtually a prisoner, all information withheld from him. Frances could have arranged this, alarmed that his brother's deep affection for the Earl might lead him to be involved in what so many who were loyal to the throne already feared would, before long, take place, the meetings at Essex House and Drury House having by Christmas attracted considerable attention.

The only contemporary of Anthony's who ever spoke against him in later years was Henry Wotton, who had entered the Earl's service in 1595. Dislike between the two men seems to have been mutual, jealousy no doubt the basic cause. In 1651, with Anthony in his grave for half a century and Sir Henry himself twelve years dead, his memoirs, *Reliquiae Wottonianae*, were published. In them he said, "The Earl of Essex had accommodated Master Anthony Bacon in partition of his house, and had assigned him a noble entertainment. This was a gentleman of impotent feet, but of a nimble head; who being of an improvident nature, contrary to his brother the Lord Viscount St. Albans, and well knowing the advantage of a dangerous secret, would many times cunningly let fall some words as if he could amend his fortunes under the Cecilians with whom he was near in Alliance and of blood also, and who had made some great proffers to win him away."

Henry Wotton, who by the time he wrote these words was past fifty years of age, had obviously drawn upon backstairs gossip. There was nothing very improvident about Anthony at Essex House, where he complained to his mother of the damp even in summer. Also, his dislike of the Cecil faction was well known. It was brother Francis who wrote courteous letters to their cousin Sir Robert Cecil. Henry Wotton continues, "My Lord Henry Howard flies presently to my Lord of Essex and tells him that, unless that gentleman [i.e. Anthony Bacon] was presently satisfied with some round sum, all would be vented. This took the Earl at that time ill-provided, whereupon he would fain suddenly to give him Essex House; which the good old Lady Walsingham did afterwards disengage out of her own store with £2,500: and before he had distilled £1,500 at another time by the same skill. So as we may rate this one secret, as it was finely carried, at £4,000 in present money, besides at the least £1,000 of annual pension to a private and bedrid gentleman. What would he have gotten if he could have gone about his own business?"

The story is an extraordinary one, and prompted by malice. There is no trace of any pension paid to Anthony amongst his papers, but that he often was obliged to pay foreign agents and others from his own pocket is very evident. He was pressed on all sides by creditors, as the Earl was himself when his fortunes sank. Nor does it seem probable that "good old Lady Walsingham" could suddenly lay her hand on some thousands of pounds to satisfy either her son-in-law or his friend Anthony, when her own husband Sir Francis had died so deeply in debt in 1590 that it was feared his creditors would steal his coffin for the sale of the lead.

It is significant that Henry Wotton was safely on the continent when the Earl's friends and supporters were gathering, significant, too, that his word was never relied upon in later years by those well-known gossips John Chamerblain and Dudley Carleton. Nevertheless, the omission of Anthony's name from all letters and State papers during the fateful period December 1600 to February 1601 is baffling. That his brother Francis was at last free, or almost free, from debt is indicated in a letter to Michael Hicks, secretary to Sir Robert Cecil, written on January 25th 1601 by Francis himself.

"I am now about this term to free myself from all debts which are in any ways in suit or urged, following a faster pace to free my credit than my means can follow to free my state, which yet cannot stay long after, I having resolved to spare no means I have in hand, taking other possibilities for advantage, to clear myself from the discontent of speech or danger from others. And some of my debts of most clamour and importunity I have this term and some few days before ordered and in part paid. I pray you to your former favours which I do still remember and may hereafter requite, help me out with £200 more for six months. I will put you in good sureties, and you shall do me a great deal of honesty and reputation. I have writ to you the very truth and secret of my course, which to few others I would have done, thinking it may move you.

"Your assured loving friend,

"Francis Bacon."

So, although in need of a further loan, yet the main part of his debts had been paid. No revelation as to the source of payment. No mention of his ailing brother.

During the first week in February someone from Essex House either sent or took a message to the Secretary of State, Sir Robert Cecil, saying that a conspiracy had been formed, led by Essex, whereby the Council was to be overthrown, the Queen's person seized, and a new parliament called to change the form of government. The name of the informer was never given; it was said to be a man who had been at Trinity College with Essex as a student, and had remained close to him ever afterwards.

The Secretary of State was now thoroughly aroused, and the rest of the Council too. On the morning of Saturday February 7th the Earl was summoned to appear before them. He refused, pleading illness, but the summons alerted him and all his supporters at Essex House. If there was to be action, it must take place within twenty-four hours; surprise was essential if action was to succeed. Zero hour was fixed for Sunday morning, when people would be at church and the Earl would ride into the city, arriving at Paul's Cross before the end of the sermon, and there appeal to Sheriff Smith who commanded the militia, and afterwards to the Lord Mayor, asking for the support of the City of London. So confident did the conspirators feel that Sir Gilly Mericke, Essex's steward, went over to the playhouse at Southwark and offered the actors forty shillings if they would perform the play of *Richard II*. It was thought this would so rouse the spectators, showing as it did the deposing of a monarch, that they would rally to the Earl the following day. The performance seems to have fallen flat: the audience had seen the play before. But the choice was significant, showing that her Majesty had some reason to mistrust the theme when she had discussed it with Francis Bacon at Twickenham Lodge.

Sunday dawned, and soon after daybreak the courtyard of Essex House was full of armed men. The members of the Council had made their own preparations, and at ten o'clock Lord Keeper Egerton, Sir William Knollys and Lord Chief Justice Popham arrived, demanding admission. They found the Earl of Essex and his friends assembled, including the Earls of Southampton and Rutland, with more than three hundred men. The Lord Keeper ordered that everyone should disperse, and said that if the Earl of Essex had cause for complaint he would hear his case in private and report it to the Queen.

Essex replied that there was a plot against his life and he was to have been murdered in his bed; letters had been written in his name, his signature counterfeited, his friends had assembled merely to defend him. This was not believed either by the Lord Keeper or his companions, and once again he asked to speak with the Earl in private.

Then the crowds in the courtyard, supporters of the Earl, began to cry, "Kill them . . . stop them. . . .Cast the Greal Seal out of the window." Essex led Egerton and his companions into a back room of the house and told them, "Be patient here awhile, my Lords, and stay here, and I will go into London and take order with the Mayor and the Sheriffs of the city, and will be here again within this half-hour."

Then the door was shut and locked 'and the further door fastened too, and the Lord Keeper, the Controller and the Lord Chief Justice were left there as hostages, guarded by Sir John Davis and others.

The plan for the ride into the city had miscarried with the unexpected arrival of the Lord Keeper, and now the horses were not ready, so that the Earl with two hundred men was obliged to go on foot from Essex House to the city, joined by the Earl of Bedford and others. People looking from their windows stared, astonished, to see the Earl with his group of supporters, sweating their way to Sheriff Smith's house in Fenchurch, no hero of Cadiz on horseback, proud and smiling, with crowds acclaiming him. The streets were empty, and there was no sermon being preached at Paul's Cross.

"For the Queen, for the Queen, a plot is laid against my life," shouted the Earl, haggard and distraught. People turned away. The Sheriff made excuses from his house in Fenchurch Street. The whole scheme was in total disarray. Some of the supporters who had followed the Earl sensed the situation and began to disperse. There was nothing for it but to return to Essex House. In Ludgate Street soldiers were standing guard. Essex ordered a charge, but his diminishing band of followers was repulsed. Sir Christopher Blount was wounded and taken prisoner, a young friend of the Earl's named Tracy was killed, and a handful of bystanders as well. A musket-shot pierced the Earl's hat. It was a lamentable and disastrous finale for the hero who had breached the walls of a citadel and sacked the houses of Cadiz.

The Lord Keeper and his two associates were released from Essex House by Ferdinando Gorges, who now feared for his own life; and scarcely had the Earl and his remaining supporters, unable to return along the Strand because of the soldiers blocking their way, taken boat from Queenhithe and returned to Essex House, than it was surrounded by forces summoned by the Lord Admiral. The Countess of Essex, Lady Rich and other ladies of the house were allowed to leave, but the Lord Admiral would make no terms with those whom he deemed rebels. The Earl burnt all his papers, among them, it was said, a history of his troubles, declaring that he would tell no tales of his friends.

At 10 o'clock that Sunday evening Essex and his fellow-peers and knights surrendered their swords to the Lord Admiral.

The night was stormy, the river rough—it was thought too rough to proceed by boat further than Lambeth—but an order came from her Majesty that despite the weather the rebels were to be conveyed by barge to the Tower, where, nearly forty-seven years before, she herself had gone as prisoner.

Chapter 24

The Earl was committed to the Tower of London in the small hours of Monday morning, February 9th. With him were the Earls of Southampton and Rutland, the Lords Sandys, Cromwell and Monteagle, and Sir Charles Davers and Sir Henry Bromley. Their fellow-conspirators were placed in other prisons.

Ten days passed before Essex and Southampton appeared on trial at Westminster Hall before twenty-five peers of the realm, the Lord Chief Justices Popham and Anderson and seven judges. These ten days gave them time to prepare their defence, but they had no contact with each other, and no means of knowing what their fellow-peers and knights would admit or deny. Members of the Council reserved the right to examine certain of the leaders of the rebellion during their confinement, and if possible to extort confessions of guilt, which could then be read out in open court. What methods were used upon the prisoners before their private examinations, whether deprivation of food and water, or even torture, has never been stated; certainly they were neither better nor worse than the grilling of political offenders in our own time.

Sir Ferdinando Gorges, Sir John Davis, Sir Charles Davers, Sir Christopher Blount, Lord Sandys and the Earl of Rutland were all questioned, and all signed statements admitting complicity though intending no harm and no treason. Each one, though with reluctance, agreed that the Earl of Essex had been the leader of a conspiracy to surround the Palace of Whitehall, seize prominent members of the Council, "protect" the Queen's person by disarming the body guard, and gain the support of the city of London. They had unwilling joined in the plot for friendship's sake, hoping that by doing so her Majesty might be moved to restore the Earl to favour.

These confessions, or perhaps it would be kinder to say admissions, of friends close to the Earl were indictments so damning that only a supreme counsel speaking for Essex could, or might, have saved him. He had no such counsel, no witness on his behalf; the "caged bird" Anthony Bacon was not present, sent no testimony and was not even mentioned in any of the signed confessions. One man could have done it, Anthony Bacon's younger brother, but Francis Bacon was commanded by the Queen to appear for the Crown and speak against the Earl of Essex. Why he should have been chosen to speak on this supremely grave occasion, in addition to Serjeant Yelverton and the Attorney-General, is a mystery that even now, after nearly four hundred years of dispute, has never been solved. His speech was more pertinent to the case and more damaging to the Earl's cause than either of theirs, and because of it he has been condemned through the centuries for accusing the nobleman who had befriended him, and had shown him only goodwill and patronage.

It has not been suggested hitherto that he did what he was commanded to do because, had he refused, his brother Anthony would have been arrested, put into prison along with Henry Cuffe and other prisoners not considered of high enough rank to be committed to the Tower, there questioned and even tortured so as to extort confession, and, like Cuffe and Gilly Mericke later, hanged, drawn and quartered at Tyburn. This "either-or" would never have been placed on record in State papers. Nor could Francis himself have admitted it in his *Apologia,* printed in 1604, in which he excused himself for his part in the trial.

In this *Apologia,* extracts from which have appeared in earlier chapters, he said,

I never moved neither the Queen, nor any person living, concerning my being used in the service, either of evidence or examination; but it was merely laid upon me with the rest of my fellows. And for the time which passed, I mean between the arraignment [i.e. the trial] and my Lord's suffering, I well remember I was but once with the Queen; at what time, though I durst not deal directly for my Lord as things then stood, yet generally I did both commend her Majesty's mercy, terming it to her as an excellent balm that did continually distil from her sovereign hands, and made an excellent odour in the senses of her people; and not only so, but I took hardiness to extenuate, not the fact, for that I durst not, but the danger, telling her that if some base or cruel-minded persons had entered into such an action, it might have caused much blood and combustion; but it appeared well that they were such as knew not how to play the malefactors; *and some other words which I now omit.*

What these words were Francis never revealed. It seems highly possible that they related, even if only in part, to the absent witness of all the Earl's past schemes and actions through the preceding years, his brother Anthony. The tenor of the words would have been, "I have done what your Majesty commanded me to do, I spoke for the Crown against the Earl of Essex. Now I ask for clemency, not only for his Lordship, but for my brother Anthony, should any of the remaining prisoners mention his name in their confessions."

One did—Henry Cuffe, the private secretary who, in the past months, had taken over so much of the Earl's personal business and correspondence, and had been close to him in the final months at Essex House. Examined in February, prior to the day of the trial, he was questioned very closely by members of the Council as to the correspondence between his lordship and the King of Scotland, and admitted that to his knowledge it had continued for at least two years, though he avowed there was nothing in this correspondence harmful to the Queen.

"I had seen in a letter from France, mention made of a Scottish cipher, wherein were characters for the principal Councillors of this State, and besides for two private gentlemen, namely Mr Anthony Bacon and Sir Henry Bromley."

This interesting piece of evidence was not produced by the Crown at the trial itself; and in a subsequent confession by Henry Cuffe on March 2nd before the Lord Keeper and Sir Robert Cecil his words, "I have often heard that Anthony Bacon conveyed diverse letters from the Earl to the King of Scots and was an agent between them" were struck from the records.

The trial itself, held at Westminster Hall, lasted from eight in the morning until seven at night, with Sir Ferdinando Gorges the first to be examined, admitting all that had taken place at Drury House and Essex House and so immediately putting the Earl himself into a grave position. Essex, despite the initial setback, seemed very capable of defending himself and refuting the various arguments of the Attorney-General Sir Edward Coke. He led the discussion into his fears about the Infanta of Spain and her claim to the succession, which he insisted was his foremost reason for wanting to protect her Majesty and to arouse the citizens of London in her defence. Indeed, it would seem from his argument that invasion was imminent.

The Secretary of State, Sir Robert Cecil, denied that any such claim had been put to the Council by the Infanta, and the discussion, heated and lively, might have drifted on, had not Francis Bacon risen to his feet and brought both accusers and defenders back to the subject of treason. The speech he made was terse, to the point, and damning.

". . . Thus the Earl made his colour the severing of some great men and councillors from her Majesty's service, and the fear he stood in of his pretended enemies lest they should murder him in his house. Therefore he saith he was compelled to fly into the city for succour and assistance; not much unlike Pisistratus, of whom it was so anciently written how he gashed and wounded himself and in that sort ran crying into Athens that his life was sought and like to have been taken away; thinking to have moved the people to have pitied him and taken his part, by such counterfeited harm and danger: his aim and drift was to take the government of the city into his hands, and altered the form thereof. With like pretences of dangers and assaults the Earl of Essex entered the City of London, and passed through the bowels thereof, blanching rumours that he should have been murdered and that the State was sold; whereas he had no such enemies, no such dangers."

Here he was interrupted by the Earl, and for the first and only time in the trial the name of Anthony Bacon was mentioned, but not even then on his own account or as someone pertinent to the defence, but to draw the attention of the Council to the letters which Francis had written ten months before, supposedly from his brother to the Earl, and from the Earl in reply.

"To answer Mr Bacon's speech at once," said the Earl, "I say thus much, and call forth Mr Bacon against Mr Bacon. You are then to know that Mr Francis Bacon hath written two letters, the one of which had been artificially framed in my name, after he had framed the other in Mr Anthony Bacon's name to provoke me. In the latter of these two he lays down the grounds of my discontentment and the reasons I pretend against mine enemies, pleading as orderly for me as I could do myself . . . If those reasons were then just and true, not counterfeit, how can it be that now my pretences are false and injurious? For then Mr Bacon joined with me in mine opinion, and pointed out those to be mine enemies and to hold me in disgrace with her Majesty, whom he seems now to clear of such mind towards me; and therefore I leave the truth of what I say and he opposeth unto your Lordships' indifferent conclusions."

Francis made a brief reply. "These digressions are not fit, neither should they be suffered. Those letters, if they are there, would not blush to be seen for anything contained in them; I have spent more time in vain studying how to make the Earl a good servant to the Queen and State than I have done in anything else." He then sat down and the hearing continued, with the confessions of Sir Charles Davers, Sir John Davis and Sir Christopher Blount being read aloud, their statements confirming the evidence already given by Sir Ferdinando Gorges.

These admissions by the Earl's friends, and above all that of his stepfather Sir Christopher Blount, not only impressed the Court with the gravity of the situation but shook the confidence of the Earl. He fell back upon protestations of his religious faith and his nightly practices of devotion, upon which the Attorney-General immediately attacked him for hypocrisy. Sir Edward Coke's attitude was so aggressive, and the Earl's manner so sincere, that the assembled peers began to feel some stirring of sympathy for him, which increased after the examination of the second prisoner, the Earl of Southampton, who also protested his innocence and that of his dear friend the Earl of Essex, the object of the consultations at Drury House having been simply to obtain some means of access to her Majesty, without any thought of treason.

The assembled peers then asked to be satisfied on a

point of law. Was it, they demanded, necessarily treason
for the Earl of Essex to go to Court with his company and
present his complaints, without doing violence to her
Majesty or any other? The judges gave opinion that it *was*
treason. The Attorney-General pursued the point with
much relish, and might have continued for some time de-
bating intention of violence and intention of conscience,
had not Francis Bacon once more risen to his feet.

"I have never yet seen," he declared, "in any case, such
favour shown to any prisoner; so many digressions, such
delivering of evidence by fractions, and so silly a defence
of such great and notorious treasons."

"If I had purposed anything against others than my
private enemies," replied the Earl, "I would not have
stirred with so slender a company."

"It was not the company you carried with you," returned Francis, "but the assistance you hoped for in the
city, which you trusted unto. The Duke of Guise thrust
himself into the streets of Paris, on the day of the barri-
cades, in his doublet and hose, attended only with eight
gentlemen, and found that help in the city which, God be
thanked, you failed of here. And what followed? The
King was forced to put himself into pilgrim's weeds, and in
that disguise to steal away to escape their fury. Even such,"
and he turned to the peers, "was my Lord's confidence too;
and his pretence the same—an all-hail and a kiss to the
city. But the end was treason, as hath been sufficiently
proved."

The prisoners were withdrawn shortly afterwards. The
verdict was unanimous: the Earl of Essex and the Earl of
Southampton were both found guilty of high treason.
When they were brought back to the bar they saw that
the axe had been turned towards them by the bearer, sig-
nifying sentence of death. Both prisoners were then asked
if they had anything to say against the judgement. The
Earl of Southampton threw himself upon the Queen's
mercy. The Earl of Essex asked pardon for past offences,
admitted no guilt, craved her Majesty's mercy with all
humility, "yet," he concluded, "I had rather die than live
in misery."

His last request was that he might have his chosen
preacher with him in the Tower, and receive the sacrament
there before his execution.

The Earl's bearing in Westminster Hall, after hearing his sentence, was noble and courageous; once outside he was heard to break out in bitter anger against those friends of his who had so betrayed him, and back in the Tower he sent for Lord Thomas Howard, the Constable, for the Lord Keeper and for Sir Robert Cecil, desiring, so he said, to tell the truth now about his companions who had so misled him. The insurrection had not been his idea but theirs. It was Davis, Davers, Blount, not Essex, who had been the instigators. Since August last they had incited him to force.

The *volte face* was embarrassing to all. He accused everyone, including his own sister Lady Rich, and most especially his secretary Henry Cuffe. Total collapse of moral fibre came when his chaplain, Mr Ashton, told him that far from being guiltless his fault had been an ambitious seeking of the crown for himself, and that unless he made a full confession of this sin and everything else he would carry out of the world a guilty soul before God and leave an infamous name to posterity.

Death the Earl was prepared to face, but not the everlasting flames of hell. The Puritan divine thus succeeded in extracting a full and abject confession which neither the Attorney-General nor Francis Bacon had been able to obtain. It was evidently after this, or even the same day, that Francis sought his audience of the Queen and asked for clemency for the broken man. That clemency was not forthcoming. Her Majesty relented in one respect only, in that the Earl's execution should take place privately inside the precincts of the Tower of London and not in public upon Tower Hill.

Although the Earl had broken down during those final days, when the moment of execution came he did at least face death like a commander. He came out of his cell at about seven o'clock on the morning of Ash Wednesday, February 25th, and walked to the scaffold dressed in black and wearing a black felt hat. He was attended by three priests and sixteen guards and the Lieutenant of the Tower. Some hundred persons, peers, knights, gentlemen and aldermen of the city, stood by to watch.

The Earl took off his hat and addressed them, admitting all the evil he had done, yet protesting he had never meant any violence to the Queen's person. He then approached the block and forgave the executioner, who by custom asked for pardon. "Thou art welcome to me, I forgive thee; thou art the minister of true justice." After which he prayed, "Lift my soul above all earthly cogitations, and when my soul and body shall part, send Thy blessed angels to be near unto me, which may convey it to the joys of heaven." The words have a familiar ring:

> "Now crackes a Noble heart:
> Goodnight, sweet Prince,
> And flights of Angels sing thee to thy rest."

The Earl of Essex next removed his black doublet and stood in a scarlet waistcoat with scarlet sleeves, his redgold hair framing his face. He lay down upon the boards before the block, stretching out his arms, and said, "O Lord, into thy hands I commend my spirit." His head was severed in three strokes. So Robin Devereux died, aged thirty-three years and three months. His head and body was buried by the Earl of Arundel and the Duke of Norfolk, and by the express command of the Queen his banner and hatchment of the Knight of the Garter were not removed from St George's Chapel, Windsor.

The five prisoners who had admitted complicity were tried on March 5th and condemned to death. Sir Christopher Blount and Sir Charles Davers were beheaded on Tower Hill. Gilly Mericke and Henry Cuffe were hanged at Tyburn. Sir John Davis was spared, and after a year's imprisonment obtained a pardon from the Queen. He was the only one of the five to be examined by Francis Bacon at this trial, the others being questioned by Serjeant Fleming and the Attorney-General. Whether Francis appealed to her Majesty for clemency, and it was granted, seems very probable.

Once again she commanded the use of his pen. He was to draw up for her, as he had done the year before in June, a full account of the entire proceedings in a "Declaration of the Practices and Treasons Attempted and Committed by Robert Late Earl of Essex and his Complices". He obeyed her command, but said later, in his *Apologia*, that what he had written was much altered by the Councillors and the Queen herself.

When a popular hero dies, and in such tragic circumstances, fiction grows up about him and is embroidered throughout the years. Some twenty years later, when negotiations of marriage were entered into between Charles, Prince of Wales, and the Infanta of Spain, "Essex's Ghost" was said to have appeared, warning England against the perils of such a match. Here, it was said, had been the true patriot, the great commander, who had been put to death by evil slanderous men. By mid-century the story of a ring, sent by Essex in the Tower to her Majesty and never delivered, turned from whispered rumour to asserted truth. It has never been proved. One of those who spread it on the continent was Aubéry du Maurier, son of that Benjamin Aubéry du Maurier who had been secretary to du Plessis Mornay in the 1590's and later French ambassador in Holland.

Then there was the black purse, said to contain the cipher used by the King of Scots, the Earl of Essex and Anthony Bacon, which his lordship, according to Henry Cuff, always wore upon his person; this was never found, and was certainly not about him when he was executed. So myth becomes tradition, but never history.

As to the Earl's final confession of guilt to his Puritan chaplain Mr Ashton, an anonymous letter, dated some three months after the execution, declared that Essex had been persuaded to confess solely from fear of eternal damnation. The writer of the letter claimed that he had been told this by Ashton himself, "a man base, fearful, and mercenary". The letter was dated May 30th 1601, was addressed to Anthony Bacon, and was never delivered. The anonymous writer had evidently been a correspondent of Anthony's during the period of the Earl's imprisonment in the Tower, for he says, "Sir, I perceive by your letters, many strange reports are spread of a confession my Lord of Essex should make before his death, wherein his honour hath, as you say, been much touched, and your desire is to receive some satisfaction concerning the same. And surely, I confess, you cannot give me a more pleasing subject to write of, than the discovery of that truth, by which any unworthy aspersion of dishonour may be removed from his memorial, whose life was so dear unto me, and of whose noble virtues I had so great experience."

The writer then gives a full account of the chaplain's visit to the cell and how the Earl was broken into confession. But the letter was never delivered, and Anthony Bacon never had the consolation of reading it; by the time it was written, on May 31st, he was dead.

Chapter 25

How he died, where he died, and where he was buried has remained unknown throughout the centuries until the present day. A book of pedigrees of Suffolk families states that he died in Essex House. This is unlikely. He left there in March of 1600, and there is no record of his ever having returned. In a previous chapter it has been suggested that his place of retreat might have been in Sir William Cornwallis's house in Bishopsgate, but this has not been proved. One last asylum for the caged bird remains possible—the house belonging to Lady Walsingham, mother of the Countess of Essex, and widow of Anthony's first employer, Sir Francies Walsingham. This house was not the old Walsingham house, known as the Papey, off Bishopsgate, but was situated in Seething Lane, close to St Olave's Church, Hart Street. In this church the Earl's two sons, Robert and Walter, were baptised in 1591 and 1592; therefore it was known and used by the Devereux and Walsingham families. Search in the Harleian MS. at the British Museum led to an examination of the register in St Olave's Church. And here at last, unnoticed for centuries, the entry states: "May 17th, 1601, Mr Anthonye Bacon buried in the chamber within the vault."

The fact that the entry is so brief, that Francis makes no mention of the death amongst his papers, that no will has been traced, suggests that Anthony may have been buried secretly, at night, though the good offices of Lady Walsingham or the Countess of Essex. But the reason for the secrecy must remain surmise. It is even possible he died by his own hand. During the weeks that elapsed between the Earl's execution on February 25th and his own burial on May 17th, Anthony waited for the letter that he did not receive. All he knew was that the Earl had confessed, thus leaving a stain on his honour. Christopher

273

Blount, Sir Charles Davers, Gilly Mericke, Henry Cuff had all confessed and died. Crippled, helpless, the bird in the cage no longer had the will to live. He would have known, too, the part that his brother Francis had taken during the trial, the story doubtless made more damning by members of the Essex family; and if Francis had told his brother that he had been commanded to put the case for the prosecution by her Majesty herself, in return for sparing Anthony from accusation, this very fact would have brought him to despair.

On May 27th John Chamberlain, writing from London to his friend Dudley Carleton, said, "Anthony Bacon died not long since but so far in debt, that I think his brother is little the better by him." This was all the contemporary world heard of the death, then or afterwards. The administration of his estate was not granted to Francis until June 23rd 1602, over a year later. "On the last day but one a commission was granted to Francis Bacon, esquire, natural and legal brother of Anthony Bacon, formerly of the parish of St Olave in Hart Street in the City of London, for the good administration of the goods, rights and credits of the deceased in the person of Francis Walleys, notary public, who took oath on his behalf."

The month of Anthony's birth in 1558 is still unknown, but, dying in 1601, he was either forty-three or approaching his forty-third birthday. His brother Francis would live on to become Lord Chancellor and Lord Keeper like their father Sir Nicholas Bacon, to live at York House and at Gorhambury, to win fame as a writer and philosopher, a fame that has endured through the centuries; and although towards the end of his career he too, like the Earl of Essex, was to fly with waxen wings and fall like Icarus, he was able to retire, after the first blow of shame and humiliation, to his private world of literature, science and philosophy. "For my name and memory, I leave it to men's charitable speeches, and to foreign nations, and the next ages." King James's ex-Chancellor, the little "Lord Keeper" who had danced attendance on Queen Elizabeth as a small boy when she visited his father's house at Gorhambury, knew very well that he had won fame in his lifetime; as to the rest, he left it to posterity.

It was otherwise with his brother. Anthony may have stared down at the Queen from an upstairs window when she paced the long gallery and young Francis bowed before her; there is no tradition that she ever smiled upon him too. Adult, he refused to seek an audience—indeed, he made every excuse to avoid her presence. The sonnets he sent back from France have never been named. The shame of his arrest at Montauban went unrecorded, save in the French archives. The esteem of Michel de Montaigne escaped notice. The eulogies of the idle pens in Gray's Inn and elsewhere were passed over. Even the hopes of so unlikely a person as his mother's chaplain pastor Wyborn, who wished him "success in literature", repose dustily at Lambeth Palace. Two men knew him for his worth—Henri of Navarre, later Henri IV of France, and Robert Devereux, Earl of Essex. Also, it seems probable, the future James I of England.

What his private dreams were, his personal ambitions, we do not know. Once he returned from France they were all centred on the Earl of Essex. And in those last months, crippled not only bodily but by his debts as well, he lost faith in God and in mankind. The loose threads of his life remain untied. No more is heard of Tom Lawson, of Jacques Petit, or of those other nameless pages who acted as messengers between Essex House and Gorhambury.

We do not know who was at his bedside when he died. His mother had nine more years to live, lonely, confused, and according to a later report "little more than frantic in her age." Forever without "children's childer", perhaps, in her moments of lucidity, she recalled earlier, happier days, when instead of warning her elder son that "strong drink breedeth strange fancies" she bade him "ride not fast for yourself, and the horses being greys will quickly take hurt in this heat, one is especially very fast, which Mr Selwyn will like and use well". No gout then, no sudden attack of the stone, but hard exercise and Ned Selwyn for companion on the road to the bachelor establishment at Redbourne. Supper to follow, some of the home-brewed ale; then the music that he loved, played upon the lute, and the virginals, sent down to the country with special care by George Jenkyll from Gray's Inn.

Finally to bed, and whether then in Hertfordshire, or later in London, or even during his last unhappy hours after Ash Wednesday of the year 1601 until May 17th, he could turn to the bedside book of essays, not his brother's with the dedication, but those of his friend, that Frenchman long since dead, Michel de Montaigne.

"Democritus and Heraclitus were two philosophers, of whom the first, finding the human race ridiculous and futile, never appeared in public without a laughing mocking face. Heraclitus, having pity and compassion for this same human race, wore a continuously sad expression, his eyes filled with tears. I prefer the first, not because it is more pleasing to laugh than to cry, but because it is more scornful so to do, and it seems to me that according to our deserts, we can never be sufficiently condemned."

Postscript

St Olave's church, Hart Street, was bombed in 1941 and almost destroyed. The coffin of Samuel Pepys, buried in a vault in 1703, was discovered beneath the communion table in the chancel. If there were others beside it, they were unrecorded. The area is now totally sealed. The church itself was rebuilt and restored, and looks as gracious today as it did four centuries ago.

When the present writer visited St Olave's on October 6th 1973, the church was empty. It was very silent, very peaceful. Then softly, from the organ in the gallery above, an unseen musician, unaware of an intruder below, began to play the sixteenth-century melody of "Green-sleeves"—that well-loved air, sung by courtier and commoner alike, known to King Henry VIII, danced to by his daughter Queen Elizabeth, and surely strummed upon the virginals by Anthony Bacon himself.

Just as suddenly as it began, the music ceased. The quest that had taken the intruder to Montauban, Bordeaux, Gorhambury, Redbourne, Twickenham, and through many a dusty document, had ended too. The caged bird was at rest.

Bibliography

The main source for reseach into the life of Anthony Bacon from the year 1579 until his death in 1601—indeed, one might say the only source—is his correspondence, which is housed today in sixteen volumes in the Lambeth Palace Library. This correspondence was used extensively by Thomas Birch in his *Memoirs of the Reign of Queen Elizabeth*, published in 1754, and some hundred years later by James Spedding in *The Life and Letters of Francis Bacon*, published between 1861 and 1872. Hepworth Dixon, in his *Personal History of Lord Bacon*, also quoted from the family letters.

For the purpose of the present work, over three hundred original letters in the collection were transcribed for me, by kind permission of the officials of the Lambeth Palace Library, by Mrs St George Saunders and her team of helpers in her Writers' and Speakers' Research. Many of these letters have never before been transcribed. Other original letters relating to the Bacon family, housed by the Folger Library in Washington, were photocopied for me by Mrs Yeandle, the Manuscript Librarian, and transcribed by Writers' and Speakers' Research. Bacon letters are also to be found in the Harleian and Cotton MSS. in the British Museum, and these have been read.

The Bacon correspondence in the Lambeth Palace Library does not give the reason for Anthony Bacon's prolonged stay in Montauban, Tarn-et-Garonne, during the years 1586-88, nor does Thomas Birch in his *Memoirs of the Reign of Queen Elizabeth*. The State Papers of the time are also silent on this subject. Letters to Monsieur Méras, Director of the *Archives Départmentales* at Montauban, and my visit there in 1973, produced the answer, with a document and letters never before published. I believe that his reason for remaining so long in Montauban was concealed from his family and friends at home in England, as well as from his employer, Sir Francis Walsingham, Secretary of State, and his uncle, Earl Burghley, the Lord Treasurer.

Facts concerning Gorhambury and Redbourne, Anthony Bacon's properties in Hertfordshire, were obtained through the family records at Gorhambury and in the Herts and County Records Office, St Albans. Through the great kindness and courtesy of the Countess of Verulam and the librarian at Gorhambury, Mrs King, I was shown books, portraits and busts of Sir Nicholas and Lady Bacon and their sons. These my son was permitted to photograph, as well as the ruins of the original Gorhambury house.

The original of Sir Nicholas Bacon's will was viewed at the Public Record Office in London, as was the document relating to the lawsuit between John Shakespeare and William Burbage.

Finally, Anthony Bacon's place of burial, searched for in vain by Thomas Birch in the eighteenth century and by James Spedding in the nineteenth, was discovered by Mrs Saunders in 1973, in the parish records of St Olave's Church, Hart Street, in the City of London.

SELECT BIBLIOGRAPHY OF PRINTED SOURCES

BACON, FRANCIS, *Works*, 5 vols. (A. Millar, 1765)

BALLARD, GEORGE, *Memoirs of Several Ladies of Great Britain* (T. Evans, 1775)

BARNS, STEPHEN, *The Cookes of Gidea Hall* (Essex Review, Vol. XXI, 1912)

BEVAN, BRYAN, *The Real Francis Bacon* (Centaur Press, 1960)

BIRCH, THOMAS, *Memoirs of the Reign of Queen Elizabeth*, 2 vols. (A. Millar, 1754)

BOWEN, CATHERINE DRINKER, *Francis Bacon* (Hamish Hamilton, 1963)

BROWN, IVOR, *London* (Studio Vista, 1965)

CALENDAR OF STATE PAPERS, DOMESTIC SERIES

CECIL, DAVID, *The Cecils of Hatfield House* (Constable, 1973)

COWPER, FRANCIS, *A Prospect of Gray's Inn* (Stevens, 1951)

DEVEREUX, W. B., *Lives and Letters of the Earls of Essex*, 2 vols. (Murray, 1853)

Dictionary of National Biography

DIXON, W. HEPWORTH, *Personal History of Lord Bacon* (John Murray, 1861)

—*The Story of Lord Bacon's Life* (John Murray, 1862)

Encyclopaedia Britannica, 1947 edition

ESSEX, 2ND EARL OF, *An Apologia Penned in 1598* (1603)

GRIMBLE, IAN, *The Harington Family* (Cape, 1957)

HAMPSHIRE FIELD CLUB, PROCEEDINGS OF, VOL. III, *Pedigree of the Pagets and other Families of Grove Place* (1894-1897)

HEADLAM, CECIL, *Inns of Court* (A. & C. Black, 1909)

HERTFORDSHIRE, VICTORIA COUNTY HISTORY, *The Burbage Family and the Manor of Theobalds*

—— *Hertfordshire*

HOTSON, JOHN LESLIE, *Shakespeare's Sonnets Dated* (Hart Davis, 1949)

—— *The First Night of Twelfth Night* (Hart Davis, 1954)

—— *Mr W. H.* (Hart Davis, 1964)

KINGSTON, C. L., *Essex House, Formerly Leicester House* (Archaeologia, Vol. 73)

MCCLURE, N. E., *The Letters of John Chamberlain* (Philadelphia, 1939)

MACDOWALL, H. C., *Henry of Guise and Other Portraits* (Macmillan, 1898)

MAUROIS, ANDRÉ, *A History of England* (Cape, 1937)

MÉRAS, MATHIEU, *Châteaux de France* (Paris, 1971)

—— *Receuil de l'Académie de Montauban* (Montauban, 1967)

MINNEY, R. J., *The Tower of London* (Cassell, 1970)

MOLET, ANDRÉ, AND ISAACS, JULES, *Histoire de France* (Paris, 1923)

MONTAIGNE, MICHEL DE, *Essais* (Paris, 1965)

MORNAY, CHARLOTTE DE, A *Huguenot Family in the XVI Century* (Routledge, 1926)

NORSWORTHY, LAURA L., *The Lady of Bleeding Heart Yard* (Murray, 1953)

ORWICK, WILLIAM, *Nonconformist Worthies of St Albans*

OUDRÉ, HENRI, *Vie de B. Aubéry du Maurier* (1853)

PATRY, RAOUL, *Vie de Philippe du Plessis-Mornay* (Paris, 1933)

PREST, W. R., *The Inns of Court under Elizabeth I and the Early Stuarts* (Longmans, 1972)

RIDLEY, JASPER, *The Life and Times of Mary Tudor* (Weidenfeld & Nicolson, 1974)

ROGERS, JOHN G., *Gorhambury and Old Gorhambury* (St Albans and Herts Architectural and Archaeological Society, 1933)

—*The Manor and Houses of Gorhambury* (Ibid., 1936)

ROWSE, A. L., *The England of Elizabeth* (Macmillan, 1964)

—*Bisham and the Hobys in the English Past* (Macmillan, 1951)

—*The Elizabethan Renaissance* (Macmillan, 1971)

SHAKESPEARE, WILLIAM, Complete Works. Text of First Folio with quarto variants, 4 vols. (Nonesuch Press, 1953)

SIMPSON, ALAN, *The Wealth of the Gentry, 1540-1660* (Cambridge University Press, 1961)

SPARKES, I. G., *Gidea Hall and Gidea Park* (Romford, 1966)

SPEDDING, JAMES, *The Life and Letters of Francis Bacon,* 7 vols. (Longmans, Green & Ryder, 1861-72)

STOW, JOHN, *Survey of London,* 1595 edition

STRACHEY, LYTTON, *Elizabeth and Essex* (Chatto & Windus, 1928)

TARN ET GARONNE, DEPARTEMENT DE, *La Revue Geographique et Industrielle de France*

URWIN, ALAN C. B., *Twickenam Parke* (Hounslow, 1965)

VERULAM 5TH EARL OF, *The Bacon Family* (Privately printed, 1961)

WILLIAMS, NEVILLE *All the Queen's Men* (Weidenfeld & Nicolson, 1972)

WILLIAMSON, HUGH ROSS, *Catherine Medici* (Michael Joseph, 1973)

Sources

CHAPTER 1

Dictionary of National Biography
Encyclopaedia Britannica
Memoirs of Several Ladies of Great Britain   Ballard
The Life and Times of Mary Tudor   Ridley
The Cecils of Hatfield House   Cecil
The Wealth of the Gentry, 1540-1660   Simpson
The Cookes of Gidea Hall   Barns
Gidea Hall and Gidea Park   Barns

CHAPTER 2

Calendar of State Papers
All the Queen's Men   Williams
The Life and Times of Mary Tudor   Ridley
The Wealth of the Gentry   Simpson
Dictionary of National Biography
The Bacon Family   5th Earl of Verulam
Worthies of St Albans   Orwick
Memoirs of Several Ladies of Great Britain   Ballard
Gorhambury and Old Gorhambury   Rogers
Bisham and the Hobys in the English Past   Rowse

CHAPTER 3

Archbishop Whitgift's College Pupils   Master of Trinity's
    Book, 1573-75
Dictionary of National Biography
The Cecils of Hatfield House   Cecil
A History of England   Maurois
All the Queen's Men   Williams
Bisham and the Hobys in the English Past   Rowse

The Wealth of the Gentry   Simpson
Pedigree of the Pagets and Other Families of Grove Place
   Hampshire Field Club
The Pension Book of Gray's Inn
The Inns of Court under Elizabeth I   Prest
Inns of Court   Headlam
A Prospect of Gray's Inn   Cowper
Lady Bacon's Letters   Lambeth Palace
The Manor and Houses of Gorhambury   St Albans &
   Herts. Society
Catherine Medici   Williamson
The Life and Letters of Francis Bacon   Spedding
Letters of Edward Bacon   Folger Library, Washington
The Story of Lord Bacon's Life   Dixon
Sir Nicholas Bacon's Will   Public Record Office

CHAPTER 4

Bacon Correspondence   Lambeth Palace
The Burbage Family and Theobalds Manor   Victoria
   History of Herts
Memoirs of the Reign of Queen Elizabeth   Birch
The Wealth of the Gentry   Simpson
Letters of Edward Bacon   Folger Library
Calendar of State Papers
The Life and Letters of Francis Bacon   Spedding

CHAPTER 5

Châteaux de France   Méras
Histoire de France   Molet & Isaac
Vie de B. Aubéry du Maurier   Oudré
Henry of Guise and Other Portraits   MacDowall
Catherine Medici   Williamson
Receuil de l'Académie de Montauban   Méras
La Revue Geographique et Industrielle de France   Méras
Memoires de Madame du Plessis-Mornay   British
   Museum
The Life and Letters of Francis Bacon   Spedding
Procés Anthoine Bacon, Archives Départementales de
   Montauban. Préfecture de Tarn et Garonne

CHAPTER 6

Procés Anthoine Bacon
Receuil des Lettres Missives de Henri IV Collection de
Scorbiac, Archives Départementales de Montauban
Histoire de France Molet & Isaac
The Life and Letters of Francis Bacon Spedding
Memoires: Du Plessis-Mornay British Museum
Calendar of State Papers
Bacon Correspondence Lambeth Palace
Henry of Guise and Other Portraits MacDowall

CHAPTER 7

Histoire de France Molet & Isaac
Châteaux de France Méras
The Cecils of Hatfield House Cecil
Memoirs of Several Ladies of Great Britain Ballard
Bacon Correspondence Lambeth Palace
Henry of Guise and Other Portraits MacDowall
Memoirs of the Reign of Queen Elizabeth Birch
Essais Montaigne
Vie de Philippe du Plessis-Mornay Patry
Memoires: Du Plessis-Mornay
Archives Départementales de Montauban
Archives Municipales de Bordeaux

CHAPTER 8

Bacon Correspondence Lambeth Palace
Memoirs of the Reign of Queen Elizabeth Birch
Lives and Letters of the Earls of Essex Devereux
Bisham and the Hobys in the English Past Rowse
Romeo and Juliet, 1st Quarto

CHAPTER 9

The Life and Letters of Francis Bacon Spedding
Memoirs of the Reign of Queen Elizabeth Birch
Bacon Correspondence Lambeth Palace
Vie de B. Aubéry du Maurier Oudré
Archives Municipales de Bordeaux

Transactions of the St Albans Architectural and Archae-
ological Society
Romeo and Juliet, 1st Quarto
Burbage v. Shakespeare   Court of Common Pleas, Public
Record Office
Shakespeare's Sonnets Dated   Hotson

CHAPTER 10

Memoirs of the Reign of Queen Elizabeth   Birch
Bacon Correspondence   Lambeth Palace
Twickenam Parke   Urwin
Henry of Guise and Other Portraits   MacDowall
Memoires: Du Plessis-Mornay
The Life and Letters of Francis Bacon   Spedding
Essais   Montaigne

CHAPTER 11

The Life and Letters of Frances Bacon   Spedding
Bacon Correspondence   Lambeth Palace
Dictionary of National Biography
Memoirs of the Reign of Queen Elizabeth   Birch
London   Brown
Essais   Montaigne
Henry IV, Pt I, 1st Folio

CHAPTER 12

The Life and Letters of Francis Bacon   Spedding
Bacon Correspondence   Lambeth Palace
Mr W. H.   Hotson
Memoirs of the Reign of Queen Elizabeth   Birch
Henry of Guise and Other Portraits   MacDowall
Essays   Francis Bacon

CHAPTER 13

Henry of Guise and Other Portraits   MacDowall
Memoirs of the Reign of Queen Elizabeth   Birch
Bacon Correspondence   Lambeth Palace
The Life and Letters of Francis Bacon   Spedding
Essex House, Formerly Leicester House   Kingston

Survey of London Stow
Henry V, 1st Quarto

INTERLUDE FOR JACQUES PETIT

Bacon Correspondence Lambeth Palace
The Harington Family Grimble

CHAPTER 14

Memoirs of the Reign of Queen Elizabeth Birch
Bacon Correspondence Lambeth Palace
Vie de B. Aubéry du Maurier Oudré
Lives and Letters of the Earls of Essex Devereux
Henry IV, Pt. I, 1st Quarto

CHAPTER 15

Memoirs of the Reign of Queen Elizabeth Birch
Lives and Letters of the Earls of Essex Devereux
Bacon Correspondence Lambeth Palace
Henry of Guise and Other Portraits MacDowall
Henry V, 1st Quarto

CHAPTER 16

Memoirs of the Reign of Queen Elizabeth Birch
Bacon Correspondence Lambeth Palace
Essex House, Formerly Leicester House Kingston
The Life and Letters of Francis Bacon Spedding

CHAPTER 17

Essays Francis Bacon (taken from the edition printed in
  1625)
Memoirs of the Reign of Queen Elizabeth Birch
Lives and Letters of the Earls of Essex Devereux
The Wealth of the Gentry Simpson
The Life and Letters of Francis Bacon Spedding

CHAPTER 18

Memoirs of the Reign of Queen Elizabeth Birch

Henry V, 1st Quarto
Bacon Correspondence   Lambeth Palace
Gorhambury Collection   Hertfordshire County Records
The Life and Letters of Francis Bacon   Spedding
Lives and Letters of the Earls of Essex   Devereux
The Cecils of Hatfield House   Cecil

CHAPTER 19

An Apologia Penned in 1598   Earl of Essex, British
   Museum
Memoirs of the Reign of Queen Elizabeth   Birch
Lives and Letters of the Earls of Essex   Devereux
All the Queen's Men   Williams
The Life and Letters of Francis Bacon   Spedding
The Merchant of Venice, 1st Quarto
The Letters of John Chamberlain   Philadelphia
Bacon Correspondence   Lambeth Palace

CHAPTER 20

Memoirs of the Reign of Queen Elizabeth   Birch
Dictionary of National Biography
Lives and Letters of the Earls of Essex   Devereux
The Life and Letters of Francis Bacon   Spedding
Calendar of State Papers

CHAPTER 21

The Life and Letters of Francis Bacon   Spedding
An Apologia   Francis Bacon
Lives and Letters of the Earls of Essex   Devereux
Memoirs of the Reign of Queen Elizabeth   Birch
The Merchant of Venice, 1st Quarto

CHAPTER 22

Hertfordshire Manorial County Records
Memoirs of the Reign of Queen Elizabeth   Birch
An Apologia   Francis Bacon
Lives and Letters of the Earls of Essex   Devereux
All the Queen's Men   Williams

CHAPTER 23

Henry V, 1st Quarto
Memoirs of the Reign of Queen Elizabeth   Birch
Richard II, 1st Quarto
Love's Labour's Lost, 1st Quarto
The First Night of Twelfth Night   Hotson
Lives and Letters of the Earls of Essex   Devereux
The Life and Letters of Francis Bacon   Spedding

CHAPTER 24

Lives and Letters of the Earls of Essex   Devereux
Memoirs of the Reign of Queen Elizabeth   Birch
Works of Francis Bacon
Elizabeth and Essex   Strachey
Hamlet, 1st Quarto

CHAPTER 25

Memoirs of the Reign of Queen Elizabeth   Birch
Lives and Letters of the Earls of Essex   Devereux
The Cecils of Hatfield House   Cecil
Harleian MSS.   British Museum
Records of St Olave's Church
Public Record Office
The Letters of John Chamberlain
The Life and Letters of Francis Bacon   Spedding
Bacon Correspondence   Lambeth Palace
Essais   Montaigne

Index

THE HOUSE ON THE STRAND	09456	$1.25
REBECCA	23010	$1.75
THE GLASS-BLOWERS	09878	$1.25
FRENCHMAN'S CREEK	06833	95¢
HUNGRY HILL	10074	$1.25
JAMAICA INN	08516	$1.25
KISS ME AGAIN, STRANGER	10330	$1.25
MY COUSIN RACHEL	22640	$1.50
THE FLIGHT OF THE FALCON	10447	$1.25
DON'T LOOK NOW	10470	$1.25
THE SCAPEGOAT	14969	$1.50
THE KING'S GENERAL	10181	$1.25
THE LOVING SPIRIT	10686	$1.25
THE PARASITES	08540	$1.25
THE BREAKING POINT	15479	$1.25
I'LL NEVER BE YOUNG AGAIN	14472	$1.25
THE INFERNAL WORLD OF BRANWELL BRONTE	18473	$1.50
MARYANNE	16709	$1.50
RULE BRITANNIA	19547	$1.50

Include 25¢ for handling; allow 3 weeks for delivery.
Avon Books, Mail Order Dept.
250 West 55th Street, New York, N. Y. 10019
DM 2-76

THE SUPERB GOTHIC EPIC

A TOWERING MANSION
AND ITS TANGLED LEGACY
OF EVIL AND DESIRE

THE STORMY ROMANTIC SAGA BY

FLORENCE HURD
ROMMANY

It began with Eustacia, first mistress of Rommany, whose love for Duncan Blackmore was not to be denied. But the innumerable rooms and sins of Rommany drew her into the grip of a sinister plot that spread its evil stain across seven decades. . . .

Until, in the life of Constance, her granddaughter, three generations of mystery converge in a fateful decision to love the hypnotic Leonard, a man cruelly linked to the shadowy past.

Suddenly, the gloom of Rommany is punctuated by ominous thumpings in the night, and Constance must pierce the veil that enshrouds her hopeless passion—so the ultimate secret of Rommany can be unmasked at last!

 28340/$1.75

THE SWEEPING ROMANTIC EPIC
OF A PROUD WOMAN
IN A GOLDEN AMERICAN ERA!

PATRICIA GALLAGHER

Beginning at the close of the Civil War, and sweeping
forward to the end of the last century, CASTLES IN
THE AIR tells of the relentless rise of beautiful, spirited
Devon Marshall from a war-ravaged Virginia landscape
to the glittering stratospheres of New York society and
the upper reaches of power in Washington.

In this American epic of surging power, there unfolds a
brilliant, luminous tapestry of human ambition, success,
lust, and our nation's vibrant past. And in the tempestu-
ous romance of Devon and the dynamic millionaire Keith
Curtis, Patricia Gallagher creates an unforgettable love
story of rare power and rich human scope.

27649 $1.95

AVON

CIΛ 5-76

THE END OF AN EMPIRE . . .
THE BURNING HOPES OF TEEMING MASSES . . .
THE BLAZING DAWN OF A NEW NATION!

THE THUNDERING INTERNATIONAL BESTSELLER

FREEDOM AT MIDNIGHT

LARRY COLLINS/DOMINIQUE LAPIERRE
authors of IS PARIS BURNING?

In a story of epic scope and sweeping grandeur, the bestselling Collins and Lapierre recreate the endless bloodbaths, the frenzied riots and the brutal assassinations that climaxed with the end of British rule in India.

The raging tumult of an era comes alive in the towering figures of Mountbatten, Nehru, Churchill and Gandhi, as FREEDOM AT MIDNIGHT unfolds against the world's most exotic backdrop.

"The song of India . . . illuminated like scenes in a pageant."
TIME

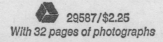

29587/$2.25
With 32 pages of photographs

FAM 7-76

The rousing, unforgettable saga of
beautiful young Lady Elysia Demarice
and Lord Alex Trevegne—and the
impetuous, searing passion which
blazed in their hearts!

Laurie McBain
Devil's
Desire

Out of the turbulence of these two lovers' clashing wills
comes one of the greatest love stories ever written . . .
a rapturous, monumental tale of love lost and won,
for the millions of readers who thrilled to
SWEET SAVAGE LOVE and
THE FLAME AND THE FLOWER.

30650/$1.95

THE BLAZING, TUMULTUOUS NOVEL
OF A LOVE AS OLD AS TIME,
AS TIMELESS AS FOREVER...

JOYCE VERRETTE

DAWN OF DESIRE

*In a faraway time, by the shores of the ancient River
Nile, they stand, possessed by a single naked desire,
in the dawning light of their eternal love. The un-
bounded passions of the incomparably beautiful
Princess Nefrytataten and the tawny-skinned Prince
Ameni sweep across the torrid landscape of Egypt
as the two lovers, wrenched asunder by treacherous
events, must brave peril, degradation, and intrigue
before their twin desires can find release once more
in a surging tide of full-blooded joy!*

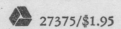 27375/$1.95

DOD 6-76